The Psychology of Death

Third Edition

Robert Kastenbaum, PhD, completed his doctoral studies in clinical psychology at the University of Southern California in 1959, a year that also saw the publication of Herman Feifel's pioneering book, *The Meaning of Death*, to which Dr. Kastenbaum contributed the chapter: "Time and Death in Adolescence." From that time to the present, Dr. Kastenbaum has been studying the encounter with death in many of its forms. These studies include a major research and demonstration project with hospitalized geriatric patients, the National Hospice Demonstration Study, and, currently, explorations of death-bed scenes in reality and in fantasy. He has worked closely with terminally ill, grieving, and suicidal people and their caregivers, and served as director of a geriatric hospital. Dr. Kastenbaum has been honored for his contributions to death education and research by the Association for Death Education and Counseling, and the National Center for Death Education. He has served as president of the American Association of Suicidology and held offices in the American Psychological Association and Gerontological Society of America. Dr. Kastenbaum served as editor of *Omega, Journal of Death and Dying;* is senior editor of *Encyclopedia of Death*; and has written numerous articles, chapters, books, and plays. He is a professor in the Department of Communication, Arizona State University.

The Psychology of Death

THIRD EDITION

ROBERT KASTENBAUM, PhD

Springer Publishing Company, Inc.
536 Broadway
New York, NY 10012-3955

Acquisitions Editor: Helvi Gold
Production Editor: Pamela Lankas
Cover design by James Scotto-Lavino

00 01 02 03 04 / 5 4 3 2

Library of Congress Cataloging-in-Publication Data

Kastenbaum, Robert.
    The psychology of death / Robert Kastenbaum. — 3rd ed.
      p. cm.
    Includes bibliographical references and index.
    ISBN 0-8261-1300-1 (hardcover)
    1. Death—Psychological aspects. I. Title.
  BF789.D4K372 1999
  155.9'37—dc21   99-43555
                                         CIP

Printed in the United States of America

Contents

Contents

Preface

There were doubters back in 1972 when people learned that a book was to be published on *The Psychology of Death*. How could there be a psychology of *that*? Dead people don't think, feel, behave, or interact, do they? And if there is a life some place else, how would an earthbound psychology know about it? I think now that perhaps these doubters were right, even though the book was well received and is now in this third edition. Psychology has not really told us anything about death. It is telling us a lot, though, about the way we live. As this understanding grows, so does our ability to live wisely and love well our fellow mortals.

Take *death* ("Please!" as Henny Youngman might have said). Whatever else death might be, it is surely a conception that has been shaped by the human mind—and repeatedly reshaped as we try to become more comfortable with it. We begin, then, with an exploration of "The Psychologist's Death: A Work in Progress" (chapter 1). In this updated chapter we see how psychology has continued to make some progress in dealing with a topic that it had ignored or avoided for many years. I think we still have a long way to go, but it is good to have some progress to report.

Everybody has some progress to report. None of us come into this world with a firm concept of death when we still have so much to learn about life. "How Do We Construct Death? A Developmental Approach" has become a chapter of its own (chapter 2) in this edition, giving us more opportunity to focus on the remarkable experiences and changes that take place from infancy through later childhood. Insights from cognitive and linguistic theorists such as Maxine Sheets-Johnstone and Michel Foucault suggest that the child's construction of death may be even more crucial a facet of mental and emotional development than previously recognized.

We keep on thinking and rethinking about death after we have passed through childhood's hour. Accordingly, "Reconstructing Death in Adolescence and Adulthood" now has its own chapter as well (chapter 3). Here we learn more about the subtle and pervasive ways in which we manage both to face and turn away from death at the same time. We also draw on additional contributions to the understanding of possible changes in cognitive structure as we move from adolescence through the later adult years and the implications of these changes for our relationship to death. The idea that "I should just die and get it over with" comes in for discussion and leads us to reconsider both suicide and physician-assisted death from that standpoint. New sections on regret theory and denial are also offered. This chapter stops at Nothing. An emerging branch of theoretical physics suggests that everything adds up to nothing. We stop at Nothing, therefore, to glimpse its possible implications for our cognitive understanding of death. However, this stop is only a pause to ready ourselves for a detailed examination of "Death in the Midst of Life" (chapter 4).

Most of the time most of us are not dying. This does not mean, however, that we are free from concern. Some theorists hold that practically everything we do is prompted by fear of death, either directly or by the attempt to conceal and deny such fear. The most influential theories about death anxiety in everyday life have a rather uneasy relationship with the research literature. Here we not only update research contributions, but also examine newer approaches to the role of death anxiety in our psychological functioning: terror management theory and edge theory (the latter in print for the first time). Both terror management and edge theory approaches seem to be more amenable to empirical testing than the classic Freudian and Existential theories and may also offer distinctive guidelines to helping us cope with death anxiety. Yes, it's a long chapter, but the research and theory deserve careful attention.

"A Will to Live and an Instinct to Die?" (chapter 5) is certainly an unfashionable title for an unfashionable chapter. Freud's death instinct theory seemed to have had its heart pierced with a wooden stake years ago, but it has remained surprisingly lively in its grave. The questions dealt with in death instinct theory are too important to ignore, I think, even if we are neither satisfied with all of Freud's answers or confident of our ability to test them. In this second look at the concept of a will to live and an instinct to die, we venture further into public violence, suicide, and the quiet surrender to death ("My life has run its course; think I'll leave the night light on for death"). Freud is back in the news these days with major reviews of his life and work in museums, books, and the media. Whether or not we see a revival of interest in his death instinct theory, for our purposes what he has to suggest about Eros and a will to live is of at least equal importance.

With the final pair of chapters we move beyond the security of academic studies. We are now with the dying person. And with those who are with—or should be with—the dying person. "Dying: Toward a Psychological Perspective" (chapter 6) is new for this edition. We explore both personal perspectives on dying and those that often come with one's choice of occupation. Attention is given first to the two approaches that have been most influential: Glaser and Strauss's observations of communicational interaction in hospital settings and Kübler-Ross's stage theory. Two emerging approaches are also considered: Coping with dying as a life-span developmental task and the existential perspective on meaning in life and death. A brief critical review of these approaches includes a discussion of the main points on which they agree. Much of this chapter (not too much, I hope) is given to the introduction of a new theoretical approach that offers multiple perspectives on the dying process. This consists of no fewer than 17 partial models, so it would be madness to try to summarize them here. Additionally, it has always seemed important to me that we understand and respect the dying person's own theory. The section devoted to this approach includes a detailed case history of "A Dying Psychologist Observed by Himself." Here we draw on the journal kept by William McDougall, one of the most illustrious psychologists of his time, during the last 2 months of his life. Several briefer examples of individuals operating in accordance with their own implicit models of the dying process are also offered.

"Deathbed Scenes" (chapter 7) had been so neglected by psychological theory and research that I offered a chapter to reintroduce this topic to a contemporary readership. The revised chapter adds a section specific to the moment of death. Banjo Bill's encored farewells to life provide an example that might perhaps heighten interest in the final opportunities for interaction with a dying person. We also note that the medical establishment is becoming more active in attempting to improve the quality of life for terminally ill patients. Psychologists who are ready and willing to help in this venture may now find a warmer welcome for their services.

Thank you for your patience with these introductory comments, and welcome.

This edition has benefitted from the useful comments made by Professor Brenda Kenyon and her students at Guelph University. Helvi Gold's skill and enthusiasm has also contributed much, which is exactly what I have come to expect from the outstanding editors at Springer Publishing Company over the years. Pumpkin has enjoyed many a long nap atop the computer monitor as this book was getting itself written, so I trust it has his approval as well.

1

The Psychologist's Death: A Work in Progress

Number of editions of the *Annual Review of Psychology* before the first review of death-related topics: 27.

Number of words related to death in E. G. Boring's classic text, *A History of Experimental Psychology:* 0.

Number of words devoted to death-related topics in the *Handbook of General Psychology*, 166. This is .0001 of the total 1,128,000 words and is confined to the death-feigning behavior of opossums and the attitudes of elderly adults toward death under "Selected Areas." No death mention occurs under such major sections as The Human Organism, Perception, Learning, Language, Thought and Intelligence, or Personality.

How little attention psychology has given to death was a salient theme of this chapter in its original version (1992). As a student I had witnessed psychology's extraordinary resistance to acknowledging our relationship to mortality in the middle of a century that had experienced war, genocide, epidemic, and starvation on an epic scale, a century in which many accomplished people chose to end their lives, and in which many lived in grief-marked despair or died in agony and isolation. Later it became clear that students in other academic and professional disciplines had also completed their studies with scarcely a whisper of mortality to be heard from their mentors. Newly minted specialists in the sociobehavioral and health sciences were prepared to deal with much of life but hardly had a clue about death.

The world has changed some. A public that had long regarded death as a taboo topic (Feifel, 1959) now participates in hospice programs, peer support groups for the bereaved, and courses on death and dying. Professionals and scholars from many disciplines often provide leadership. Psychologists are well represented among service providers and researchers on death-related issues. Several scientific journals focus on death, dying, grief, and suicide, and many other journals have opened their pages to these once neglected topics. The world has changed some, then, but not entirely. There are still academic and professional education strongholds in which "never say die" continues to reign. There are still people in need of expert and sensitive care who suffer in isolation. And there is still a need to review and refine our conceptions of death.

This chapter examines some of the ways in which psychology has been constructing death. We begin with the general concept of constructing experience and then see how it might be applied to death. Attention is next given to specific constructions of death that exist in society at large and within psychology, including recent developments. We conclude with an exploration of the work that still lies ahead for psychology in reconstructing our constructions of death (and, not so incidentally, of life). The basic proposition is the one the Delphic Oracle put to Socrates a while back: "Know thyself," said the Oracle to Socrates. Well, we're trying.

IS DEATH CONSTRUCTED?

The idea that we *construct* reality has been prominent long enough to lose some of its strangeness. Naive realism comforts us by insisting that the world is out there just as a world should be. Our task is to be keen and accurate observers. Because of our limits we cannot observe all of reality, but we know it's out there and—here's the most reassuring part—reality stays real no matter how much or how little we understand it. The notion that each of us participates in the construction of reality is both alarming and liberating. Alarming because it threatens to dissolve our everyday view of things. If there is only your reality, my reality, and their reality, where is *the* reality, *our* reality? Liberating because it acknowledges the contribution of human

thought, imagination, and desire in the continual creation and re-creation of the world. Not only does reality need us, but we can come up with as many versions as there are "constructors."

The Child Shall Guide Us: Psychology Becomes Aware of the Constructivist Approach

One cannot name the precise moment when psychology first attended to the constructivistic claim. Perhaps no book was more influential, however, than Jean Piaget's *The Construction of Reality in the Child* in its 1954 English translation. A growing number of psychologists found merit in Piaget's description of cognitive development from infancy through adolescence. It was not terribly disorienting to suppose that children move through several stage modalities of thought before they achieve the adult conception of reality. For the child, reality was a work in progress. Researchers could observe these constructions at various stages, and measure each child's cognitive distance from the adult model. Implicit in this developmental model was a subtle flattery of the adult mind. Here come the children, striving so hard to achieve our level of understanding!

This was actually a conservative application of constructivistic thinking. For Piaget as for many others, there was still something resembling an "out there" reality—the world as conceived by cognitively mature adults. Furthermore, this was a more or less standard model. Adults, for example, always built their worlds out of strong materials such as object constancy; it would be unheard of for a person to mature by becoming less beholden to object constancy than he or she had been as a child. Each of us was required to construct reality from the materials of our ripening cognitive abilities and our lived experience—but it was assumed to be pretty much the same reality for all.

Reality Turns Weird

By this time, though, physicists had come to terms with a more radical conception: We do not and *cannot* know reality apart from our own observations—and the observation process itself shapes and limits what can be known. We construct (or distort) "reality" even as we attempt to catch it with our observations and cage it for display within our symbolic systems. The physical scientist had become a participant-observer in the universe. Moreover, the new versions of reality were strange as can be—and kept getting stranger. Spend a little time with black holes and quarks and one begins to pine for Newton's clockwork universe, if not for medieval angels dancing ever so daintily on the head of a pin.

The new image of reality—if such weirdness could be said to have an image—encompasses not only the "out there" but also the "in here." Neuroscientists have been almost feverishly reconstructing the brain. It is not just that there is a wealth of additional information on neural functioning: the brain itself and even the individual cell seem to have become quite different creatures than previously supposed. This strongly implies that consciousness may also not be what has been supposed (Calvin, 1996; Gilbert, 1997; Hobson, 1994). In fact, consciousness, for some time a neglected topic, has become a battle-ground of scientific and philosophical controversy. Running through many of the reports from neuroscientists is the emphasis on the spontaneous and enterprising characteristics of our neural equipment. The emerging portrait of the brain is not that of a passive instrument that records objective reality and serves as an obedient switchboard. Instead, the brain is akin to an active, creative, and amazingly complex creature (or confederation of creatures) that enjoys imposing its reality claims on the universe. We are well equipped, then, to construct or coconstruct experiences, symbols, and meanings, many of which we like to call aspects of "reality." We are rather too full of ourselves to be confined to the task of tracking "objective" reality—indeed, "objectivity" is one of our most glorious constructions.

Meanwhile, apart from the blaze of discovery in the physical and biological sciences, anthropologists have been making the constructivist case from a different perspective. It is said that all we are tempted to hold as universal in human thought actually originates within the particularities of a given culture. The ideas that guide our lives do not come from a treasury of universal and infallible truths, but from cultural values and practices. Truth itself, along with beauty, love, and life are ideas shaped within the cultural milieu and best designed to function within that milieu.

Death As a Construction

So what about death?

Reason and experience rebel against the notion that we construct death. Cultures may differ in a great many ways, but death obviously is death, as real as can be. What could be more blunt, more decisive, than the difference between alive and dead? What could be more persuasive than millennia of evidence that the living must die? And why would we construct such an ominous concept as death were there not something powerfully convincing that compelled our acknowledgment?

The idea that death is an idea becomes less ridiculous upon reflection, however. We might first remind ourself that dead is not death. These are related but not equivalent concepts. All societies have come across dead bodies. Furthermore, all societies have witnessed—and inflicted—the changes that occur when a life ceases. Our ancestors everywhere and at all times had to deal with the transition from warm to cold, ruddy to pale, moving to nonresponsive. This consequential set of changes had to be represented in thought and language. The construction of *dead* involved more than any one observed element (such as cold or still). It required a complex set of mental operations. Take, for example, the expectancy shift. This warrior will not fight *tomorrow*. But wait—he will not fight the next day either. He will not fight *again*. He will not fight . . . *ever*. It is a leap of thought from "not responsive now" to "not responsive tomorrow, again, or ever. Now add the ontological surmise. *That* warrior is also still and unresponsive. But he will fight again because he is sleeping off a night of intoxicated dancing and revelry. And, possibly, that *other* warrior is *thanatomimetic*, impersonating a corpse to avoiding becoming one. Humankind has long understood that an unlively appearance could have more than one meaning, more than one set of implications for future actions.

That *dead* is a mental construction has been rousingly demonstrated again in our own era. Some biomedical experts have regarded *clinical death* as the interval between the time that vital processes have ceased and the time when permanent, irreversible damage has occurred. (This interval is usually thought to be just a matter of a few minutes, although some cases may challenge this interpretation.) *Brain death*, as demonstrated by a flat-line electroencephalogram (EEG), refers to the cessation of activity in the neural structures that support and guide life. This can take the form of whole brain death that encompasses all the neural structures above the spinal cord, or cortical death, the loss of the neural structures that support awareness, thought, and other intellectual functions.

Several points are of particular interest to us here.

• The continued development of biomedical technology is leading to new ways of assessing the condition of impaired organisms. Each new assessment technique alters our constructions of dead and death.

• New technologies can also prolong some life functions in organisms who might once have been taken for dead.

• There is room for disagreement and confusion regarding "how dead" a particular organism might be at a particular time.

• This biomedical conquest of the deathbed scene is taking place within a sociocultural context that has strong emotional, spiritual, judicial, and economic stakes in the process. It makes a lot of difference whether or not we agree that this person is dead. And the Supreme Court may or may not agree with what we decide.

• The distinction between dead and death is often blurred and confused. Although the term "death" is frequently used, usually "dead" is what is meant. *The concern is with determining whether or not a person should be considered dead under particular circumstances.* When a physician, a committee, or a judge makes this decision, we have learned nothing about *death*. We have simply had one more episode in which various meaning systems in our society have fought to establish guidelines for the transition between the quick and the dead.

Perhaps we have seen by now that *dead* can be regarded as a construct and has proven itself amenable to substantial reconstruction in our own time. Were this the place to roam through history we would find a great many other constructions and reconstructions. In Renaissance England, for example, the dead seem to have been an unusually literate and influential set (Stein, 1986), while, although dead enough, they were also presumed to be available to return and rescue the Lakota Sioux if only the ghost dance were performed persuasively enough (Hittmann, 1990).

If *dead* is a construct after all, then there can be little doubt that the same can be said about *death*—and *life*. When the first human puzzled over the mortal transition, this must have marked the codis-covery of both life and death. These two concepts have developed in tandem, each implying the other. Definitions of *life* have proven susceptible to change in accord with scientific discoveries and techno-logical innovations. One could not expect definitions of death to be uniform and constant while scientists are still puzzling over those qualities that distinguish life forms from inanimate objects.

Death was already a concept that had been pulled into radically different directions long before the advent of modern science. We will identify some of these constructions in a moment. It might be useful first to acknowledge an ambiguity in the way that the term death is used among English-speaking people and in some other language systems as well. Often death refers to an event: the passage from alive to dead. This event occurs within our everyday frame of reference: "The death of Clarinda occurred at 3:37 p. m. on the patio when a blunt instrument (Marla's fly swatter) ended her sojourn on this earth." There is nothing inherently mysterious about this usage. Death is something that happens within society's stream of life. A variant is numbered death. Here the emphasis is not necessarily on the moment of the death-event, but in the total number or rate of such events (e.g., deaths attributable to use of tobacco products). Both the moment of death and the accumulative numbers of deaths are useful sources of information, but neither takes us beyond the frame of everyday experience.

Moment and number tell us something about the circumstances of death. The problem arises when we use the same term to refer also to "the death that happens after death." The death that "begins" when a living person becomes a corpse has little to do with the externals we can track and chart (time, cause, number). Society—especially societies such as ours that so enjoy counting and recording—acquire a lot of information about death as event and number. We must be careful, though, if we are to avoid the error of supposing that all this knowledge necessarily tell us anything about what death really is or is not.

The answers to the big questions—how should we understand the nature and meaning of death?—are available in the form of competing constructions. Death is the end. Death is the beginning. Death is an end and a beginning, a pass-through state. These are among the most salient answers that have been offered through the millennia. Some answers provide further detail. We keep our individual personality, memory, and cognitions. We stay what we were, but are less. We stay what we were, but become more. We become absorbed into a universal spirit. There is no us and no anything in, through, or after death. Here it is (fortunately!) not our mission to choose among alternative constructions of death as essence and existence. Instead, we are concerned with the way that people develop and use constructions of death. How do ideas about death affect our lives? This aim directs our attention to the sphere of values and attitudes. We begin with a very brief exploration of values and attitudes prior to the emergence of psychology as a distinct field of inquiry and service.

MORAL CODES FOR MORTAL ISSUES

Moral codes have developed most powerfully around those actions and decision points that most affect human survival. How can society feed itself? Defend against enemies? Produce and rear the next generation? *Explain and come to terms with death?* There must be a right way of meeting these challenges, hence the need for a moral code. Here is a synopsis of some approaches that have been with humankind for a very long time.

Death Is Neither Wrong nor Right

Our practical dealings with mortality have often come down to the following:

I Kill

"It is good for me to kill this tasty creature. It's death is my life. My killing it proves that I am good at being who I am."

"It is good for me to kill you. It feels good to take revenge."

"It feels good to protect my people. It feels good to kill!"

I Am Killed

"It is right that I should die in this way. I have done what I knew was the right thing to do, and so my death is honorable."

I Mourn

"I am doing what I know I must do for you. It would be wrong and it would be dangerous if I neglected the sacrifices and rituals that will help you in the perilous passage from this life to the next."

I Elude Death

"It is good to live. It is right to do what I must do to stay alive. A painful ritual is good if it saves my life. Tricking a demon or deceiving a stranger is good if it saves my life. Almost anything that keeps me alive is good, because being alive is sacred and being alive is the root of all treasures."

I Refuse to Elude Death

"But, no, I will choose death over this disgrace. I will not dishonor my name or the name of my people. I will not deny what is most precious to me. I will not accept this humiliation. Death becomes the good if the alternative is to wrong my life."

I Think of Death

"There is a right way to think of death and many wrong ways. I choose to think of my death only in the right way (although sometimes wrong thoughts trouble me). I am at peace with myself when I think of death in the right way, and I trust and value those who know how to do this. I feel scorn or pity for whose who think of death foolishly, or who foolishly do not think of death at all."

All these attitudes were tutored by worldviews and guided by moral principles. (The same was true of the variant attitudes that we would need to take into account if this were the place to excavate ancestral ideas in a thorough and systematic manner.) The particular attitude is not as important here as the fact that value-laden attitudes toward death have been the rule throughout history. I might think your gods monsters and you might think my gods fools, but we would understand each other nevertheless. We would both be stunned to come on somebody who had *no* set of moral rules that governed killing, being killed, dying, and mourning. And we would know ourselves to be in the presence of a deranged mind if we were told that "right or wrong" are notions that do not apply to death.

The situation became more complex as the Judeo-Christian worldviews became articulated and recruited their faithful. The psalmist of the Old Testament was elegant in affirming a bleak view of death that had already made its deep impression.

A Moral Perspective on Death

The emergence of the Judeo-Christian tradition added another level of belief and moral code to the already ancient ideas that have already been considered.

Death Ends All

"What man is he that liveth, and shall not see death? Shall he deliver his soul from the hand of the grave?"

"As for man, his days are as grass . . . "

"Man is like to vanity: his days are as a shadow that passeth away."

"His breath goeth forth, he returneth to his earth; in that very day his thoughts perish."

These representative Old Testament utterances construct death as a sort of cancellation stamp upon all human endeavor. In this sense, death could be regarded as an evil. But the Old Testament Psychologist (if this term may be invoked) was taking aim at our *attitudes*, not at death itself. There are right and wrong ways to think of ourselves; right and wrong ways to chart our course of actions through life. Let us face our common mortality, then, and not dissipate our lives in blinkered vanity and self-deception.

The new-made Christian, of course, did not lose all the feelings and dispositions that dominated in the previous era. Instead, a powerful set of (relatively) novel ideas entered the mix. Believers would now take the following propositions as being central to their attitudes toward self and world.

Death Is My Deserved Punishment

"Then when lust hath conceived, it bringeth forth sin; and sin, when it is finished, bringeth forth death" (*Jas.* 1:15).

"Wherefore, as by one man sin entered into the world, and death by sin; and so death passed upon all men, for that all have sinned" (*Rom.* 5:12).

I May Pass Through Death to Salvation

"Verily, verily, I say unto you, The hour is coming and now is when the dead shall hear the voice of the Son of God: and they that hear shall live" (*John.* 5:25).

"Behold, I shew you a mystery; We shall not all sleep, but we shall all be changed. In a moment, in the twinkling of an eye, at the last trump: for the trumpet shall sound, and the dead shall be raised incorruptible, and we shall be changed" (*Cor.* 15: 51-52).

These constructs have served as tremendous intensifiers of the moral perspective on death. Old Testament death is nature's way of showing us that we are subject to the same laws as the grass and the ox. The psychologist and the moralist—still one person at this point—confronts the challenge of how we are to live with this prospect in mind. New Testament death is quite a different proposition. Death is more than the inevitable cessation of life. Anybody can see that flowers eventually wither and die. Christian belief incorporates this concrete and realistic view, but reframes the construct of death and its moral associations. Original sin, personal sin, guilt, hope, faith, resurrection in the flesh, and salvation are among the ideas that become intertwined with the death construct.

Consider, for example, just two implications of the Christian reconstruction of death.

Alienation from the Realm of Nature

"Yes, the grass withers, the blossom falls, and my ox grows old and dies. But I have an immortal soul. My true life is not here on earth among mortal creatures. I claim dominion over the beasts of the field and sky and sea. I take my orders from God, but everybody else takes their orders from me. My life and death are in a class of their own."

The Risk-All Game of Salvation

"What happens during my life is of little consequence when compared with the fate of my soul after death. I am tempted by the pleasures of life; these seem good to me. But I must subdue these cravings. I must keep my eyes fixed on eternity. Give me courage to risk all for salvation.

The actual interplay of dynamics that operate within the Christian death construct zone is much more complex and subject to variations. But even when limited to what has been summarized here, we can appreciate the special intensity of the Christian moral psychology. Death has become a salient construct. It is not just something that happens. We might even describe Christianized death as an *electrified construct*. Not only does it occupy a superordinate place in the hierarchy of constructs, but it requires the caution and respect one takes in dealing with a live wire. At any moment and in any situation the death construct can deliver a bolt of stinging energy to any other construct. It would not be accurate to say that death reigns as the supreme construct, however, because it is inextricably connected with other powerful ideas such as faith and salvation. A Christian as pious as Cotton Mather doubted and despaired on his deathbed. Had he really held firm to the faith? Would his mortal move bring him eternal blessing or damnation? The personal stakes are enormous in the risk-decision game of salvation: there is more than all the world to gain or lose—there is the fate of one's soul. ("Game" is not used in a derisive sense here; social psychologists have made fruitful use of the game model in approaching many significant questions.)

One cannot venture any distance within the Christian construct zone without encountering that tingling live wire construction of death. Paradoxically, perhaps, death is one of the primary sources of psychological energy here, and this can also be described as a kind of moral energy. If food seems the supreme good to a starving person, then safe passage *from* this imperfect life *through* death and *into* endless blessing is the supreme good. The essential points for us here are the consequentiality and moral urgency of the Christian death construct. We will see in a moment how much this differs from the psychologist's version.

ENTER THE PSYCHOLOGIST

Psychology as an identifiable and independent field of study has been with us for about a century and a half. A great many people had developed psychological insights long before that time, of course, and elements of psychology frequently appeared in works of medicine, natural science, rhetoric, etc. But the firm beginnings of modern psychology were made in a world that had already transformed itself. The psalmist of the Old Testament never observed the slums of a great industrial city or felt the hot breath of a steam locomotive. The authors of Corinthians and Revelation did not measure their hours by mechanical timepieces nor read pennydreadful novels. Mighty empires had risen and fallen, and religion and science had occasion to make new arrangements with each other.

The psychologist was part of the new breed. For a few rather enchanted years psychology was led by creative scholars who had the rare ability both to appreciate the past and help to bring the future into being. (William James and Wilhelm Wundt are among the names that come to mind, although one man's work scarcely resembles the other's.) Soon American academic psychology would innovate the functionalistic, pragmatic, behavioristic pattern that has contributed so much both to its triumphs and failures. The academic bastion would eventually be tested and tempted by depth psychology from Vienna and Zurich. The emergence of clinical psychology and a host of other applied fields also had its impact. Nevertheless, American psychology maintained its profile as an efficient producer of hard-nosed empirical studies and an annual crop of well-ordered graduates.

So where was death in all of this? Up in the attic and down in the dungeon. American behaviorism had little use for anything that looked, felt, or smelled like the baggage of the past. The gritty, feisty, let's-start-the-world-over-again attitude lead to the discard of virtually every scholarly context within which death might have embedded itself. The great philosophers and theologians were excluded, and with them went much of the dialogue on mortality. The weeding-out process was vigorous within psychology as well. Introspectionism and phenomenology were big losers. This was bad news for death (as well as for aesthetics and other topics once of psychological interest). Looking within our own minds was not to be the method of choice for the new psychology. The psychology of the public, observable and countable, was not devised as a clever way to dispose of death. But it did the trick, nevertheless.

At least two other influences also converged to make psychology a death-free zone. From the exciting scientific ferment of the times, psychology took hold of the concept of objectivity. It was not just that psychologists recognized the value of objective measurement and analysis. Objectivity became virtually an end in itself. This approach has had a mixed effect. The design, execution, and evaluation of psychological studies became more sophisticated; some errors of the past became less frequent. "Objectivity" is also an attitude that supposes a highly unusual if not artificial relationship between the observer and the observed. Psychology had therefore maneuvered itself into a position in which death could either be (a) ignored because it is too subjective and too embedded in moral passions, or (b) reframed to meet objectivistic specifications.

From the general American scene at the time, psychology took the cue that death was not a popular topic. There was really no call for it. Hospices were not asking for psychological knowledge to help dying patients and their families: there were no hospices. Suicide prevention centers were not knocking on the doors of academia for data-based techniques to reduce the probabilities of self-destruction: there were no suicide prevention centers. And so on. The idea of teaching a course on the psychology of death was considered peculiar in the mid-60s, when the first such offerings were made; a journal devoted to publishing scientific and professional contributions would not begin until 1970. There was little to prompt American behavioralists to include death among their studies, and there was the prevailing sociocultural attitude ("Don't talk about it and it may go away") to discourage such thoughts if they did happen to arise. Psychology had fashioned an objectivistic, utilitarian, atheoretical perspective whose many strengths did not include either the conceptualization or the study of death. Death was irrelevant to the systematic study of psychology and irrelevant to most of what psychologists do in the applied sphere. Death as an event became of some interest when people violated social norms, as through suicide. Parental bereavement received some attention as psychologists became aware of its impact on child development. Both suicide and parental bereavement in early childhood are norm-violating, therefore upsetting events. Psychology responded somewhat to these inappropriate and disturbing deaths. Death as number became of interest occasionally, for example, did those who died in the course of a longitudinal study differ from those who survived in ways that are relevant to interpreting the findings?

Death as a core part of the human condition, however, was beyond the self-imposed limits of psychology. "What man shall live and not see death?" Perhaps the psychologist . . . until recent times.

There is probably a connection between the psychologists' perceived irrelevance of death and two other variables: (a) the psychologist's separation from phenomenological and natural time; and (b) the preference for aggregated rather than individual (nomothetic) types of quantitative analysis. Experimental psychology is strong on establishing its own designer time frameworks—reinforcement schedules are one familiar example. Statistical psychology is strong on analyzing data on the basis of techniques and assumptions that have an underlying spatial or other atemporal foundation. This tendency expressed itself in the early days of statistical treatment of behavioral data when research designs were borrowed from agricultural experimentation. (The "hort" in cohort bears witness to its horticultural roots.) Investigators became adept at studying the effects of treatment A, treatment B, and control conditions on "crops" of rats or undergraduates who had been assigned to these various conditions, much like sweet peas to Mendellian garden patches. The results are analyzed by aggregated clumps (Group A, Group B, Group C). We are not really much interested in what happened to this particular sweet pea. Furthermore, natural time (in this case, the growing season) is replaced by quantitative outcome. True, there is the appearance that time has really been taken into consideration. But the statistical analysis merely compares two sets of numbers based upon aggregated performance. The growing season might have been a month or an hour. The process might have been linear or geometric, smooth or discontinuous. We'll never know.

Natural time is seldom treated as natural time in psychological research. It is replaced by outcome measures that are indifferent to the actual temporal course. Similarly, the typical research program concentrates upon aggregated numbers. Individuals disappear as individuals almost as soon as they are fed into the computers. Combined, the tendency to dispose of both the individual and of natural time comprises a splendid way to make death appear irrelevant. Without individuals and the actual passage of time, how is this unpleasant topic to intrude itself? Furthermore, the already mentioned dislike of introspective studies has pretty much taken care of phenomenological time as well. Psychologists may not have any extraordinary ways to maintain social stability and continuity, but they can create little time- and death-free worlds in their studies and theoretical models.

It is not surprising that clinical psychologists and others who relate to people on an individual and intimate basis have had more difficulty in regarding death as irrelevant. The psychotherapy client does introspect and has been known to speak of both time and death. On these occasions, the psychologist is not likely to find much to draw upon from the general body of academic theory and data.

Death Responses Destabilize

Despite its slow and hesitant beginning, psychology, as we have seen, has shown some interest in death as a shadowy sort of background stimulus that elicits destabilizing responses. Most of the psychological contributions to the area that some call "thanatology" has centered around cognitive, affective, and behavioral responses to the construct of death. This gives rise to implicit replacement constructions: (a) "Death is that which elicits destabilizing responses." (b) "Death is that which serves as an alarm function to indicate a destabilizing situation." The death construct therefore has been replaced by the responses-to-death construct. This is not a completely satisfactory solution. Responses to death remain in a conceptual vacuum if we have no clear conception of what these responses are in response to! Should we be concerned about this sleight-of-mind maneuver? I think so.

Each construction has its favorite or most convenient source of data, as the following examples are intended to illustrate.

Brooke's mirror presents her with unassailable evidence of a white hair among her raven locks. "I am old!" she laments. "Nobody will love me. Young twerps will call me Ma'm! And—oh, my God—this must mean that I'm mortal after all! Why me?"

The realization of our personal mortality can come about in many ways. Acknowledging signs of physical aging is one of the more common reminders that if youth is but a temporary gift, then life itself may also not be ours to hoard forever. The death of an old friend ("But he wasn't really old—why, he was my age!") is another frequent *memento mori*. These are examples of private encounters with death. There is also the "brush with death." A reckless driver roars through the intersection and nearly broadsides your car. Angry and relieved at the same time, you realize afresh how vulnerable we all are, how quickly a life can end.

The implicit construction, "Death is that which elicits destabilizing responses" applies to all these situations and many more. Perceived encounters with death disturb our equanimity. We no longer feel safe in the world. We dread. We might become so disorganized with anxiety that we cannot act effectively in our own self-interests. Some activities of everyday life may become so aversive to us that we fall into a pattern of functional disability, such as, afraid to travel, afraid even to answer the telephone. But we might also take quite the opposite approach. Nothing scares us. We double-dare death to catch us. And there are, of course, many variations between these extremes.

Some of psychology and psychiatry's most useful contributions have come in this sphere: recognizing that disturbed or distorted behavior patterns can be interpreted as responses to mortal fears. There is no doubt that some people develop either temporary or enduring disturbances that can be linked to death-related anxieties. But does everybody suffer from a basic anxiety that has fear of death at its root? This question is examined at some length in our chapter on death anxiety. It is not the answer to this question that most concerns us here. What interests us is the plain fact that psychologists often conceptualize death primarily as a stimulus for destabilizing responses. In other words, we "read" death from the way the individual recoils. For the psychologist, death is that-which-we-recoil-from. Death does not have its own direct symbolic construction.

Death Is a Task

This is perhaps the strangest psychological construction of death that we have yet considered. It is also the most popular view within the vigorous new area of life-span developmental psychology, and is also well represented among psychologists who provide services to people with life-threatening or terminal conditions. Few people think of this view as being strange, and that may be the strangest thing of all.

Developmental psychology was once almost synonymous with child psychology. However, a growing number of psychologists have taken the entire life-span as their framework, curious about processes that unfold in real or natural time. They are also sensitive to variations in the sociocultural contexts of development. The passage from childhood to adolescence is not the same in the Navajo nation as it is on the sidewalks of New York. Furthermore, the people who are reaching their 40th or 80th birthdays today are different in many respects from all past and future generations because their life experiences have been so distinctive in a nonrepeatable way. There are many intellectual and personal rewards to be discovered in the textured, culturally-aware, and time-conscious world of life-span developmental research.

The death constructions that have already been described on these pages are less likely to claim the allegiances of the life-span developmental psychologist. This is especially true for those who primarily study or provide services for elderly adults. Some years ago I was starting to perform both clinical and research activities in a hospital for the aged. The morgue was two doors down from my office. Any inclination I might have had to consider death as an irrelevant variable was quickly overcome by the unrelenting force of reality. Others have also become too conversant with time, age, and death to find death either irrelevant or unusual.

As I write these words I think of some of the old men and women I have known as their lives approached the end, and I also think of other psychologists and health care providers who have had similar experiences. "Harriet died just as she had determined to, and just how she lived." "Allan was terrified that he would die alone. And he did. That was not a good death." "Thelma was always dying in her mind. When death actually came, it was so swift and smooth that she probably felt very little at all. I wonder if that's the easy death she earned by rehearsing harder deaths so often?"

It would take some effort on my part to regard these deaths as neither right nor wrong, and I have not even mentioned those that stir up the strongest feelings. This involved and judgmental attitude is common among those who have come to know many lives and deaths. We cannot help but feel that some people died too soon or too late, too painfully, or too clouded by drugs, and so forth. We are also aware that some of our clients, research participants, and friends were convinced that they were passing through death to a better life, while others were equally convinced that "dust unto dust" is the way the story must be told. Whatever we felt, it was not as highly objective and distanced observers.

Life-span developmental psychologists may agree with their colleagues that death-related responses are often associated with a destabilizing psychic condition. But they are perhaps less inclined to conclude that this constitutes an adequate psychological construction of death. They observe that some people seem remarkably at peace with the idea of personal death. These same people often have a view of life in which death is seen as part of the totality, rather than as an unexpected and unfair intrusion. Even as their health deteriorates, there is little or no concern about death as such. (They may have a variety of concerns about various aspects of *life*, including their ability to engage in self-care activities, the status of insurance policies, etc.)

Having made observations of this type, the life-span developmentalist along with some practitioners in psychology and related fields may feel the need for a more encompassing and value-friendly death construct. Although there has been no official contest to select such a construct, there has been an uncrowned winner for more than three decades. Life-span developmentalists know what death is. Death is a task.

Where did this idea come from? Straight from the heartland. The life-span developmental vision emerged a few years after the end of World War II. Some far-sighted people recognized that industrial nations would be accumulating ever greater numbers of elderly adults. Psychological theory and social planning both would require greater attention to old age as a part of the total life-course. The "can do" spirit was still vital in the United States. Anybody could become successful by working hard and demonstrating some courage and ingenuity along the way. The Vietnam War and the protest movement, Watergate, the loss of U.S. dominance in several major fields of manufacturing, escalating drug problems and other "downers" had not yet enveloped us.

This conjunction of influences gave us the irresistible concept of the *developmental task*. Life's journey is not for the dawdler or idle wanderer. We are to pause at each of life's work stations just long enough to perform the task that awaits us. Early childhood, late childhood, early adolescence, late adolescence, and so on were conceptualized as work stations. The work was primarily "psycho-social" (another term that was in full bloom, either as given or daringly hyphen-free). We needed to make ourselves competent to take our places as decent, well-adjusted, and productive citizens.

There was rapid acceptance of the theory that our life is a series of tasks to be accomplished, all strung out across the time dimension from infancy through old age. It was quite an attractive proposition at the time. The task image accorded well with the work ethic that had contributed much to this nation's rise to power. Moreover, this seemed to be a much more positive alternative to conceptualizing the human life-span than anything else that was readily available. Psychoanalytic theory was still influential, although struggling against its critics and the changing times. The newly hatched life-span developmental psychology did not want to attach itself too closely to a pessimistic Old World theory that gave more attention to neurosis than to health. Soon there were many variations on the theme of developmental tasks. Help also arrived from mildly renegade psychoanalysts such as Erik Erickson. Psychological textbooks swarmed with lists of developmental tasks, and the fervor spread as well into social work, nursing, and other adjacent fields.

It was not long before living into dying and dying into death had been transformed into a developmental task. The burning task faced by task psychology was to find something for old people to do. The very young had the task of developing trust. Later one had to accomplish the task of becoming independent, and so on. By the time we reached old age there was not much left on the bottom of the developmentalist's sack. Well, why not death? This would kill the proverbial two birds with the same proverbial stone. Old age and death could be wrapped up together in an attractive philosophical and poetic package. Theorists differed in their terminology and emphases, but the basic view was broadcast with rare unanimity: old people should be occupied psychologically in preparing themselves for death.

This influential view did not derive from systematic research. In fact, at that time there had been very little research on the ways in which older people orient themselves toward death. Furthermore, the construction of death as a developmental task did not lead to a great deal of hypothesis-testing research either. The theory just sounded good and seemed to meet the needs of the life-span developmentalist. And what kind of research would have provided an adequate test of this theory? Most life-span developmental studies are descriptive rather than experimental, and the same holds true for most studies of death-related behavior. Although it would be useful—indeed, essential—to describe the ways in which mature adults cope with the prospect of death, this information would not necessarily tell us how they *should* cope. And developmental task theory is about "shoulds" as well as "ises." Although developmental tasks are no longer as dominant in life-span theory as they were a few years ago, the construction of death as a developmental task is still invoked more frequently than any other view. Until further notice, then, preparing one's self for death remains the old person's primary developmental responsibility. (Perhaps it's a good thing that many elders are not aware of this assignment! Some seem to be having rather too much of a good time.)

Death task theory does offer a view of our relationship to death that is not couched within a psychopathology model. It also brushes aside the machine-is-broken-and-useless model that is so influential in our produce-use-and-discard society. Death task theory proposes that it is normal (or normative) to confront the prospect of death as our lives draw to an end. There may be stress, challenge, and conflict involved in this confrontation, but coping with difficulty is something that humans are equipped to do. As we grow older, it is normal for us to reflect upon the shape our lives have taken and to consider what options remain to us. As the prospect of death comes into the closer horizon, it would be mature rather than neurotic to consider how we can best manage "final things" (living will, disposition of estate, funeral arrangements, etc.). The fact that a person is taking death into account is seen as a continuing fulfillment of one's responsibility to self and others.

A second distinctive feature is also worth noting. In life-span developmental psychology, the death construct tends to be much more integrated into the overall theoretical structure. Developmental task theory does not consider itself complete without taking old age and death into account. We could pare death-related discussions from most other psychological theories and find that we have had little if any impact on their overall structure. By contrast, developmental task theory would miss its final pages without its death construct. This would represent not only an abridgement of the theory, but a serious distortion as well.

There is still another welcome contribution of developmental task theory. Psychotherapists and counselors can draw upon this approach to establish their own guidelines for intervention. Many a potential helping person has been hesitant to approach people who seem marked for death because of uncertainty about what they might expect themselves to achieve "What can I do—really? This person will die soon, no matter what I do or how I do it." Task theory suggests that one might help people on both sides of death—the dying and the bereaved person—to review their life-course achievements and "work through" whatever barriers stand in the way of completing their final assignment. This kind of makes sense, enough sense to encourage psychologists and other helping persons to enter the situation.

This appealing theory has its limits and difficulties, however:

1.   Developmental task theory is a way of looking at human behavior:it has not been firmly supported through systematic testing with rival hypotheses.

2.   There is no adequate data base for advocating that older people *should* select death as their number one "task," or that they should approach this task in the particular way favored by the particular theorist.

3.   Unfortunately, this theoretical approach has made it even easier to treat death as though a specialty of the aged, and therefore of only academic interest to the young. Confining death to the geriatrics department was not part of the life-span developmentalist's plan, but the outcome has drifted in that direction. The "let-the-old-people-do-all-the-worrying-about-death" implication has been drawn mostly by popularizers and consumers to accord with society's wishes.

4.   Conceiving the entire human life span as a series of developmental tasks is a bourgeois artistic creation that has been "standing in" while the field awaits a more adequate theoretical framework. As already mentioned, the idea of developmental tasks was congenial to American tradition and especially to the historical period in which it emerged. It feels as comfortable as an old pair of bedroom slippers, and, generally speaking, offers about as much precision and predictive power. I do not intend to throw my old slippers away, nor do I urge that the like be done with developmental task theory. What I do urge is that we bear in mind that this is a model of human development that selects one predominant image—Man the Worker—over all others. There are worse images, to be sure.

There are also a variety of other images that might be enshrined in their own theories of development. These include theories of some antiquity and demonstrated appeal such as the Hindu, Buddhist, and preindustrialization Judeo-Christian conceptions. It does not preclude the development of new models of the course of human life (which may already be struggling to find expression).

The crucial point here is that the life-span developmentalist's construction of death as a task to be completed flows from our sociocultural dispositions, not from any compelling scientific perspective. I have yet to hear anybody ask, "But why is death a *task?*" Perhaps we should start asking this question. This might be preferable to the docile acceptance of a comfortable image whose place might be occupied by a more encompassing, rigorous, and productive theory.

Pop Psych and the Death Meld

Many people receive their psychology through the popular media. Prominent among these are the talking heads of television and the numerous books and tracts that propose to liberate us from the disappointments and cares of everyday life through a heightened (or deepened) spiritual experience. Perhaps the intensely authentic psychic hotlines should also be included. Even the diligent student of official psychology might turn to some of these sources after a hard day of being Skinnerized or multivariated.

Death has become a salient topic in pop psychology where a bold construction of death has found its most receptive home. What is death? Death is a kind of life. Death is the other side of life. Death is the ecstatic fulfillment of life. Death is everything life should be, but isn't. The pop psychologist's construction of death includes some elements that can be found in other views, but seldom in as pure or dramatic a form. The construction has been assembled from selected elements of Eastern and Western thought, rearranged to suit one's own preferences.

Essentially, pop psychology's construction regards death as a phenomenon that is positive in both senses of the term: Death is really "something" (not simply the absence or end of being), and it is something that is desirable. One hopes to attain the degree of spiritual enlightenment that makes possible a kind of meld between life and death. Opposites disappear. Life and death appear as a single, united reality. Rhapsodies on the near-death experience are often introduced to explicate and support this view.

The life/death meld occupies the furthest extreme from the behaviorist's indirect and minimalistic offering. Melders are very much interested in *death*—not just in cognitive and behavioral responses to death. They would not find much satisfaction in the behavioral corollaries that death is pretty much irrelevant and is devoid of moral attributes. The view that death can best be conceived as a source or signal of a destabilization is shared by both academic and clinical functionalists and by many others who have intervention on their mind. Life-span developmentalists do find more use for the death construct within their overall theoretical structure. Our concern with death is also regarded as serving an approved, nonpathological purpose (assuming we keep to our developmental task schedules).

The pop psychology construction of death as the secret and delightful room just a breath away from life is enticing to some people who have found that neither orthodox religion nor orthodox psychology offers them a satisfying image. The death meld construction might be considered too far out by mainstream psychology—but then, some independent-minded spirits might consider the behavioral, clinical, and developmental conceptions to be too far in. (Is it better to die with a workman's satisfied grumble: "There, now that's a good job if I say so myself?" or with the sense of ecstatic union with the Allness of All?)

THE PSYCHOLOGIST'S DEATH: STILL UNDER CONSTRUCTION

Today there are more psychologists than ever who have placed their own feelings at risk by entering into relationships with the terminally ill, the grieving, and the suicidal. More psychologists have also explored their own attitudes toward death and loss in preparation for services to others. Additionally, there seem to be more of us who are not deterred by disciplinary boundaries, either inside or outside of psychology. From psychologists who recognize the significance of death in human experience and who value the contributions of other branches of learning we might well expect more resourceful and valuable constructions of death in good time.

Three approaches that might prove especially useful are the cognitive-linguistic, the embodied, and the emic.

The *cognitive-linguistic approach* would focus on the structures and functions of the specific ways in which we construct or reference death. We would inquire into what might be distinctive in forming concepts such as nonbeing, nothing, and absence. This project should prove useful to psychologists whose major interest is in general cognitive and linguistic development and the influence of ecological context. Piaget's familiar concept of constancy, for example, calls for an understanding of our constructions of variance, change, and transience. Psychologists and others with a special interest in orientations toward death should be in a position to learn more about the ways in which our feelings, actions, and relationships are shaped by the symbol constructions through which death is represented. Just how and how much our thoughts and actions are influenced by characteristics of our language has been a prime subject of controversy ever since Benjamin Lee Whorf (1956) entered his claims. The battle has waged back and forth for some years. It is fairly clear now that Whorf's evidence for the influence of language over thought was not as persuasive as it might have seemed at first. Nevertheless, the overall pattern of research findings now indicates that our construction of reality does depend much upon both universal and culture-specific facets of language (Bloom, 1998). Perhaps some of our difficulties in understanding and coping with mortality can be traced to the limits and quirks of our cognitive-linguistic systems.

The *embodied approach* would foster an organismic psychology. We would not focus solely on thoughts, feelings, behaviors, and relationships, important though they be. Instead we would always have the body in mind, the total organism adapting both to the outer and inner world. Many psychologists have become expert in physiology, contributing to knowledge about sensory, motor, and brain functioning. There have also been theoretical frameworks in which organismic concepts were salient (e.g., Werner, 1961). An organismic psychology with systematic interest in life-and-death issues, however, has been slow to develop. Now would seem to be a favorable time to see what might be accomplished with a serious application of the organismic approach to the psychology of death, dying, and grief. Foucault's (1967, 1973, 1986) discourses on history have heightened awareness of the extent to which even such bedrock concepts as "body" and "mind" are social constructions. Frank (1995) and others have analyzed "illness narratives" that demonstrate the usefulness of the embodied approach even when dealing with words rather than symptoms. There are hints of a sociology of embodiment and death in the making (Seale, 1998). Perhaps psychological approaches will not lag far behind. Some possible elements of an embodied approach will be found throughout this book.

The *emic approach* would counterbalance the natural tendency of practitioners, researchers, and theorists to proceed on the basis of their own ideas. We have the anthropologists to thank for emphasizing the distinction between etic and emic methods of inquiry. We would have a choice of approach if, as outsiders, we entered a culture for purposes of study. We could observe, describe, and interpret this culture on the basis of the ideas that are already in our mind from our education and previous studies. This *etic approach* has drawn much criticism in recent years: we might well be forcing the host people into our preconceived categories, missing their actual themes, patterns, and meanings. The emic approach is more difficult because we must be able to set aside the ideas and assumptions that guide our actions in our own society. Our challenge here is to try to understand the culture as the insiders do. It is *their* stories we want to hear, told in their own way, and not edited to meet our preconceptions. Ideally, one might want to integrate etic and emic perspectives for a better-rounded view.

"The psychologist's construction of death" could therefore be put aside long enough to learn how each individual as well as each group understands death. As psychologists we might protest that we do this all the time—listen to what others say, observe how others think and act. Frequently, however, we make these observations in order to compare them with our standards and to test our theories. A devoutly emic approach would be receptive to the other person's constructions of life and death rather than just using those constructions as data points to fill in our own charts.

REFERENCES

Bloom, P. (1998). Some issues in the evolution of language and thought. In D. D. Cummins & C. Allen (Eds.), *The evolution of mind* (pp. 204–223). New York: Oxford University Press.

Calvin, W. H. (1996). *How brains think*. New York: Basic Books.

Feifel, H. (1959). (Ed.). *The meaning of death*. New York: McGraw-Hill.

Foucault, M. (1967). *Madness and civilization: A history of insanity in the age of reason*. London: Tavistock.

Foucault, M. (1973). *Birth of the clinic*. London: Tavistock.

Foucault, M. (1986). *History of sexuality, Part II*. London: Allen Lane.

Frank, A. W. (1995). *The wounded storyteller*. Chicago: University of Chicago Press.

Gilbert, S. F. (1997). *Developmental biology* (4th ed.). Sunderland, MA: Sinauer Associates.

Hittman, M. (1990). *Wovoka and the ghost dance*. Lincoln, NE: University of Nebraska Press.

Hobson, J. A. (1994). *The chemistry of conscious states*. Boston: Little, Brown.

Seale, C. (1998). *Constructing death. The sociology of dying and bereavement*. Cambridge, UK: Cambridge University Press.

Stein, A. (1986). *The house of death*. Baltimore: Johns Hopkins University Press.

Werner, H. (1961). *Comparative psychology of mental development*. New York: Science Editions.

Whorf, B. L. (1956). *Language, thought, and reality*. Cambridge, MA: MIT Press.

2

How Do We Construct Death? A Developmental Approach

Certainly we know death when we see it and certainly, by definition, our death-recognizing ancestors knew death when they saw it. What we do not know in the least, and what they did not know either, is what death is like . . . even if it is nothing. How, then, could we or they possibly come to have a concept of it?
—Maxine Sheets-Johnstone, *The Roots of Thinking*

Perhaps there exists in speech an essential affinity between death, endless striving, and the self-representation of language. Perhaps the figure of a mirror to infinity erected against the black wall of death is fundamental for any language from the moment it determines to leave a trace of its passage.
—Michel Foucault, *Language, Counter-Memory, Practice*

We have seen that psychology was once among the disciplines that considered death to be only of peripheral interest. North American society in general consigned and confined death to the category of special topic. One could—and should—ignore death except for those occasions when it takes a form too intrusive, too compelling, too immediate. Even then, the rule was to "deal" with death as quickly as possible and restore the previous order of our lives and illusions. Within this sociocultural context it is not surprising that

29

we had little curiosity about the child's curiosity. It would be so much better for us all if children were protected from awareness of mortality.

The opening quotations offer a marked contrast to the once-prevailing attitude of ignoring death in our scholarly endeavors, public practices, and interpersonal communications. Both Sheets-Johnstone and Foucault argue that awareness of death is at the root of thought and language. There is no way of escaping from this connection, even if we call upon thought and language to conceal death from us. Neither of these authors are psychologists per se; rather, they are philosophers with a broad range of historical, cultural, and scientific knowledge. In this chapter, we start within the framework of developmental psychological and making such explorations into the humanities and other sciences as seem useful.

"YOU ARE DEAD" AND "I WILL DIE": TWO SIMPLE CONCEPTS THAT ARE VERY DIFFICULT

We begin with two basic concepts that might at first appear simple and self-evident. As we come to appreciate the complexity of these ideas, we will also become more sensitive to the challenges that children must overcome in their efforts to comprehend death.

"You Are Dead"

One of most fundamental distinctions occurs between our conceptions of the death of the other and the death of the self. The first of these constructions can be expressed as "You are dead." It is more concrete and therefore more within the young child's grasp to begin with "dead" rather than "death." "Hammy the Hamster is dead" literally makes more sense—especially when one is looking at or touching Hammy—than "Death has taken our beloved hamster as it must all mortal beings."

There is reason to believe that "You are dead" develops earlier and more rapidly than the inward-looking, "I will die." But the child must know, guess, or imagine several not-so-simple concepts in order to arrive at the conclusion: "You are dead"?

1. You are *absent.* But what does it mean to be absent? We must appreciate the observer's frame of reference. For a young child, the frame of reference is largely perceptual. Absence means *not here-and-now.* The younger or less developed the child, the more that here-and-now are condensed into the same global unit. Spatial and temporal dimensions are not yet treated independently. Suppose that you are "away," in another city. From an adult frame of reference, you have a spatial existence at the present time, even though you are not within my own personal space. But the child experiences your total absence. You are not in the child's perceptual space at this moment, therefore, you are *not.*

2. I am *abandoned.* This statement is the organismic reciprocal of the first proposition. Your disappearance from my perceptual frame of reference has destroyed my sense of security. As the child, I am not merely aware of your absence, but also of the presence of dysphoric feelings within myself. Your absence and my anxiety are intimately related. We see that the child has an organismic, embodied response. There is a cognitive core, but the stress and fear run through and through the child's state of being.

3. Your absence plus my sense of abandonment contributes to the general sense of *separation.* I have been isolated from the contact and support that I need to feel safe in the world and good about myself. This separation may also lead me to experience a pervasive sense of having lost contact with the environment, not just with you. I am nowhere. I am anxiety. Furthermore, my distress may have been intensified by the feeling that I was *forcibly* separated from you, wrenched away. This trauma could intensify the already bleak picture of absence and abandonment. Sheets-Johnstone (1990) maintains that this sense of sundering between the observer and the observed is crucial to forming the concept of death. She focuses on the perception of a dead person or animal, how different it is from the living version. In our view, this sense of alarming separation also has its roots in the infant and young child's awareness that the mother–self bond has been violated.

4. The separation has *no limits.* Young children do not grasp the concept of futurity nor of a general time that flows directionally through all lives everywhere. They live in a world of what might be called "local time" that is limited to its overall egocentric organization of experience. Therefore, the immediate experience of separation

cannot be modulated by future expectations. The infant or young child cannot say to itself, "Mother has gone away . . . but she will return Wednesday and have a nice present for me." The young child cannot distinguish among short-term, long-term, and final, irreversible separations. Once the separation experience has been induced, the child has no dependable way of estimating or anticipating its conclusion. What the outsider may regard as a brief separation may be indistinguishable in the child's mind from the prospect of prolonged separation. Is not-here-now the same as never-again? Even very young children experience the former; it is more difficult to determine just when they start to comprehend the latter.

5. The child's involvement in *recurring psychobiological rhythms* complicates its relationship to separation and death. You and I have accepted the existence of "objective" or "external" time that moves unit by standard unit from the past, through the present, to the future: a clockwork universe that does not much care about our own wishes and priorities. It is different for the child whose time begins afresh each morning when he/she awakens. Midday nap signals a "time-out." The child's experience of time is strongly influenced by its internal rhythms of hunger-satiation, sleep-activation, and so forth, as well as the recurring rhythms of night and day.

How does this relationship to time affect the child's construction of death-of-the-other? The vulnerability to separation has already been emphasized. For example, the child cannot distinguish well between the prospects of brief and extended or final separation. Now we must give more attention to an apparent contradiction within the child's experiential world. The sense of limitless separation and the endlessness of any experience conflicts with the recurring rhythms, the periodicity that characterizes infancy and early childhood. As a child who feels abandoned, I have no way of establishing a future limit upon my present experience. The intensity of my distress suggests that I fear that this will go on and on without relief. Nevertheless—and this is the more difficult part to grasp—my psychobiological state is always in transition. I am always becoming hungry or sleepy or curious or . . . something! And the environment in which I am embedded is also in transition. The sun is coming up or it is going down. Various periodic household routines are being started or completed. If the cat has just jumped on the ledge of the living room window, this means that the sound of Daddy's or Mommy's car will soon be heard; those rattling sounds in the kitchen suggest that food is again on the way, and so forth.

As a cyclical creature in a cyclical environment, I do not maintain a constant frame of reference over a protracted period of clock or calendar time. There are breaks and interruptions in even my most steadfast thought and behavior patterns. In other words, I do not have a continuous experience. Periodic changes in my inner state and in my relationship with the external environment rest, refresh, and distract me. This means that my experiential world is subject to both rules: (a) the lack of limits or boundaries within which to place a separation experience, but also (b) the inability to maintain a steady frame of reference over an extended period of time.

As a young child I might misinterpret your temporary departure as being a consequential separation. By this same token, however, I may *under* estimate a consequential separation—even your death. My cyclical pattern of functioning has lead me to anticipate that *every* end has a fresh beginning, just as *every* beginning has an end. But there is no end to ends. You have been away a long time now. I measure "long time" arbitrarily by my own feelings—long enough to make me feel uncomfortable, abandoned. And I have deeply rooted within me the expectation that the familiar pattern of separation-reunion will be repeated.

Two opposite responses can testify to the young child's special relationship to time: (a) The child may respond in panic or despair over what is objectively a brief and insignificant separation because to the child this feels like total and unmoderated abandonment or (b) the child may respond as though expecting a dead parent, sibling, or animal companion to return any minute now.

6. *You do not respond.* This applies to the specific situation in which an infant or young child is in close contact with a dead person or animal. It can also involve a "dead toy" that does not do what it was supposed to do. The most characteristic behavior I have observed in this kind of situation involves the child's attempt to persuade the dead other to respond. Nonresponsiveness, of course, remains an important constituent of the death construct for adults as well. This includes death in the literal sense: "The eyes did not respond to light; there was no response to pressure or pain stimuli, or to words." It also includes death in the figurative sense: "Alas, Percy was dead to my pleas." For the young child, it is clear that the concept of

nonresponsiveness arises from an interactive context. "I will make you move. I will make you talk to me. I will make you smile." It is only through the expectation of responsiveness and through failed attempts to elicit responsiveness that the child can generate this facet of the "You are dead" concept. Very early in development, then, an infant or young child will have considerable difficulty in grasping the concept of nonresponsivity. Experience with the world as well as maturational changes in the central nervous system will soon teach the child that it is characteristic of living things to respond, and, therefore, a discomfirmation of expectation when they do not. But precisely what—and how—are children thinking when they puzzle over a nonresponsive being or toy? There is an emerging controversy here that we will take up when we review empirical studies on the child's constructions of death.

For children as well as adults it is much easier to *realize* (Weisman, 1974) death when one has had the evidence of one's own senses to support this conclusion. Again, this is an embodied response: one *feels* as well as thinks. The need to realize death is perhaps the most frequently cited reason for advocating open caskets at memorial services: there really is a body in that casket, and it is the body of our deceased friend. The young child's direct experience of a dead person or animal will differ appreciably from an adult's, but in either instance this kind of contact does provide a firmer reality base for one's response. A 2-year-old does not think of death the way his/her parents do, but the encounter with a cold, still, unresponsive form conveys vital, if still mysterious information.

"I Will Die"

This proposition requires even more of the child. We are not in a position to make this statement in a meaningful way until we have mastered a number of related concepts. These include the following:

1. *I* am a person with a life of my own, a personal existence.
2. I belong to a *class* of beings, one of whose attributes is mortality.
3. Using the intellectual process of logical deduction, I conclude that my personal death is a *certainty*.

4. There are *many possible causes of my death*, and these causes might operate in many different combinations.
5. Although I might overcome or evade one particular cause, *I cannot overcome or evade all causes.*
6. My death will occur in the *future*. By future, I mean a time-to-live that has not yet elapsed, a time that I have not previously experienced.
7. But I do not know *when* in the future my death will occur. The event is certain; the timing is uncertain.
8. Death is a *final* event. My life ceases. This means that I will never again experience, think, or act, at least as human being on this earth.
9. Accordingly, death is the *ultimate separation* of myself from the world.

"I will die" implies self-awareness, logical thought operations, conceptions of probability, necessity, and causation, of personal and physical time, of finality and separation. It also requires bridging a tremendous gap: from what I have actually experienced of life to a construction of life's negation. I have not been dead (the state). I have not experienced death (the event). Therefore, the mental operations that I call upon in my efforts to fathom death tend to falsify as they proceed. If death implies lack of movement, then my eyes conspire against this fixed image by moving restlessly as I scan the environment (your eyes do the same). If death implies emptiness or silence, my mind again rushes ahead to fill in the void with its own operations, just as people in sensory deprivation experiments manufacture their own stimuli to satisfy our need for cognitive activity. Our mind's own *modus operandi* equips us for interpreting life, not life's negation. This will continue to be a problem for adults, and probably contributes to the child's difficulties in comprehending cessation of life.

Brock Haussamen (1998) argues that the rules of our language systematically falsify the propositions we articulate about death. More specifically, our syntax often produces a denial rather than an acknowledgment of death.

Language does not have much respect for the dead, in the sense that it does not treat them any differently than it does the living. Some of the ways we refer to the dead—not euphemisms but the most ordinary statements—are incongruous, on the fact of it. The verb in the sentence *John is dead*, for instance, is in the present tense, as if the statement were a variation on *John is sick*. And the other ordinary announcement of death—*John died*—has the same structure as any other in which John did something intransitive, such as *John fell* or *John slept*. John may have died, but in saying so we present him as the same source of action that he always was. Simple sentences about a person's death cannot help but cast the person in the mold of the living. (p. 313)

The more rapidly children master language, then, perhaps the more rapidly they learn to present their discoveries about death in a way that subtly contradicts their insights into the fundamental disconnect between being and nonbeing. Perhaps, as Foucault (1984) suggests, the very act of speaking or writing about death achieves a triumphant denial:

Death is undoubtedly the most essential of the accidents of language (its limits and its center): from the day that men began to speak toward death and against it, in order to grasp and imprison it, something was born, a murmuring which repeats, recounts, and redoubles itself endlessly, which has undergone an uncanny process of amplification and thickening, in which our language is today lodged and hidden. (p. 55)

To put it another way: the dead are not dead if we can retain and revive them through words, and we will not die as long as we are speaking, listening, writing, or reading. Again, Foucault: " . . . discourse has the power to arrest the flight of an arrow" (p. 53).

Children, through their avid observations and compelling discoveries, are less likely than adults to thicken and hide their constructions of death. Improving our understanding of the child's growing awareness of death may be essential to understanding how we manipulate these ideas as adults.

There is a further difficulty as well. Children's conceptions of death often are influenced by encounters with a dead person, animal, or plant. Yet these perceptions do not truly bridge the gap. The deadness is perceived from the outside only. *What it feels like not to feel* eludes me. In the language of phenemonology, the *Otherness* of the dead startles us into awareness of the chilling distance between life and death. However, under some circumstance both children and adults are vulnerable to misinterpretations, taking the living for dead, or vice versa. Experiences with the dead and with the transition from alive to dead must be taken into account as we attempt to understand the development of death conceptions.

THE CONSTRUCTION OF DEATH IN INFANCY AND EARLY CHILDHOOD

Two assumptions have been with us since the earliest explorations of the development of the understanding of death in childhood:

1. Infants and very young children are incapable of understanding death.
2. The aim of the developmental process is to achieve the mature conception of death that is held by adults.

These propositions are by no means unreasonable, but we will see that they fall short of characterizing the actual course of development.

The Piagetian Perspective and Its Limits

Developmental psychologists have often told us that very young children (from birth to about 2 years) can have no understanding of death because they lack the ability to grasp *any* abstract conception. Jean Piaget (1954; Piaget & Inhelder, 1959), for a prime example, offered a fine-grained analysis of mental development from infancy through adolescence. Within the period of infancy alone, Piaget identified six stages of mental development. Formal operations (abstract thinking), however, do not emerge until early adolescence. Although the 10-year-old is adept with concrete operations—thinking about the actual—it is not until adolescence that a person is able to think about thought and bring to bear the full intellectual powers required for a mature comprehension of death. A Piagetian analysis would reach the same basic conclusion as our examination of the proposition, "I will die," although differing in some particulars and emphases.

Piaget's influential theory that has contributed to a lack of interest in the young child's conception of death. Piaget and his colleagues devoted much attention to clarifying the development of the concept of constancy, conservation, or invariance (three ways of saying pretty much the same thing). Many innovative studies were devised for this purpose. These experiments have contributed much to our understanding of early cognitive development and honed our observational powers. However, there is a strong bias in this approach. Piaget's emphasis upon that-which-does-not-change has diverted attention away from the significance of actual transience transformation. Yes, it is useful to know when a child has achieved the concept of conservation and can therefore tell us with absolute certainty that pouring water from the long, tall beaker into the short, squat glass has had no effect on the amount of water involved. But reality includes real change as well as real constancy. There is a tendency in developmental theory to treat the evanescent or mutable circumstances as a kind of error variance. The developmental psychologist is in danger of forgetting that children cannot truly grasp that-which-does-not-change unless they also have an acute appreciation for that-which-perishes (the goldfish floating at the surface of the water) and that-which-becomes-something else (the ice cream cone on a hot day). It is as though psychology had decided to create an idealized universe in which constancy and invariance rule supreme: but this is not the world we know, and children are quick to find this out.

There are other problems with relying entirely on the Piagetian approach. Carey's (1985) studies suggest that children draw increasingly more refined and accurate inferences from their experiences. They do not leap from one stage of development to another, quite different stage. Instead, they become more and more adept at making judgments as they have more and more information at their disposal. Young children can draw accurate partial inferences about life and death before they have acquired a sufficient knowledge base to comprehend the most fundamental differences. For example, children are likely to realize that dead people do not eat or ride bicycles before they can put together the whole picture. The child's incomplete understanding of the difference between life and death, then, can be attributed to its limited knowledge of biological processes. Carey found that within the limits of their biological knowledge, children as young as 4 years could discriminate between characteristics of alive and dead or nonliving, a finding consistent with Atwood's (1984) study. We will encounter another interesting alternative view when our exploration of the research literature takes us to the work of Sandor B. Brent and his colleagues. And now—to the research.

EARLY EXPOSURE TO DEATH-OF-OTHERS

We begin with young children's responses to the death of a person who has been important to them. One of the earliest researches into the psychology of death touched on this question. G. Stanley Hall and Colin Scott (reported in Hall, 1922) asked adults to recall their earliest experiences with death. Analyzing the questionnaire responses, Hall tells us that:

> The first impression of death often comes from a sensation of coldness in touching the corpse of a relative and the reaction is a nervous start at the contrast with the warmth that the contact of cuddling and hugging was wont to bring. The child's exquisite temperature sense feels a chill where it formerly felt heat. Then comes the immobility of face and body where it used to find prompt movements of response. There is no answering kiss, pat, or smile. . . . Often the half-opened eyes are noticed with awe. The silence and tearfulness of friends are also impressive. . . . Children of from two to five are very prone to fixate certain accessions of death, often remembering the corpse but nothing else of a dead member of the family. But funerals and burials are far more often and more vividly remembered. Such scenes are sometimes the earliest recollections of adults. (pp. 439–440)

Despite Hall's stature as a founder of American psychology, there was no evident follow-up to this study. A few later studies of early memories (e.g., Costa & Kastenbaum, 1967; Tobin, 1972) also found that death experiences are often reported. I am still finding that early childhood experiences of loss, separation, and death are often mentioned when elders offer their life narratives.

We cannot assume, however, that the young child's experience of death is the same today—in this era of violence-drenched television—as it was in the early years of this century. Nevertheless it is worth listening to Hall's further comments on the children of his own time:

> Little children often focus on some minute detail (thanatic fetishism) and ever after remember, for example, the bright pretty handles or the

silver nails of the coffin, the plate, the cloth binding, their own or others' articles of apparel, the shroud, flowers and wreaths on or near the coffin or thrown into the grave, countless stray phrases of the preacher, the fear lest the bottom of the coffin should drop out or the straps with which it is lowered into the ground should slip or break, a stone in the first handful or shovelful of earth thrown upon the coffin, etc. The hearse is almost always prominent in such memories and children often want to ride in one. (pp. 440–441)

And Hall even has an explanation to offer. He refers to the "well-known laws of erotic fetishism by which the single item . . . (finds) room in the narrow field of consciousness (and is) over-determined and exaggerated in importance because the affectivity that belongs to items that are repressed and cannot get into consciousness is transferred to those that can do so." This is a remarkable interpretation to come from an academician writing in the twilight of his own life and at a time when the psychoanalytic approach was meeting a mostly hostile response from university-based psychologists. An independent thinker, Hall decided that his data did point in the direction of an intriguing selective memory process. He dared to compare the emotions aroused by exposure to death with erotic sensations—and both in childhood!

Hall's interpretation resonates with psychoanalytic theory's emphasis on the subterranean ways in which our memories are shaped in order to reduce internal conflict. The emotion-laden experiences at the graveside could not be represented effectively through verbal/conceptual categories that had not yet developed, nor could they be forgotten. It is a reasonable working hypothesis that the recollection of a "minute detail" served as a kind of code for the total experience.

Ernest G. Schactel's stimulating essay on memory and childhood amnesia (in *Metamorphosis*, 1959) would make an excellent starting point for those who are interested in tracing adult memories back to their roots in childhood experience—or to understanding why it is so difficult to recapture our earliest memories. He makes a strong case for the proposition that the processes of memory in adulthood "substitute the conventional cliché for the actual experience." It may well be that our sense of wholeness as adults will elude us unless we can somehow liberate and integrate our early memories into our total being. If this is true, then our earliest exposures to death and other forms of loss may be significant not only for what their role in our development of death constructs and attitudes, but for understanding the entire shape of our lives.

Case histories offer many examples of significant links between early childhood experiences with death and subsequent adult behavior. Here is an example provided by psychiatrist David M. Moriarty (1967).

> Mrs. Q. had undergone severe depressive episodes for over a decade. She made three suicidal attempts and twice was treated (unsuccessfully) with electroconvulsive therapy.When Mrs. Q was three years old, her mother had died of appendicitis. She recalled standing beside her uncle at the graveside, her arm around his leg. This memory was recovered during psychotherapy after she had several panic episodes in which she reported in great alarm that "the world is coming in on me." Moriarty notes that "The thought behind this fear was traced to this graveyard scene when they threw a shovel full of dirt on the lowered coffin. . . . She (Mrs. Q) felt dead, non-existent, wanted to die, and feared dying. . . . The most impressive fact was that she talked and thought about the death of her mother as much as if it had just happened. This tragic event of forty years ago was still uppermost in her mind. (p. 88)

The sense of time described here seems more appropriate to the young child's experiential world rather than the adult's. Objective time (the passage of 40 years) was not nearly as significant psychologically as the still-fresh, still-painful feeling of losing her mother. It is not that unusual for highly anxious people to distort or compress time into idiosyncratic patterns that conform to their emotional states rather than to standard, consensual time. We should not overgeneralize from case histories, however. There is no direct and automatic connection between death of a parent in early childhood and subsequent depression and suicidality. This is a major life event, but the outcome depends upon many factors, including the type of interpersonal support available to the bereaved child and the arrangements made for the child's subsequent well-being. It is probable that parental bereavement and other significant losses, including the death of an animal companion, increase the urgency of the child's quest to understand how "alive" becomes "dead"—and what happens after that.

Many studies have relied partially or exclusively on retrospective accounts. This was true, for example, of Hall's survey and Moriarty's case report. But it is also possible to observe the death-related behaviors of infants and young children more directly. Consider the "death-exposure" responses of these two very young boys, David and Michael.

David

David, at 18 months, was toddling around the back yard. He pointed to something on the ground. Daddy looked. It was a dead bird. The boy labeled what he saw, "buh, buh" (his approximation, at the time, for bird). But he appeared uncertain and puzzled. Furthermore, he made no effort to touch the bird. This was unusual for a child who characteristically tried to touch and handle everything he could reach. David then crouched over and moved slightly closer to the bird. His face changed expression. From its initial expression of excited discovery it had moved to puzzlement: and now it took on the aspect of a grief mask. To his father's surprise, David's face was set in a frozen, ritualized expression that resembled nothing so much as the stylized Greek dramatic mask for tragedy. Daddy only said, "Yes, bird . . . a dead bird." In typically adult conflict, he thought of adding, "Don't touch," but then decided to say nothing more. In any event, David made no effort to touch.

Every morning for the next few days, David would begin his morning explorations by toddling over to the dead-bird place. He no longer assumed the ritual-mask expression, but he still showed no inclination to touch the bird. The small feathered body was allowed to remain in place until greatly reduced by decomposition. The parents reasoned that he might as well have the opportunity to see the natural processes at work. This had been, to the best of the parents' knowledge, David's first exposure to death. No general change in his behavior had been noted at that time, nor had any been expected. This concluded the first brief chapter.

But a few weeks later there was a second dead bird to be discovered. (This fatality was clearly the work of a well-known local cat whose name need not be mentioned here.) David showed quite a different orientation toward death #2. He picked up the bird and gestured with it. What was on his mind? Something—because he was also "speaking" insistence. When his parents did not seem to comprehend his wishes, the boy reached up toward a tree, holding the bird above his head. He repeated the gesture several times. Finally comprehending, Daddy tried to explain that being placed back on the tree would not help the bird. David continued to insist, accompanying his command now with gestures mimicking the flight of a bird.

All too predictability, the bird did not fly when returned to the tree. David insisted that the effort be repeated. And again! And still again! Abruptly, he then lost interest altogether in this project.

But there was to be a sequel a few weeks later. It was now a New England autumn. David and Daddy were strolling in the woods. There were many small discoveries to be made. After a while, though, the boy's attention became thoroughly engaged by a single fallen leaf. He tried to place it back on the tree himself. Failure. He gave the leaf to his father with "instructions" that it be restored to its rightful place. Failure again. When Daddy started to try once more, David shook his head, "No." Although leaves repeatedly were seen to fall and other dead animals were encountered every now and then, little David made no further efforts to reverse their fortunes.

This exposure to death seems to have called forth behavior that was unusual and unprecedented for this very young child. Whatever responses were touched off in him by the sight of the dead bird, these represented something new and consequential. The "mask of tragedy" expression suggests the possibility of an almost instinctual and archaic response to death, but this is a question raised, not a theory proven. Perhaps the most impressive feature of this experience was David's persistence in working with the dead bird image over a period of time. He already had enough experience with the world to know that birds were supposed to rest in trees or fly about, and that leaves also belonged on their branches. Some connection was made in his mind between the dead birds and the fallen leaf, and in all these instances he expressed the desire to see things set to right. In effect, David was testing the principle of commutability in the biosphere—and finding that it doesn't hold up very well.

David formed some connections and concepts through this set of experiences. He could not express his new-made death construct in words, but it seems obvious that he entertained, tested, then rejected the idea that the dead can be returned to life. Since this incident, I have collected many others from friends, colleagues, and students who welcomed the opportunity to talk about *their* own children, grandchildren, students, or patients. It is clear that other—probably very many other—very young boys and girls have made their own personal discoveries about death. It may seem foolish to suggest that a child barely 2 years of age can sometimes grasp the essence of death, but the testimony I have heard and the several examples I have seen for myself make it seem perhaps more foolish to insist that we do not comprehend the central facts of death until adolescence.

Michael

Michael had not drunk from a bottle in more than a year. As a big boy who was almost 3 months past his second birthday, he was a competent and articulate member of the family (Brent, 1977–1978). But now there was a problem. For the past several weeks, Michael had been waking up several times during the night—screaming hysterically for a bottle. He could not be satisfied unless the ingredients included both warm water and sugar. Attempts to talk him out of it were useless. He would tearfully insist, "But I have to have it!"

One night Michael had been especially upset—so desperate-sounding that his father took him out of his crib and sat with him in the rocking chair. The boy relaxed a little, but was still tense. His father asked what would happen if he didn't get his bottle. "'Then I won't (or can't) make contact!' he replied through his tears." But what did that mean—"make contact"? "If I run out of gas, I can't make contact—my engine won't go. You know!"

Within a few minutes of further discussion the mystery had been solved. Michael had been with his father on three separate recent occasions when their vehicle ran out of gas (twice in the family car, once in a speed-boat in the center of a large lake). These situations had confused and disturbed Michael (and didn't exactly please his father, either). Michael feared that "My motor won't run, and then I'll die." His father then recalled still another episode in which the engine of their old car refused to start while they were trying to sell it. The conversation at that time had included the key phrases, "Maybe it's not making contact," "the motor died," and "I guess the battery's dead." Michael had listened to this discussion and had drawn his own conclusions.

There was a happy ending to this part of the story. His father reminded Michael that a car was very different from a boy. "Lemme see. Can I turn your motor on and off?" Michael laughed. Soon Michael was reassured that he did not have to be filled up with "gas" every night: His motor would keep running very nicely anyhow. Michael kissed his father goodnight and never again awakened to ask hysterically for a bottle of warm sugar water.

The total story was more complex. Gradually Michael's parents pieced together a picture of what had happened as background to the nocturnal anxieties. The family parakeet had been found one day lying motionless at the bottom of its cage. Michael was very upset and persisted in asking what had happened to it. His father had explained: "Every animal has a kind of motor inside that keeps it going. When a thing dies it is like when a motor stops running. It's motor just won't run any more." *His father had not been satisfied with this explanation, but it was the only thing he could think of at the moment. There had also been other elements in the family's recent life-and-death adventures, and all of these had been observed by Michael and contributed both to the need to develop a death construct and to the particular form it had taken. This set of related incidents is useful in reminding us that parent-child communication has a telling influence on the development of death-related thoughts and feelings, just as it does in other aspects of life.*

These two excerpts from the early biographies of David and Michael suggest that exposure to death can contribute to emotional and behavioral disturbances in early childhood, but also stimulate intellectual curiosity. Furthermore, there was a strong sense of caring, of involvement on the part of both David and Michael for the dead birds they encountered. The death of another creature touches something within the young child. We also see that ambiguities in adult language and thought are apt to confuse young children as they attempt to make sense out of death.

INTIMATIONS OF MORTALITY: DO THEY START IN THE CRIB?

David and Michael were already up and about when they had their observed encounters with death. There is a more extreme view which asserts that intimations of self-mortality start even earlier. Adah Maurer (1966) suggests that the sleep–waking cycle sensitizes the infant to the dichotomy between being and nonbeing. This leads to the additional proposition that the infant is capable of experimentation with the states of being and nonbeing:

By the time he is three months old, the healthy baby is secure enough in his self feelings to be ready to experiment with these contrasting states. In the game of peek-a-boo, he replays in safe circumstances the alternate terror and delight, confirming his sense of self by risking and regaining complete consciousness. A light cloth spread over his face and body will elicit an immediate and forceful reaction. Short, sharp intakes of breath, vigorous thrashing of arms and legs removes the erstwhile shroud to reveal widely staring eyes that scan the scene with frantic alertness until they lock glances with the smiling mother, whereupon he will wriggle and laugh with joy. . . . To the empathic observer, it is obvious that he enjoyed the temporary dimming of the light, the blotting out of the reassuring face and the suggestion of a lack of air which his own efforts enabled him to restore, his aliveness additionally confirmed by the glad greeting implicit in the eye-to-eye oneness with another human. (p. 36)

Maurer observes that the term, "peek-a-boo" derives from an Old English phrase meaning "alive or dead?" In her view, the infant and toddler's first games are not to be dismissed as inconsequential. She believes these activities should be regarded as an integral part of the long-term process of developing a self identity. Beyond "peek-a-boo," the very young child is likely to engage in a variety of other disappearance-and-return games. These, suggests Maurer, are little experiments with nonbeing or death:

During the high-chair age, babies persist in tossing away a toy and fretting for someone to return it. If one has patience to replace the toy on the tray a dozen or twenty times, the reward is a child in ecstasy.

Gradually, the child learns that some things do not return. "All gone" becomes one of the child's most popular expressions. In fact, the child may become a diligent researcher of the all-goneness phenomenon. Maurer cites three examples:

Offer a two-year-old a lighted match and watch his face light up with demonic glee as he blows it out. Notice the willingness with which he helps his mother if the errand is to step on the pedal and bury his banana peel in the covered garbage can. The toilet makes a still better sarcophagus until he must watch in awed dismay while the plumber fishes out the Tinkertoy from the overflowing bowl.

Is Maurer reading too much into the behavior of infants and toddlers? Perhaps so. However, she has identified some common types of early behavior that do pertain to the phenomena of presence versus absence and return versus loss. A key characteristic observed by Maurer is the motivational and emotional connection between the very young child and loss-related phenomena. It is not just a cognitive task: the child expresses terror, fascination, delight.

This pattern of highly involved, affect-laden behavior is most readily comprehensible within organismic-type theories of human development such as those introduced by Kurt Goldstein (1939), Kurt Lewin (1936), and Heinz Werner (1957). Learning, interacting, and experiencing are not fragmentary activities: these occur as expressions of the total organism ("Short, sharp intakes of breath, vigorous thrashing of arms and legs . . . "). On this view, what eventually emerges as a set of verbal and conceptual formulations about life and death may begin as a highly involved participation in the wonders of immediate experience.

Death perceptions are probably the forerunners of death conceptions. Perhaps this long developmental sequence originates in the infant's experiences of the periodic alternations in its own internal states. Then, if Maurer is correct, the infant actively seeks out the experiences of coming-and-going, appearing-and-disappearing. This is a stage marked by intensive organismic participation. Later in childhood, one is able to stand a little apart from the immediate experience. The child now perceives changes, losses, disappearances that have "deathish" resonance (e.g., David and Michael with their dead birds). After some years of additional psychobiological maturation and life experience, the individual develops the type of cognitive structures to which such terms as "conceptual thinking" or "formal operations" can be applied.

This is a scenario that has not been tested through systematic research. It is worth our attention, however, because it does utilize relevant behavioral observations that we can check out and extend if we so choose. It also makes some intuitive sense—that our quest for understanding life and death begins with a lively curiosity based upon our own immediate experience of the world, and that this curiosity is charged with strong affect. The infant may not yet be a logician, but it has an excellent reason to be interested in the phenomena of loss, disappearance, separation, and return. For what is the infant, but itself a newcomer on the scene, whose hold on life is still precarious, and whose security is intimately linked with supportive human contact? "Peek-a-boo!" What an odd little theory! Do we have a better one?

CONSTRUCTION OF DEATH THROUGH CHILDHOOD

We will now look at the continuing development of death constructs throughout childhood. Some studies take all of post-toddler childhood as their span (approximately from age 3 to 12), others concentrate on a particular age level. But first let us try to capture the tone of a young child's view of death by listening into this conversation, which I did in fact eavesdrop upon on a geriatric hospital ward. A 4-year-old girl is visiting with her 84-year-old great-grandmother. "You are old! That means you will die. I am young, so I won't die, you know. . . . But it's all right, Gran'mother. Just make sure you wear your *white* dress. Then, after you die, you can marry Nomo (great-grandfather) again, and have babies."

This 4-year-old obviously has caught on to something about death. There is a connection with age. It is comforting to believe that she herself will not die, because that is something that (only) old people do. For a moment or so, the girl seems to be on track—but then she reveals her belief that death is only a temporary state of affairs, an ending that is followed by another beginning. Theory apart, we will find in children's thoughts about death an interesting and ever-shifting mixture of solid fact, wishful thinking, guesswork, and the occasional riveting insight.

Pioneering Studies

Psychological studies of death did not start appearing with any frequency until the 1960s, mostly through the activities of American researchers. However, two important investigations of children's concepts of death were conducted in Europe during the 1930s.

British psychologist Sylvia Anthony interviewed and tested 117 children and arranged for home records to be kept over an extended period of time by 13 families with children and also interviewed and tested another 117 children herself (Anthony, 1940, 1972). Her most basic finding came as a surprise to some people: normal children *do* think of death. It had previously been supposed that only emotionally disturbed or traumatized children would think of death. Most parents seemed to believe that they could and should insulate children from awareness of death. Anthony's study provided one of the first clear indications that children are quite capable of discovering death for themselves and of generating some ideas about it.

Usually, the child's conception of death was associated with the themes of loss, separation, and abandonment or violence and aggression. The children did not have to experience these catastrophes themselves in order to offer their fantasies. Children could regard death with fear, curiosity, and wonder even if they did not comprehend exactly what it meant to *be* dead. It was enough to know that loved ones had been separated from each other, or that a person had fallen victim to an act of violent aggression.

Anthony also attempted to discover the basic principles that guide the child's construction of death-related concepts. One of these, she believes, is the *law of the talion.* If the child commits—or even thinks of—an aggressive action, there will be equally severe retaliation. The talion dynamics involve a kind of psychological *oscillation* on the part of the child. First, one is the aggressor. Next, one becomes the aggressed-upon. Aggression is a constant, but the nature of one's own participation in the aggression alternates between perpetrator and victim. Anthony sees an even more primitive cognitive mechanism beneath this phenomenon:

> The idea of retaliation itself, primitive as it is, develops from a manner of thought still more general and primitive. This manner of thought is an oscillation of attention, by which a whole fantasy of thought-complex is alternately seen in primary and then in reversed aspect, and then again in primary. Thus, a mother loses her child by death, and then the mother herself dies; and then the child (or a substitute) is alive again; and then the mother comes back, too. (1940, p. 46)

Anthony further suggested that the oscillation tendency can be traced back to the mother–infant feeding interaction. First in fantasy, then in overt behavior, the infant may exchange places (oscillate) with the mother with respect to who is feeding and who is being fed. "Infants barely weaned, long before they can walk or talk, may be seen spontaneously to offer their biscuit to their mother to eat. . . ." Still another factor bears even more directly on the development of the death concept. The tendency for the child's cognitive pendulum to swing back and forth makes it natural to replace "He is dead" with

"I am dead"—and vice versa. This implies that the child does not go through two independent lines of development for personal mortality and death-of-the-other. Whenever the thought of death enters the mind of children, they are likely to put this idea through both passive and active orientations. Furthermore, the continuing alternations between self-and-other do not end where they started. The child's thoughts and feelings become increasingly enriched and refined. For example, the primitive idea of retaliation tends to be replaced by fantasies of reparation, which is a more complex and sophisticated concept.

The child's inclination to use "magical thinking" (thinking about something can make it happen) leads to emotional vulnerability when bad things happen. The death of a person or pet may lead to guilt feelings because the child has occasionally had some mean thoughts about them. By appreciating the child's back-and-forth processing of death-related events, adults may be in a better position to share their concerns and relieve their anxieties.

Anthony, like Maurer, also found that children can sometimes take pleasure in their dealings with death or all-goneness. This is most likely to occur when the child is playing out the role of the aggressor rather than the victim. I remember an incident in which delight burned in the eyes of a little girl who approached a family guest (by far the grouchiest of the adults) with a plump woolly caterpillar in hand. She displayed her find directly in front of Auntie Rosanne's eyes—and then pulled the unfortunate little creature apart. "Oooh! It's *juicy!*" the little killer squealed with undisguised satisfaction. Auntie's response was somewhat lacking in delight. Encounters of this sort may alarm some adults. If, however, we accept Anthony's frame of reference, it is natural and instructive for children to imagine themselves as both "producers" and "consumers" of death. Through a variety of experiments, some in their minds and some out in the world, the child continues to test and extend its emerging constructions of death.

Valuable if circumstantial evidence in support of Anthony's observations came later when Opie and Opie (1969) published *Children's Games in Street and Playground*. Children have delighted in playing death-related games for centuries—from ancient Rome to the present time. Opie and Opie demonstrate, for example, that hide-and-seek has many variations throughout the world (e.g., "Dead Man Arise") in which it is clear that "*It*" is the death-person who pursues the other children with a fatal tag to bestow. "Ring-around-the-rosie" became an elaborate and popular children's game during the plague years as "Ashes, ashes, all fall down" was an all too accurate representation of what was taking place about them. This line of research suggests strongly that children are, and probably always have been, fascinated by death and have attempted both to control their anxieties and improve their grasp of this mystery by incorporating death into their everyday thoughts, games, and rituals.

Despite—or because—of its wealth of observations and suggestions, Anthony's work has not fared very well. Perhaps her psychoanalytic approach has seemed too speculative for the tastes of later psychologists, or perhaps they have been discouraged by the discursive way in which her findings were presented. Nevertheless, there is much in Anthony's contributions that is still worth attention and which have yet to be tested systematically.

Nagy's Developmental Stages

The pioneering study conducted by Maria Nagy (1948/1959) has set the pattern for much of the subsequent research. She conducted this study in Budapest in the 1930s, although it did not enter the research literature until 1948 and then became more accessible when reprinted a decade later. Nagy met individually with 378 children (ages 3 to 10). The interview method was supplemented by asking the older children (6 to 10) to make drawings that represented their ideas of death and to explain these drawings. Furthermore, children aged 7 and above were asked to "Write down everything that comes to your mind about death." Her sample was almost equally divided between girls and boys, and she made an effort to include children with various social and religious backgrounds as well as with a broad spectrum of intellectual functioning.

Nagy found that her results could be categorized into three major developmental phases, although there was some overlapping:

1. *Stage one: up to about age 5*
The preschool child usually *does not recognize that death is final.* However, the child also looks upon death as being continuous with life, that is, *deadness is a dimunution of aliveness.* A close relationship is

seen between death and departure. The person who has gone away is sort of dead. And the dead person has sort of gone away. "To die . . . means the same as living on but under changed circumstances. If someone dies no change takes place in him, but rather our lives change since we can no longer see the dead person as he no longer lives with us." Given this interpretation, the child is mostly likely to be distressed by death's most palpable aspect: *separation.*

> Most children, however, are not satisfied when someone dies, that he should merely disappear, but want to know where and how he continues to live. Most of the children connected the facts and absence and funerals. In the cemetery one lives on. Movement is to a certain degree limited by the coffin, but . . . the dead are still capable of growth. they take nourishment, they breathe. They know what is happening on earth. They feel it if someone thinks of them and they even feel sorry for themselves. Thus the dead lie in the grave. However, the children realize—with a resulting aversion for death—that this life is limited, not so complete as our life. Some of them consider this diminished life exclusively restricted to sleep. (Nagy, p. 83)

In this first stage, the children often begin their remarks with the description of a death perception. The perception itself appears authentic and accurate enough. It is the mental elaboration that goes astray (according to adult standards). This characteristic of Nagy's protocols is consistent with the view that the young child can notice the essential facets of death-related phenomena, but does not yet possess a mature framework within which to interpret and contain them. The young child's egocentricity is also very much in evidence: much of the "deadness" comes from the deceased's invisibility to and distance from one's self. Furthermore, the dead are understood with reference to one's own experiences (e.g., they don't get as hungry as I do).

2. *Stage two: between the ages of 5 and 9*

The child now seems to comprehend that *death is final*. However, one does not have to die, not if one is clever and lucky. This conception was often offered by Nagy's respondent in the form of *death personifications*. Although images of death in the form of a person were reported at all ages in the Nagy study, this was the dominant view for the 5-to-9 range. Two forms of the personification were found: death seen as a separate person, and death as himself being a dead person. Some children spoke about a "death-man" who goes about at night. (Most personifications were male when gender was specified.) The death-man is difficult to see, although one might get a glimpse of him just before he carries you away. But death might also be a skeleton-man, an angel, or someone who looks like a circus clown, among other variations.

The protective feature here is evident the death-man can be avoided by an alert and resourceful person. Run faster than the death-man, lock the door, trick him. Find a way to elude Mr. Death, and you will not die.

3. *Stage three: ages 9 and 10 (and, presumably, thereafter)* The oldest children in Nagy's study usually recognized that *death is inevitable and universal as well as final*. There is no escape, no matter how clever or fast we are. The 10-year-old knows that everybody in the world will die. "It is a thing from which our bodies cannot be resurrected. It is like the withering of flowers," as a 10-year-old girl explained to Nagy. At this point it would seem that the child has attained an adult conception of death—but we should not be too hasty with that conclusion.

What Has Been Learned from More Recent Contributions?

The personifications that were reported so frequently by Hungarian children in the late 1940s have turned up only occasionally in subsequent studies. It is possible that Nagy's respondents were more influenced by folk traditions than subsequent generations of children, especially in the United States, who were far more likely to absorb their stories from television than from storytellers and books who were still mining the old traditions. We also appear to live in a media-saturated world in which technology appears more powerful and attractive than the magic and mystery of "fairy tales." Perhaps children have decided to ally themselves with the power of technology and, as a consequence, have found less place in their imagination for personifications of the old-fashioned sort. Supernatural explanations no longer seem to be popular among children—although perhaps of renewed appeal to adults!

The curious drop-out in personifications is the major difference between Nagy's original findings and those of subsequent studies.

Nagy's basic conclusion that death concepts undergo a decisive development from early through later childhood remains intact. It takes some time for the child to recognize that death is final, inevitable, and universal A useful addition was Koocher's (1973) finding that the chronological age of a child is not as important as its level of maturation. An independent measure of developmental level predicts the child's conceptions of death better than chronological age.

Research has been rather sparse in recent years and repetitive of the early studies. A series of studies by Brent (Michael's father!) and his colleagues, however, have provided new findings and ideas. These studies focused on the components of the death construct we have already discussed, but also considered *nonfunctionality* to be a separate concept. Nonfunctionality was defined as "the understanding that once a person's body is dead it cannot do *any* of the things it did when it was alive (e.g., eating, breathing, loving, learning)" (Brent, Speece, Lin, Dong, & Yang, 1996, p. 68). In a previous study (Speece & Brent, 1992) they took particular note of the children who did *not* demonstrate a maturing understanding of death at various age levels. There was a curious finding here. Fewer third graders demonstrated their understanding of the finality and nonfunctionality of death than did second graders. More than three times as many third graders thought that under certain conditions a dead person might become alive, and some also thought that, while dead, they could also do some life-like things, such as feeling sad. How could this be? Is it possible to lose an achievement in cognitive development so soon after acquiring it?

The researchers considered several alternative explanations. The explanation that seemed best to fit all the facts was the *emergence of a new level of conceptualization*:

> The third graders were exhibiting the first signs of the emergence in older children of a new awareness of some of the complexities involved in modern adults' conceptualizations of the relationship between life and death—one which differs . . . from the previously presumed mature adult conceptualization. (Brent et al., p. 69)

The emergence hypothesis was subsequently investigated in a study of Chinese and U.S. children. The finding of most interest here is the decrease of binary logic from earlier to later childhood. This type of thought may be better known as either-or thinking. Everything has to be one way or another, true or false, good or bad, strong or weak. Those who use binary logic as their primary way of interpreting the world are most likely to hold that one must be either living or dead, with no middle ground. They are also likely to give firm yes or no answers to other questions about life and death. Older children, though, are starting to appreciate that situations often are more complex, not reducible to either-or categories. Maturing cognitively and having more experience with the world seems to encourage "fuzzy logic." This type of thought will continue to develop as appreciation grows for ambiguities, uncertainties, and multiple frames of reference. It is as though leaving the world of childhood means entering a new and more complex domain in which one, perhaps reluctantly, surrenders the comfort of either-or categories in order to pursue a more mature understanding of both life and death.

Effect of Maturational and Environmental Factors

Most psychologists believe that development represents the interaction of maturational, environmental, and situational factors. Anthony, Nagy, and Piaget are among the many who share this general view, although differing in their specific approaches.

Powerful life experiences do affect the children's cognitions of death. Myra Bluebond-Langner found that all the children who were 3 years of age or older became aware that they were dying before death was close. The following sequence usually appeared: "the children moved from a view of themselves as 'seriously ill' to 'seriously ill but likely to get better,' and then to 'always ill but likely to get better.' This was followed by a perception of self as 'always ill and not likely to get better' and, finally, to a view of themselves as dying" (Bluebond-Langner, 1989a, p. 47).

This sequence of cognitive formulations depended upon the child's opportunity to make certain kinds of observation. For example, children would notice that parents and other adults had started to treat them differently after the diagnosis was made. At first the diagnosis itself did not mean much to the children, but the change in adult behavior did convey a message that they needed to decode. They did not draw the conclusion that they were dying until they had undergone a sequence of experiences, including awareness of the death of another sick child they had known. Basically, they seemed to learn a series of events that can happen to children with leukemia and then figure out where they fit into that sequence. Clearly, the endangered children's thoughts about death had been influenced by their circumstances. And it is also clear that the children had been working hard at trying to understand their situation: after some time and experience they "take all of these isolated bits and pieces of information and put them into a larger perspective, the cycle of relapses and remissions."

At various times the same child might express several different views of death:

> . . . as separation, mutilation, loss of identity, the result of a biological process that is inevitable and irreversible. Death comes across as many things, even contradictory things at once. For example, one 5-year-old concerned about separation who talked about worms eating him and refused to play with toys from deceased children was the same 5-year-old who knew that the drugs had run out and demanded that time not be wasted. . . . We find views of death that one would expect for children their age as well as ones we would not. . . . When a child is dying, his or her experiences are very different from other children of the same age, and hence the accepted developmental model of children's view of death is not as applicable for the dying child as it would be for healthy children. (Bluebond-Langner, 1989b, p. 9)

These children's increasing understanding of death seem to demonstrate points made by Carey (1985) through their rapidly improving knowledge of biomedical facts and Brent et al. (1996) through their recognition of complexity.

The siblings of dying children also face special challenges, as studies by Bluebond-Langner (1996) and others have found. Both dying children and their siblings are under intense pressure to understand what is happening and what it means to them. It would be a seriously flawed developmental theory that could not incorporate such vital situational dynamics as life-threatening illness into its scope.

Understanding and Helping Marjorie

Let us take one example in which knowledge, theory, and practice were brought together. What should be done—if anything—when one of the 3-year-olds participating in the activities of a children's center becomes terminally ill? This was the question faced by the instructors in a Pittsburgh preschool program (Pohlman, 1984).

Marjorie was a 3-year-old enrolled in this preschool program. She had already been under treatment for cancer. The two instructors experienced "dismay and fear with a touch of anger" when they first saw Marjorie: She had lost her hair as a result of chemotherapy, and the tumor had caused the loss of one eye, which had been replaced by a prosthesis. The instructors faced the challenge of coping with their own personal anxieties as well as the effects on the other children if Marjorie was accepted into the class. They decided to accept Marjorie and to integrate her into the group "as normally as possible and . . . deal with her differences as they came up in the normal context of the program" (Pohlman, 1984, p. 125).

The instructors were well prepared for this challenge. They knew that (a) children did think about death, and in a distinctive way that intertwined reality and fantasy it was normal for them to have some personal anxieties; this did not have to be denied, but could be worked through; (b) the children would probably have a variety of concerns that would be expressed over time and in many different ways; and that (c) the teachers would need to be good listeners and observers who were able to respond to subtle meanings as well as to the surface communications. In finding the courage to accept this challenge, the instructors drew not only upon their personal resources, but also upon readings in the dying and death literature. Perhaps the most essential fact was simply that the topic of children and death had been legitimatized. In the past, the implicit message had been that one should pretend children are unaware of death, and that adults can really protect them from all death encounters. Now it was not only acceptable to face death together with children, but a potential growth experience for everyone involved. Furthermore, the prevailing philosophy in the new death-related literature asserted the rights of the dying person. People who are facing death should not be isolated and rejected because of society's own anxieties.

The instructors integrated Marjorie's wig into the category of the different types of clothing that the children wore (red shirt, green shirt, blond wig). The discussion eventually expanded to include illness and medicine. It turned out that many of the other children had their own concerns about doctors, hospitals, injections, and so forth. Had

Marjorie not been in the program, the other children probably would not have had the opportunity to express their own health-related concerns and have some of their questions answered.

The children became especially concerned about Marjorie when she came to class with a patch over one socket. Her prosthetic had been removed to be enlarged. This led to discussion about "pretend eyes."

> The children were given bandages, gauze, cottonballs, old syringes, and stethoscopes as part of their free play equipment. The intensity of their play indicated the impact of our discussion. There was not a sound in the room as the children administered medicine and cared for their babies. Many of the babies' eyes were covered with bandages, and during the play several children, including Marjorie, tested the problems of eye loss by covering first one and then the other of their own eyes. This play continued for several days. When we held back the materials thinking it was time to move on, the children asked for them. Children most often played the roles of parent, nurse, or doctor. . . . The doctors always were able to make these babies better. . . . Soon the children's interest in the hospital play waned, and they returned to the usual preschool activities. (Pohlman, 1984, p. 127)

We can see in this description some evidence of the oscillation phenomena that were reported by Anthony: the children first chose to play the role of the patient, then became competent adult caregivers. We also see the value of allowing the children themselves to decide how much time they need to experiment with loss before moving on to something else. Furthermore, through the group activity and the instructors' approval, the children had the opportunity to learn that it was acceptable to notice and respond to loss: they didn't have to keep all their fears to themselves or their curiosity under wraps.

Marjorie died rather suddenly during the 7th week of school. She was one of several children who had been ill, apparently with the flu. The class had been acknowledging the absence of the sick children during each day's "sharing time." During the next day's sharing time, the instructors introduced the topic by talking about Marjorie's eye. Some of the children hoped that she would be able to see again. When the instructors said that this was not so, the class began to come apart. The children showed a high level of anxiety and started to talk to each other about other things—anything but Marjorie and her pretend eye. "We had to insist on quiet and attention, assuring the children they would have their turn to talk later." The instructors explained that the doctors had done everything they could, but that Marjorie had died. They described cancer as "being inside of you where no one can see; so we had not known how sick Marjorie was." They also emphasized that many people with cancer do get better, and then they spoke of their sadness that Marjorie would not come back to school, and that they would not see her again.

Over the next several days the children expressed curiosity and concern about many aspects of Marjorie's illness and death. The teachers attempted to answer the questions simply and specifically; they also tried to help the children differentiate between her illness and other illnesses that they or their family members had experienced. Some questions were asked over and over again, such as, "Is cancer like a cold in your eye?" The children seemed to be checking the instructors out to see if the answers were still the same. Some information the teachers had previously given to the children now made it more difficult for them to integrate the facts associated with Marjorie's death. For example, they had learned that shots and medication and doctors help to keep you from getting sick: but look what had happened to Marjorie!

The pattern of response to Marjorie's death extended over time and took many forms. Hospital play resumed, but now the doctors could not always make the babies well. In other games, such as cops and robbers, people also died sometimes. Some sad-looking children seemed to wait for others to express the feelings they could not put into words themselves. Returning to the same preschool program a year later, the children spoke occasionally of Marjorie and raised further questions about her. Throughout all this time, the teachers and the program director had remained in frequent contact with the parents and kept them informed of what was taking place.

Pohlman remarks that their own anxiety-motivated evasion of Marjorie's impending death interfered with opportunities to offer preparatory experiences for the children. "For example, when a gerbil died . . . we did not talk with the children about it. Talking about death at this point would have given them an experience to build upon later." She also felt they might have had more open communication with the parents in advance of Marjorie's death, thereby perhaps reducing subsequent anxieties.

Adult anxiety in death-related situations is common, and so are the effects of anxiety on our thought processes. We do not "deny" most of the facts. We do not deny the situation is serious. We cope with many of the changes and challenges. However, we allow ourselves the secret comfort of holding back that further concession to reality, that chilling conclusion, "Yes, it is so: death." The preschool instructors were just being normal human beings in leaving themselves the hidden mental escape hatch, the thought that "Marjorie is not really going to die—not now, not soon, not while I'm teaching this class" (p. 129). This was not only a private arrangement within the mind of each participating adult, but also seemed to be the group's strategy.

We have looked at this sequence of experiences in some detail because it emphasizes the importance of sharing death-related experiences with children. Even very young children are sensitive to absence, separation, disfiguring changes, loss, and other phenomena associated with death. It is also evident that children hone their minds on death-related phenomena as part of their general grasp of the world: curiosity and concern are engaged when they observe disappearances, decay, nonresponsiveness, and so forth. As adults we will not succeed in protecting them from all such experiences—and, as adults, we will be modeling attitudes toward death that are either open or closed, consistent or inconsistent, anxious or comforting.

Marjorie's peers in the preschool program probably experienced some anxieties that would not have entered their lives at that moment if she had been excluded from the class or if the instructors had worked diligently to deceive them. However, they probably also drew some valuable lessons about life and death, including the feeling that people have the strength to cope with sad and frightening things; we do not have to keep all these bad feelings and confused thoughts to ourselves. But the instructors were handicapped to some extent by the relative lack of attention to death-related issues in teacher education. The major theoretical orientations and data bases that are influential in schools of education still resemble Marjorie's "pretend eye" when it come to death-related phenomena. The instructors had come across some relevant literature, and this proved useful. But they had not been given much opportunity to explore their own thoughts and feelings about death and to develop skills specific to the challenging situation that confronted them here. It may not be realistic to expect teachers and other human service providers to be expert in helping children cope with death when this issue has been neglected in their own educational background.

REFERENCES

Anthony, S. (1940). *The child's discovery of death*. London: Routledge & Kegan Paul.

Anthony, S. (1972). *The discovery of death in childhood and after*. New York: Basic Books.

Atwood, V. A. (1984). Children's conceptions of death: A descriptive study. *Child Study Journal, 14,* 11–29.

Bluebond-Langner, M. (1989a). Children, dying. In R. Kastenbaum & B. K. Kastenbaum (Eds.), *Encyclopedia of death* (pp. 46–48). Phoenix, AZ: Oryx Press.

Bluebond-Langner, M. (1989b). Worlds of dying children and their well siblings. *Death Studies, 13,* 1–16.

Bluebond-Langner, M. (1996). *In the shadow of illness*. Princeton, NJ: Princeton University Press.

Brent, S. B. (1977–1978). Puns, metaphors, and misunderstandings in a two-year-old's conception of death. *Omega, Journal of Death and Dying, 8,* 285–294.

Brent, S. B., Speece, M. W., Lin, C., Dong, Q., & Yang, C. (1996). The development of the concept of death among Chinese and U.S. children 3–17 years of age: From binary to "fuzzy" concepts? *Omega, Journal of Death and Dying, 33,* 67–84.

Carey, S. (1985). *Conceptual changes in childhood*. Cambridge, MA: MIT Press.

Costa, P. T., Jr., & Kastenbaum, R. (1967). Some aspects of memories and ambitions in centenarians. *Journal of Genetic Psychology, 110,* 3–16.

Goldstein, K. (1939). *The organism*. New York: American Book.

Hall, G. S. (1922). *Senescence*. New York: Appleton.

Haussamen, B. (1998). Death and syntax. *Death Studies, 22,* 307–320.

Koocher, D. (1973). Childhood, death, and cognitive development. *Developmental Psychology, 9,* 369–375.

Lewin, K. (1936). *Principles of topological psychology*. New York: McGraw-Hill.

Maurer, A. (1966). Maturation of concepts of death. *British Journal of Medicine and Psychology, 39,* 35–41.

Moriarty, D. M. (1967). *The loss of loved ones*. Springfield, IL: Charles C Thomas.

Nagy, M. (1959). The child's view of death. In H. Feifel (Ed.), *The meaning of death* (pp. 79–98). New York: McGraw-Hill. (Original work published 1948)

Opie, I., & Opie, R. (1969). *Children's games in street and playground.* London: Oxford University Press.

Piaget, J. (1954). *The construction of reality in the child.* New York: Basic Books.

Piaget, J., & Inhelder, B. (1959). *The growth of logical thinking from childhood to adolescence.* New York: Basic Books.

Pohlman, J. C. (1984). Illness and death of a peer in a group of three-year-olds. *Death Studies, 8,* 123–136.

Schactel, E. G. (1959). *Metamorphosis.* New York: Basic Books.

Seale, C. (1998). *Constructing death.* Cambridge, UK: Cambridge University Press.

Sheets-Johnstone, M. (1990). *The roots of thinking.* Philadelphia: Temple University Press.

Speece, M. W., & Brent, S. B. (1992). The acquisition of a mature understanding of three components of the concept of death. *Death Studies, 16,* 221–229.

Tobin, S. (1972). The earliest memory as data for research in aging. In D. P. Kent, R. Kastenbaum, & S. Sherwood (Eds.), *Research, planning, and action for the elderly* (pp. 252–278). New York: Behavioral Publications.

Weisman, A. D. (1974). *The realization of death.* New York: Jason Aronson.

Werner, H. (1957). *Comparative psychology of mental development.* New York: International Universities Press.

3

Reconstructing Death in Adolescence and Adulthood

Three teens are lounging after school before heading home. They have seen a video on death and grief in one of their classes.

Brent: I never think about that stuff.

Martina: There's nothing you can do about it, any how.

Alicia: I think about it all the time.

Brent: Yeah, well . . . me, too. But I'm never going to die, you know.

Alicia: Me, too, not as long as I keep thinking about it.

Martina: Isn't there anything else to talk about?

Author's observation

There's a certain amount of denial in swordfishing. . . . Once you're in the denial business, it's hard to know when to stop. Captains routinely overload their boats, ignore storm warnings, stow their life rafts in the wheel house, and disarm their emergency radio beacons. Coast Guard inspectors say that going down at sea is so unthinkable to many owner-captains that they don't even take basic precautions.

—Sebastian Junger, The Perfect Storm

I can recall the hour in which I lost my immortality, in which I tried on my shroud for the first time and saw how it became me. . . . The knowledge of my dying came to me when my mother died. There was more than sorrow involved. Her vanished voice echoes in my head and the love she bore me struggled painfully to stay alive around me. But my heart did not claw at the emptied space where she had stood and demand her return. I accepted death for both of us. I went and returned dry-eyed from the burial, but I brought death back with me. I had been to the edge of the world and looked over its last foot of territory into nothingness.

—Ben Hecht: A Child of the Century

Children take a lively interest in death, loss, change, and separation. This interest ranges from high-spirited curiosity to panic and terror. Their understanding of death-related phenomena grows rapidly under the influence of sociocultural values, their distinctive personal life experiences, and the force of maturation. As we have seen in the previous chapter, one can either emphasize children's imperfect grasp of death or their resourceful attempts to comprehend the nature of mortality.

Now it is time to consider cognitive and attitudinal orientations toward death throughout the adolescent and adult years. It is generally held that the basics of mental development are accomplished during adolescence. Brent, Martina, and Alicia, for example, should all be capable of understanding that death is universal. The seasoned mariner who has become captain of a swordfishing vessel should certainly understand the life-threatening hazards of his occupation. The reporter Ben Hecht, having written many newspaper articles about murders, suicides, and funerals, should have accepted death long before his mother's passing (although we are not always clear about what we mean by "accept").

There is a lesson here: We cannot focus on basic cognitive operations alone. Instead we must try to understand how adolescents and adults apply their thinking abilities to death-related issues. Perhaps the central question here is the following: *Why do people who "know all about death" from a cognitive standpoint so often behave as though they didn't have a clue?* A related question also demands attention: *Assuming that we all understand the basics of life and death, why do we differ so much in our death-related attitudes and behaviors?* Why did I shave my skull, adorn my flesh with those nasty deathhead tattoo's, and sail forth as a skinhead while you were preparing yourself for a life-saving career as nurse or physician? Why do some of our neighbors diet, jog, and load up on health-store formulations to extend their lives as long as possible, while other neighbors drink, drive, and smoke as though impatient to coil off this mortal shuffle as soon as possible? We will not be able to answer such questions with naive confidence, but we will heighten our awareness of how death often is reconstructed in adolescence and adulthood.

DEVELOPING A MATURE VIEW OF DEATH

There is a more or less standard story about mental development. Some important elements remain in doubt, and theoreticians differ in their emphases. Nevertheless, it will be useful to remind ourselves of this story before turning specifically to the understanding of death through the adult years.

Parallels Between Physical and Mental Growth

There are relatively clear guidelines for physical development from conception through adolescence. Children grow taller, transform their proportions, become more coordinated, and become pubescent. Developmental psychologists have attempted to chart a similar course for mental growth. In its simplest form, this approach would establish criteria for cognitive performance at various age points. School systems cherish this approach because it provides standard expectations for performance at a given grade level.

Even in its simplest form, though, this concept of a uniform progression in mental development is complicated by a myriad of influences that affect cognitive achievement and performance. The home and school environments can make a tremendous difference, as can sensory or linguistic problems that interfere with learning. The method of instruction may also have differential effects, encouraging some students and discouraging others. Furthermore, we have already seen that chronological age is not identical with developmental level. Children in the same classroom may differ markedly in both their specific cognitive skills and their overall comprehension of the world.

The parallel between physical and mental growth becomes increasingly undependable as time goes by. Children who are relatively undersized for their age may be endowed with keen intellectual and social skills, for example. For all of its powerful organismic effects, the onset of puberty does not necessarily boost overall cognitive functioning. There is still another reason to avoid thinking of physical and mental development as proceeding in lockstep. Intelligence takes many forms and employs many styles. Sternberg's (1988) influential theory of intelligence, for example, distinguishes among three kinds of cognitive ability: those involved in (a) academic performance, (b) dealing with practical life situations, and (c) creative or novelty-seeking thought. Other researchers and theoreticians have also argued persuasively that we have a broad range of abilities and, therefore, a given person may excel in one sphere but not necessarily another. By contrast, few are likely to argue that "Joanna is tall in some ways, but not in others."

The challenge of tracking cognitive development becomes even greater beyond childhood. This challenge requires us to let go of the expectation that mental growth obligingly chugs along with physical development. We have a much better idea of "how tall is tall enough," but a much less secure idea of "how insightful/creative/wise is enough." The problem becomes more complex, but also more interesting, when we inspect the supposed outcome of cognitive development that is most relevant here: the "mature" view of death.

What Is the Mature View of Death?

There are two obvious streams of theory and research from which to draw in formulating the mature view of death: Piaget's extensive work on the development of thought from infancy to adolescence and studies of children's ideas about death, as reviewed in the previous chapter. Actually, these two streams flow together much of the way, as many studies on death constructions have either been guided by or interpreted within Piaget's framework (Piaget, 1972; Piaget & Inhelder, 1959).

The most salient idea is that with adolescence comes the emergence of *formal thought operations*. One can now think abstractly and go beyond what is apparent in the immediate situation. The adolescent discovers new connections among people, events, and processes. One can play with thought more resourcefully. Instead of taking things as they seem to be, the adolescent can take them apart and, if so disposed, put them together in a different way—repeating the young child's play with blocks, perhaps, but at a much higher conceptual level.

Of particular interest is the adolescent's ability to imagine alternative futures. Things could happen this way or that way. One can invent both delicious and appalling future scenarios. This new ability to escape into the future can provide the foundation for a distinctive and rewarding adult life, for temporary diversion and relief, or for episodes of apprehension and depression—and sometimes for all of these outcomes, and more!

Piagetian-oriented studies conclude that children have acquired the adult conception of death when they realize that mortality is universal (everybody dies), personal (me, too), inevitable (can't hide from it), and final or irreversible. These would seem to be the characteristics of a mature view of death. However, there are some questions worth considering.

How Stable Is the Standard Adult Construction of Death?

It is often assumed that a concept, once grasped, remains in our grasp. (An exception is sometimes made for the possible decline of intellectual abilities with advanced age or as the effect of illness and trauma). There is surprisingly little evidence, however, to support this assumption. We cannot say with confidence that people who comprehend and utilize formal operations in adolescence are still doing so at midlife. This means that we also cannot say that the 13-year-old's insights about death remain within his or her active intellectual repertoire even a few years later.

Is this a strange notion—that a developmental achievement can be diminished, lost, or squandered, perhaps in just a few years? Yes, but not so strange when we recover from our initial surprise. A distinguished lifespan developmental psychologist observes that:

> The intellectual processes required for the acquisition of cognitive structures and functions in childhood are not necessarily relevant to the maintenance of functions and the reorganization of structures that may be needed to meet the demands of later life. (Schaie, 1995, p. 513)

We may have a strong need for certain intellectual structures at a particular time in our lives, but it is possible that these structures could become less relevant or even the source of difficulty at a later point. It is also likely that after childhood there are much greater individual differences in how we think. Personality, life experiences, and task demands could shape our thinking into divergent patterns. One child may become an adult whose thinking is dominated by the desire to develop and maintain crucial interpersonal relationships. Another may become engrossed in an occupation that requires sustained painstaking attention to objective details (e.g., numbers or design and operation of complex equipment). Neither may be called upon to exercise abstract thinking and might even find themselves subject to snubs and resistance if they engage in creative and imaginative thought.

Perhaps, then, the standard cognitive model of mature death construction is of less value to adults than it is to older children and adolescents who have urgent problems of identity to solve. Death is a different kind of threat to those who have yet to become the person they hope to be, as compared with the arrived adult who has tasted much more of life and found a more or less settled place. Perhaps some of us need only a brief period of intense stewing over death. With a mixture of intellectual triumph and emotional stress we come to terms with universality and the other primary cognitive elements of a mature construction of death. But who needs to think so rigorously about death all the time? *The intellectual conquest of death in adolescence may also be the signal to stash this insight away so it will not interfere with continued enjoyment of life.* Mad Magazine's Alfred E. Neuman contributed a once very popular phrase to our culture: "What, me worry?" Were Alfred a flesh-and-blood personage, though, he probably would have done a lot of worrying *before* he could shrug off concerns about life and death.

We might, then, advance the proposition that the standard mature concept of death must accord with the individual's total life situation if it is to stay on active duty. If, for example, I feel I must put my life at exceptional risk for some purpose, I might deactivate my understanding of death. Action in an emergency situation might be delayed and confused if I stop to think about the meaning of death. If a person very dear to me has died, I may also choose to believe that she is still with me somehow, and that I will see her again in the next life—wishes that are not easily reconciled with the purely cognitive model. This hypothesis must include the corollary that we can maintain a potential repertoire of cognitive structures or models but keep some of them on the inactive list when they do not seem to accord with our needs of the moment. I need a guiding principle that will help me deal with a difficult situation. Thinking about death might not seem to be the most useful guide when there are crucial life decisions to be made. This approach may lack something in logic, but it is steeped in psycho-logic.

Does Everybody Develop a Mature Construction of Death?

No.

Some people do not have the intellectual endowment for abstract thought. This does not mean that they are insensitive to crucial facets of death—separation, loss, grief, progressive illness. The judicial system recognizes that people may have various levels of competence to make decisions on their own behalf. Residents in a facility for people with significant development impairments may have the competence to make a number of everyday life decisions for themselves and often will be encouraged to do so. There will be a sequence of due process steps taken, however, if a life-or-death medical decision arises. It may be judged that this person does not have a sufficient understanding of death or of the relative risks and benefits of alternative procedures, thereby passing the decision to people who have a more adequate understanding of the decision.

The issue is not always clear-cut. I have known institutional residents who were regarded as incompetent to manage their affairs, but who seem to have had insight into the basic meanings of death. I have also known people leading apparently normal lives in the community who showed no grasp of abstractions, including universality and finality. At this point we know very little about how many adults have ever have developed the standard mature conception of death, nor of the personality characteristics of those who do and those who don't.

Is There Only One Mature Way to Think of Death?

Everybody who lives dies and stays dead. It is difficult to dispute this conclusion while we are wearing the cap of objectivistic and rational thought. Obviously, though, there are a great many people who believe otherwise, as well as those who hold at least two sets of apparently contradictory beliefs. There have been more believers than disbelievers in survival of death since the beginnings of human society. This view cannot be dismissed as a foible of the immature. Some of the wisest and most intelligent people have cherished beliefs that are not countenanced within the standard model.

Furthermore, there have been and still are many cultures in which death is not seen as it is through the eyes of Western logic. For example, anthropologists have often told us about societies in which most if not all deaths are the result of sorcery. This is a consequential difference in belief, because the death of an important member of the group must then be revenged by attacking the supposed culprit. Cultural differences extend to the basic conception of life and death. In the Euro-American sphere, we tend to see life and death as sharply divided. Some cultures see more of a continuity. There may even be differences in the deadness of the dead (with the newly dead not as removed from the living as the long-dead).

There is a tension, then, a conflict between developmental psychology's claims for a mature model of death and the broader spectrum of belief that does not find a comfort zone within that model. This conflict will not be resolved here, especially since much of it centers around issues of religious belief that are best considered within a theological context. There are, however, some matters of concern within the psychological sphere as well.

1.   *Personal conflict between the claims of logic and belief.*

It is a little misleading to separate logic and belief: there are logical sequences within belief systems, and faith in reason is a form of belief. Nevertheless, many people have undergone personal crises as they attempt to resolve experiential conflicts between reason and faith. St. Thomas Aquinas is but one of many major figures in religious history whose intellect raised painful doubts about the faith he cherished. Youth is perhaps the prime time for religious crisis, a phenomenon that is sometimes underestimated because sexuality and independence are also under construction at the same time. Others experience a religious crisis later in life as the consequence of personal catastrophes, such as the death of a child. The issue is seldom restricted to the meaning of death per se. People may find themselves rethinking their assumptions about God and the purpose of life.

Psychologists might give more attention to intrapsychic struggles in which "cold logic" and the "heart's desire" both assert their claims to construct the most persuasive model of death. A challenge here is our ability to respect both forces. An additional challenge is to avoid imposing our personal views on those who we may be in a position to counsel and help. It might also be useful for us to become more comfortable with the fact that people can alternate between one conception and another. It may be recalled that Anthony (1972) observed an oscillation phenomenon in children's attempts to understand death (e.g., playing the killer one moment and the victim the next moment). As adults we may also experiment with alternative constructions of death and achieve personal growth by so doing.

2.   *Maturity: an established scientific fact or a concealed value judgment?*

Maturity is generally considered to be a positive value. To call people "immature" is to downgrade them and discredit their ideas, beliefs, and achievements. This unfortunate usage can not only be harmful in our personal relationships, but can also muddle our understanding of theoretical issues.

May I suggest that we exercise caution in characterizing a person's views of death as either mature or immature. It is all too easy to ignore or dismiss another person's perspective by labeling it as immature. A more useful approach would be to try to understand the other person's perspective on its own terms and within that person's total life context. Biologists tend to use terms such as "maturity" in a qualified sense— qualified by very specific rules and observations. Social and behavioral scientists tend to be looser and more variable in their definitions. It may still be "premature," then, to speak of an established mature construction of death as though we are working from a tightly defined and well-supported data base. If we are not to get too far ahead of ourselves, perhaps it would be wiser to leave open the possibility that *intelligent adults may have several ways of conceptualizing death.* In particular, we should leave open the possibility that some people may develop new and perhaps more sophisticated conceptions of death in their later adult years as a facet of deepening wisdom. With advancing age and experience some of us may become more adept in the interpretation of life's challenges and contingencies.

This does not necessarily mean that long-lived people have all the answers. In my own interactions with aged people I have more often found an attitude of equanimity about the days that have "dwindled down to a precious few." The cognitive side of this attitude is seldom encountered among youth. A man in his late eighties, burdened with several life-threatening conditions, put it this way:

> Yes, I've thought about all of that. Of course I have. But I don't *know.* Nobody does, whatever they say. But, you know, not knowing doesn't bother me any more. Why should I expect to know everything? (Q: So how do you think about life and death today?) Today—that's how I think about it—today. That's the day it always is, isn't it?

To some extent, what we call "wisdom" may be the ability to discover what we can about life and death and come to a state of equanimity about what remains a mystery. Perhaps we can find our own balance between the quest for knowing and the acceptance of unknowing as we now undertake a brief exploration of thoughts of death throughout the adolescent and adult years.

WORKING AND PLAYING WITH THE THOUGHT OF DEATH FROM YOUTH THROUGH OLD AGE

I have noticed several types of cognitive operation that we often call upon when we either work or play with our constructions of death. Four of these operations—or mental gymnastics—are worth identifying at the outset.

1. *Awareness versus habituation or denial.* This represents a complex set of perceptual and cognitive operations, but it comes down to the choice between accepting or dismissing a signal. When reading the newspaper this morning I experienced so familiar a conflict that it almost went without notice. Yes, I wanted to learn what was happening; but no, I did not want to read about any more murders, accidents, or ecological disasters. My information processing system was all set to read about everything of possible interest. At the same time, my anxiety-reduction system attempted to shield me from the worst of the day's crop of bad news. If this were a particularly stressful time in my life I might rely so heavily on my antianxiety shield that today's news glances off without touching me. If I am feeling more secure and ready for challenges, I will lower (but never quite deactivate) my antianxiety shield so that I might continue my contact with ongoing realities. Chances are that at least one signal of human distress will get through. I will again become aware of our common vulnerability and mortality. I will lose my distance. I will feel something

2. *Activation versus inactivation of a death construct.* If I have become "alive to death," then I must do something with this signal. Should I activate or deactivate the various death constructs that are within in my repertory? Most theories assume that if we have concepts we will use them. I don't think so. Instead, I think we have linking mediating operations that give us the flexibility either to call upon or ignore the concepts we have developed at various points in the past. Perhaps, then, tomorrow morning I will allow myself to be pierced

by a death signal, but will not go so far as to think through its implications. So, like a self-repairing tire, I may have patched over my intense but momentary exposure to death by the time I have finished with the newspaper. I did not engage this signal with my death construct system, therefore I did not let it make a lasting impact on me. (Echo of Alfred E. Neuman: "What, me worry?")

3. *Reframing the signal.* This is a technique that can be used in an almost infinite variety of ways. I become aware of a death-related signal and I accept it as such. I now make a set of perceptual, cognitive, and symbolic arrangements that will have the effect of transforming the original meaning to something else—usually something less threatening. Perhaps I substitute professional or ideological jargon for the earthy emotional words that first rush to mind. I witnessed many examples of this legerdemain while I was a hospital director who met frequently with other health officials. Almost never was there discussion of real people really dying—but there were frequent bureaucratic rhapsodies that surrounded this theme (bolstered by references to "the bottom line"). I soon learned it would be a violation of the rules and offensive to tender bureaucratic sensitivities if I dared to speak of dying, death, and grief as the actual perils these posed for the actual (aged) patients in my charge. But if I would join in the reframing game, then I might accomplish something now and again by exchanging coded messages. Reframing can also accomplish its mission by making the urgent seem routine, the preventable seem out of our hands, or the tragic seem quaint and humorous. Unlike denial or habituation, reframing does acknowledge the existence of a death signal, but it transforms the original encounter to something that appears less threatening, more controllable.

4. *Interpreting death signals as special but compartmentalized phenomena.* People sometimes are able to cope with death signals in a highly focused and effective way. This efficiency, however, may be purchased at the cost of excluding the event from one's overall view of self and world—in other words, compartmentalized. Paramedics repeatedly find themselves in situations that encourage this approach. Unlike most other people, paramedics have been well trained to respond to life-and-death emergencies in the community. They often constitute the front line in the battle to save a life. Paramedics are not likely to shy away from a death-relevant situation: they do not deny what meets the eye; on the contrary, close and attentive observa-

tions will be made. Their basic death constructs will be activated as part of the recognition that this is a consequential situation. It is no time to indulge in the luxury of the antianxiety shield. Although paramedics frame life-and-death situations in a distinctive manner, this does not represent an evasion of reality, but, rather, a preparation to function effectively and with a minimum of wasted effort. The one "luxury" the paramedic has at this moment is to focus all attention on the job to be done. In fact, paramedics may experience emotional suffering if their thoughts are invaded by the broader implications of the situation.

Growing realization of the paramedic's burden of unresolved grief has led to increased attention to intensive discussion sessions after such experiences. By contrast, a person who has the time to reflect may interpret a particular death (even his or her own) as only one aspect of a larger pattern. Death is given its place, but it is not allowed to dominate one's entire thoughts and values (as will be seen in William McDougall's journal entries in the last weeks of his life, chapter 7).

Some Death Thought Games in Youth and Early Adulthood

The following examples of thought operations involving death are usually found more often in youth and early adulthood, but they are not practiced by all young people nor are they entirely neglected by their seniors.

"I Die, Therefore I Am"

This game, like all the others, is serious—that is why it is such a good game. During adolescence we reconstruct the ideas and attitudes that served us through most of childhood. It is during this process that some young men and women write poetry for the first and only time in their lives, and even characteristically unreflective people wonder why we are born to die and why girls (or boys) are so hard to figure out. Equipped with the ability to think more abstractly and flexibly than before, the adolescent and young adult also has a more vivid awareness of the dialectic between being and non-being (Kastenbaum, 1986). This is intensified by interest in futurity. "I might be this or I might be that—or, I might not *be!*"

A transitional, fragile, but very intense sense of selfhood may emerge at this time, formed around the dialectics of being and non-being. "This is who I am. I am the one who is torn by conflict. I am the one who wants to go back and go forward and not move at all. I am the one who has everything, I mean nothing, I mean everything to live for. I am the one who will live forever but who may die tomorrow." This kind of dialectic seems to be especially common in adolescence as active young minds recognize and attempt to cope with the inherent ambiguity of the future (Noppe & Noppe, 1996). It might be said that every future scenario proposes another version of one's self, and every imagined version of one's self proposes another future scenario.

The solution to both challenges may be found—temporarily—by drawing upon the power of metaphor. Dying is an especially potent metaphor during transitional situations and when one must cope with extremes of stimulus overload and deprivation. The same person may feel "bored to death" and slain by excitement ("I just died!") in passing from one unmodulated experience to another. Furthermore, one may also feel he or she is dying from the past of childhood without having yet reached the relatively secure ground of adulthood. In short, "I am the dying person" or "I die, therefore I am (still alive)." The adolescent, in this sense, *needs* the thought of death. It provides an image that resonates with core experiences. In a paradoxical way, the sense of dying is enlivening and the uncertain destination offers direction.

The rules that distinguish metaphorical from literal meaning, however, may collapse under pressure. For example, "if my life is like dying, then maybe dying is like my life. And if sleep is like death, then death should be like sleep. And if sex is so exciting I could just die, then death might be even more exciting than sex!" Do these metaphor-driven ideas seem strange to us—or oddly familiar from our own youthful meditation?

Often adolescents have little opportunity to try out their more lavish death-related thoughts on more experienced minds. A feeling may therefore spark an image that enlists a thought and encourages a course of action that actually threatens life. The three leading causes of death in adolescence—accident, homicide, suicide—are closely related to the victims' own behavior; it is probable they are also related to the intense, imaginative, but "unseasoned" mix of death-related constructs at this time of life.

"The Future Can Wait"

This mind game becomes appealing when one feels rushed—unprepared—toward an uncertain or alarming destination. It has been suggested that the catatonic form of schizophrenia is a strategy for controlling annihilation anxiety by controlling time and motion. "I do not act. I do not change. Therefore, time is suspended and death must wait." Adolescence is not catatonia. But many teenagers do feel themselves accelerating toward the future, hurtling rapidly from the known to the unknown. These were among my findings when I studied future time perspective and orientations toward death in high school students (Kastenbaum, 1959, 1961):

1.   Typically, the teenagers directed their thoughts to the future—but only to the near future. Almost everything important in life was just about to happen. By contrast, the second half of their projected life span was almost barren. Seldom did anybody mention even the fourth or fifth decade of their own lives, let alone the inconceivable years of advanced age.

2.   Much of the past was neglected or blanked out as well. They expressed a sense of uneasiness when asked to turn their thoughts toward their own childhood. "I wasn't anything!" is the way one high school senior put it, and he seemed to be speaking for most of his peers.

3.   The sense of rapid movement from the present to the future has already been mentioned. However, most of the teens had little idea about that future to which they were so rapidly hurtling. In reading the responses I could not avoid the impression of a person at the wheel of a hot sports car, tearing along a road without knowing—without *wanting* to know—what might lie beyond the next curve.

All these adolescents could conceive of futurity. They also had the intellectual ability to think about their lives as a whole: who they had been, who they were now, who they might become. Nevertheless, most seemed to have erected psychological barriers between their momentary selves and both their past and their adult selves. Subjectively, they existed in an intense, narrow chamber or tunnel that, despite its hectic pace, did not actually take them anywhere.

Two other studies may help us to put these findings into perspective. College students (males only) were asked a set of direct questions about death, such as, "I think about my own death . . . more than once a week, once a week, once a month, every few months." They were also given a time perspective task and the Picture Arrangement subtest of the Wechsler Adult Intelligence Scale, which some clinical psychologists regard as a measure of the capacity to anticipate future events. Dickstein and Blatt (1966) found that those who reported the most thinking about death showed a more limited tendency to project into the future. This finding is based upon correlational techniques and, like my studies, cannot demonstrate causality. Nevertheless, it does suggest that apprehension about death may be a major factor in the tendency of adolescents to allow themselves relatively little attention to their extended future. Perhaps one does not care to gaze too far down the road because he or she just might see something (i.e., *nothing*) there.

If death concern does restrain one's view of the future, then it may also impair the ability to plan ahead, to anticipate both hazards and opportunities. Somes teenagers might appear to be impulsive or short-sighted when in fact they are thoughtful people who have averted attention from all but the near future because the feared annihilation of self is "out there, someplace." The fact that adolescents have had a relatively limited opportunity to learn how to schedule and organize events in time may also make it difficult to "finesse" the future. Midlife adults are more likely to protect themselves from naked encounters with the thought of death by arranging their minds and schedules so that the "plannedness of time" serves as a subjective shield against the pricklers of mortality.

In a sense, then, adolescents have:

- More to lose from death because their desires and identity depend upon the uncertain and risky future for fulfillment
- Less experience in shaping and scheduling subjective time
- A sense of rushing (or being rushed) without a strong sense of destination
- Often, little opportunity to discuss life and death issues with mature adults who might serve as guides or models (because many adults are busy in being busy, that is, avoiding thoughts of death).

Given these circumstances, it might be comforting to let the future wait. Keep the excitement, keep the sense of motion and acceleration, but don't actually venture out too far into that murky place where annihilation is but one of the terrors. In reporting my earliest study on this topic (1959), I tried to make sense of the pattern of findings by suggesting that there may be a close link between the adolescents' rejection of their childhood past and their avoidance of their extended adult futurity. So similar were the statements they made about past and remote future that they seemed to come from the same psychological source. It was as though the dysphoric who-I-was-is-not-who-I-want-to-be past was hurled as far away as possible—into the formless future. This sets the individual up for more difficulty. Eventually, the comforting sense that time is holding fairly constant will be destablized, and the future become more real: such as, parents die or move to Florida, the first gray hair is discovered on one's own head. When forced to recognize the reality of change and futurity, one may encounter the anxious, dysphoric feelings that had been projected from childhood to the remote-seeming zone of middle and later adulthood.

The other study that may help some in understanding the adolescents' thoughts of death requested college students (all women) to write a set of six personal essays. These were to describe pleasant and unpleasant future events, pleasant and unpleasant past events, the earliest memory, and the day of one's death (McLaughlin & Kastenbaum, 1966). They were also asked to rate each of their essays on a scale of engrossment or self-involvement. Those who felt objective and detached, as though they had been writing about somebody else, would have low engrossment scores.

The young women described their own deaths in a tranquil and distant-manner, almost as though they were speaking about somebody else. This unruffled emotional tone and the omission of symptomatology had much in common with the imagined deathbed scenes I have collected during last several years and summarized in chapter 7. These young women placed their days of death well off into the future, usually into the "unimaginable age of 60!" as one commented, or beyond. Graceful, peaceful acceptance and resignation were the general themes. The self-engrossment scores were lower than for any of the other essays they were asked to write.

It would appear that these young women were not nearly as concerned with death as we might have expected from the preceding discussion. Furthermore, they did project ahead into the remote future (the modal death was seen as taking place in their sixth decade).

But this was only half the story. After completing all the essays, the respondents were asked to imagine the day of their death in a different way. We did not specify what was meant by "different."

The second projected day of death was not only different, it was radically different. Death was now much closer. Many of the young women described deaths that would occur within the next few years. For the total group, the distance between one's present situation and death decreased by more than 20 years. They also died in a different way. Accidents and acts of violence became much more frequent. Furthermore, the death situations were described more vividly, in greater detail, and with more use of emotion-laden words. The writing style became less restrained and "proper." The young women expressed themselves more spontaneously and idiosyncratically. Emotional conflicts—almost completely absent from the first stories—were abundant in the second set. Judges who read both sets of stories ("blind") rated the second set as conveying more emotional impact and a greater sense of involvement on the part of the authors.

Yet the respondents themselves reported, through their self-ratings, that they were even *less* engrossed in these essays than they had been in the first version! The self-ratings and the judges' ratings were contradictory. At the same time that these young women were depicting their deaths as being closer to them in time and more vivid, disturbing, and emotional they were also reporting that they had felt very little involvement! How strange can things get?

Methodologically, this study underscores the importance of going beyond the respondent's first or most accessible response. But what does it suggest about the relationship between concepts of death and futurity in young adults? *The future was at first used as insulation between one's present self and the self that eventually must die.* In other words: *I am the person who writes, not the person who dies.* The success of this insulation may be judged by the fact that the other aspects of the personal death essay were neutral and tranquil. The respondent could rely upon readily available stereotyped expressions: a sort of greeting card view of one's own death.

The requirement to deal twice with the same question forced the respondents to find an alternative organization of thought and feeling within themselves. It was especially interesting to see the compensatory dynamics at work. One's death became closer in time, but was correspondingly separated by an even greater psychological (self-involvement) distance. Somebody will die pretty soon, but it won't be me.

SUPPOSE: NOBODY DIES, EVERYBODY DIES, OR THAT I JUST DIE AND GET IT OVER WITH?

There is another set of mental death games that are best considered together. The first is one that I have introduced as a thought experiment. The other two occur spontaneously among youth more often than adults at midlife or beyond. The games are not entirely innocent amusements, although they can be such on occasion. Some players step, out of the game into an early death.

Nobody Dies: A World Without Death

It can be instructive to imagine the world as being different in some respect from the world we know—for example, suppose that the law of gravity were replaced by the law of levity, everything floating up? I have asked people to imagine something that is no less unusual: a world without death. The specific instructions:

> Suppose that the world is just as we know it, with one exception: Death is no longer inevitable. Disease and aging have been conquered. Let us also suppose that air and water pollution have been much reduced through new technologies. Take a few minutes to imagine the implications and consequences. What will happen? How will people respond to this situation, individually and as a society? How will the quality of life change?
>
> Think first of the effects of the no-death scenario on the world at large. Write down the changes you think would be likely to happen. Next think of how the no-death scenario would influence your own thoughts, feelings, wishes, needs, beliefs, and actions. Describe some of the major ways the no-death situation would be likely to influence you.

Data were collected from more than 629 respondents (482 women, 119 men, and 28 who did not report their gender). These were people who had attended conferences, workshops, or enrolled in courses focusing on death.

What was found?

Most respondents judged that a world without death was an attractive proposition at first thought, but not to be desired after second thought (Kastenbaum, 1996). Let us consider first the positive general characteristics of a world without death:

1. Society would be able to keep its wise and experienced people. ("We could have Gandhi's living example still with us." "Great minds could get even greater.")
2. Money would not be tied up in life insurance or wasted in funerals. ("People could use their money for life, not death." "We wouldn't have to worry about cemeteries . . . there are a lot better things to do with land.")
3. Societies could become more flexible and sensitive to each other and to their own subgroups because more people could learn about alternative forms of life. ("We would all have time to learn Chinese, and the Chinese to learn English." "You could have a dozen different careers and really learn how the other guy lives.")
4. Religious institutions would have less social power because they would not be supported by fear of death. ("If people were still religious it would be because they really believed, not because they were just scared of death.")
5. Some career opportunities would improve. ("Sounds good to me. I'm a leisure studies major, and people would have lots of leisure." "There'll be lots of time to study this and that, and that means new jobs for teachers.")

The most frequently mentioned negative general consequences of a world without death were the following:

1. Overcrowding and its effect on the quality of life. ("Full-time turf wars." "People every place—it would be a zoo!")
2. Birth control would be enforced. ("There wouldn't be much room for the next generation." "You'd have to get a license to make babies.")
3. Discrimination, elitism, and power politics would become even more oppressive. ("Only people in power could have a little private space to call their own." "And who do you suppose would be approved to have children? The poor and powerless?")

4. Society would become overly conservative and lose its adaptability. ("There'd be more old people than anybody else; society would get stuck in its ways." "We'd be controlled by the past.")
5. Economic structures and processes would change drastically, and mostly for the worst. ("There'd be no more inheritance because nobody would die.")
6. Moral beliefs would be undermined, with destabilizing effects on social institutions. ("Society would be like a ship without a rudder, if it isn't already." "Would people even think of sins as sins if there wasn't punishment after death?" "People would think, hey, what's the point of being married to just one person forever and ever." "People might get tired of the mess they make of their lives, and try to get themselves killed, one way or another.")

The general effect of a world without death was seen as predominately negative on society in general. What about the effect on the respondent's own lives? Here, again, there were positives and negatives.

Three ideas predominated in the positive reaction toward a personal world without death:

1. *Liberation from the fear of death.* This was by far the most frequently acknowledged benefit. ("I would just give a real long sigh of relief." "I'd be free to enjoy life a lot more without that dark shadow hanging over me.")
2. *Preservation of valued relationships.* ("I hate good-byes, even at airports when you're going to see them again in a few months." "I have the greatest husband. I'd like to keep him forever.")
3. *Opportunity for continued personal growth.* ("I'm a marketing major, so I'm going to get filthy rich, ha-ha. But I more enjoy nature photography. If I didn't have to die, I could do both things, and maybe even more." "I could spend just centuries learning and learning.")

The most frequently expressed negative themes center around the meaning of life. Respondents often mentioned more than one of the following:

1. *Abundance of time would be too much of a good thing.* Unlimited time would take the edge off pleasure and achievement. ("I hate the pressure of time, but I need it. If I had forever, I'd probably take it." "I'm terrific in getting things done at the last minute. But there wouldn't be any more last minutes if I had all the time in the world.")

2. *Religious faith and guidance would be undermined.* ("Would there still be heaven, and how would you get there?" "Jesus died for us. What would that mean now?" "This whole business of life could start to feel pointless if there were no real purpose or destination.")

3. *Death is necessary as part of God's plan.* Although related to the preceding theme, this variant is an affirmation of faith rather than a fear that faith would be undermined. ("We were meant to die. I think we should try to prevent and treat diseases, but I don't think we should try to defeat God's plans for us." "We shouldn't even think of living forever because that would make us little imitation gods ourselves!")

4. *Prolonged life would lead to continued aging and deterioration.* ("I've worked in nursing homes. Spare me! I'd never want to be so helpless and dependent on others." "I wouldn't look forward to just getting older and older.")

We might have expected people to welcome a world without death—and they did. However, on reflection, most of these mostly young adult respondents found more negatives than positives in this prospect. Some of the negatives were of ecological nature, such as overcrowding. Others, though, dealt with issues of purpose, meaning, and the basic structure of experience (such as having too much time and perhaps no sense of direction other than making one's way through the relentless repetition of daily rounds). At the least, a world without death would challenge us to change some of our most fundamental attitudes and practices. Research has consistently found, however, that attitudes and habits can be extremely resistant to change, even when that change is favorable (e.g., Heatherington & Weinberger, 1994). But the challenge seems to go even deeper. We may feel like "strangers in a strange world." Even though many things seem the same, their meanings and relationships will have become altered.

Who would we be in a world without death, and what would life mean? Perhaps in due time we would learn how to live in such a world. The discomfort felt at this prospect, though, suggests that much as we may lament the loss of loved ones and the impending final curtain in our own lives, we still need death as a structuring principle for individual and society. As alarming as it might be for youth to recognize the universality and finality of death, this realization soon permeates one's total view of life and probably could not be eradicated without provoking a crisis of destabilization.

Everybody Dies—Soon!

Few believe that there could be life on earth without death. But what about a belief at the other extreme: everybody will die—or should die—soon? This proposition is not included in mainstream theories that assume a layer of protective insulation between the child's discovery of mortality and the execution of the death sentence. Sadly, Mom and Dad will die some day, but probably not for a long time, and a longer time still before the child's turn comes. Nevertheless, some people hold the compelling view of imminent and/or catastrophic death. Their lives may be organized around the expectation that everybody on earth soon will be destroyed as punishment for their sins. In such visions, the human race does not perish with peaceful acceptance but in panic and terror as we are swept by earthquake, fire storm, or other overwhelming events. In some versions, all are destroyed. In other versions, the pure and the faithful are spared while millions of others perish.

Death here takes the form of a cleansing agent, a powerful detergent that removes the stains of sin and guilt from the human race at the cost of the human race itself. Unlike, for example, the scientist's functionalistic death constructions, catastrophic death is lodged within a framework of values and morals. Bad people—or people who are not good enough—must pay with their lives.

This view is not held by most people who are guided by the major religious traditions. Nevertheless, it is a key element in the beliefs of some people within the larger panoply of religious belief. With a little searching, one often can find groups of people who are united in the catastrophic death vision and hear their ideas at firsthand. Alternatively, one can cruise the internet and read the messages of impending doom. These messages are almost always supported by references to

Biblical or other sacred writings and to current events that seem to document the moral decline of the human race.

We would be mistaken to regard these beliefs as recent developments in a troubled world. Visions of catastrophic death were at a high point a millennium ago. Many believed the year 1000 or 1001 would surely produce universal destruction. Perhaps today's millennianists are drawing somewhat upon that tradition, but the tradition of expecting imminent widespread death has had a number of other periods of peak influence over the centuries. Imagining a fiery end to human life has long been a capability of the human mind. Furthermore, at times—such as The Holocaust—the human race has behaved as though it were dedicated to giving catastrophe a helping hand.

It is difficult to escape the impression that many of those who believe fervently in the imminent destruction of life on earth are responding to their own private terrors rather than to religious teachings. I recall, for example, a freelance photographer who would spend his evenings at a traffic circle notorious for its high accident rate, hoping to capture a fiery and fatal crash on film. He told me this was the best he could do until all the sinners on earth (he did not exclude me) perished in the inevitable fire storm of judgment which would take place any day now. What makes this impression so compelling is the note of triumph: the cataclysmic destruction of most or all of the human race will prove the moral superiority of those who prophesy this ending: the ultimate, "I gotcha!" The photographer proved to be psychotic. People in a psychotic state have also committed murder in the belief they were acting on God's command. Nevertheless, a belief in ordained megadeath does not necessarily signify a disordered mind. Scriptural basis can be found for this belief, and it is held by people of sound as well as people of unsound minds.

Although there is often a strong component of religious/moral belief in doomsday thought, the impending destruction of life on earth is sometimes fueled by alarmist interpretations of scientific facts and theories, which may or may not be understood. There are also situations in which some people believe that the chaos seen about them signifies widespread death and the end of civilization, a conviction that is not necessarily related to religious doctrine. We should bear in mind that the great majority of people whose lives are guided by religious principles do not expect, much less advocate, the imminent destruction of life on earth.

I Should Just Die and Get It Over With

Adults are supposed to understand that death is the end of life, although there are differences of opinion about what, if anything, happens after death. It is not surprising that fear, anxiety, and depression often accompany this cognition. Some people experience these negative feelings keenly for a while, then come to a private arrangement with their awareness of mortality. "I will die" is put away, perhaps like an old photo album, for another day's reconsideration. Others must exert continual effort to keep death-related fears from disturbing everyday life. These people tend to score higher on self-report anxiety scales, and may also have a number of death-related phobias (see also chapter 4).

We must also acknowledge another orientation, however, even though it may seem to go against logical expectations. The idea that "I should just die and get it over with" can serve to reduce intrapsychic tension, at least for the moment. A recovering alcoholic in his forties offers one version of this strategy:

> Every day, I mean every day, I thought about killing myself. I knew I *was* killing myself every day, and I'd think, why not just get it all over with. (*Your life or your death?*) (*Laughs*) Both! I've seen alcoholics die. I could tell you about it. I'd a lot sooner pick my own way to go and not leave a disgusting mess for somebody else to clean up. My life was not the best, then, but I didn't want my death to be the worst. I'd think—when I was sober, that it would be best to get rid of my life and my death, and that wonderful thought (*laughs*) made me feel a little better! I tried it, too, five times. But I was always a little or a lot drunk and didn't get the job done. (*Now?*) I'm still a suicide risk. I still think death is a great way out, even though I'm still scared to death of death. Funny thing is, this screwed-up thinking really makes sense to me!

This man's thought processes are not unique. Counselors experienced in helping suicidal individuals have often discovered that their clients have cherished the intention of ending their lives as an option that could be exercised if the situation becomes really desperate (e.g., Heckler, 1994). Furthermore, some people—especially depressed and anxious youths—take unnecessary risks with their lives as a way of testing out their partially formed suicidal intentions. The thought of suicide, coupled with risky living, paradoxically can reduce otherwise unbearable tension between the wish to escape psychological pain and the fear of death. Unfortunately, this strategy can also fail, leading to an impulsive and fatal suicide attempt.

The "let's get death over with" solution is often considered by people with chronic or life-threatening conditions. In point of fact, though, most people who live with such conditions do not attempt suicide. Competent health care, support from significant others, and one's own sense of purpose and values are important shields against suicide. A woman in her fifties with progressive kidney disease reflects:

> It took a while for the diagnosis to sink in; I mean, how serious it really was. I was too young for this to be happening to me—but it was happening. So then, I guess I panicked. Actually, I don't have to guess—I *did* panic. That's when I might have overdosed or something. Then I sort of got used to it, not really, but sort of. And there was so much going on with the family that I didn't want to miss anything. I guess—and this *is* guessing—that getting myself dead is such a good way of getting rid of death. I hate, really hate, having to life the way I do, and knowing what's coming, but I want to life as long as . . . well, as long as I want to live.

The controversies that swirl around physician-assisted death have brought this intense personal dilemma into the public scene. The issues involved are medical, legal, economic, subcultural, sociological, and philosophical as well as psychological. Nevertheless, there is one point of special relevance here.

Most of the people who died with Dr. Jack Kevorkian "in attendance" were neither terminally ill nor suffering from organically based pain. Most, however, were depressed and, as a group, resembled a general population of suicide-attempters far more than a general sample of terminally ill people (Kaplan, Lachenmeier, O'Dell, & Uziel, in press). The high proportion of women to men is a reversal of the general gender-related rate of completed suicides, but consistent with estimates of suicide attempters. This pattern suggests that the availability of a "death doctor" may have contributed to the deaths of some people who otherwise might have found other solutions to their anguish while keeping suicide as a cognitive tension-reducing option. Meanwhile, many people with similar medical conditions continue with meaningful lives because they are confident that palliative care will control their symptoms, and that death itself need not be feared.

Other sociocultural phenomena can also serve either to increase or decrease the likelihood that a person will press the suicide button. Legalized gambling, for example, has been found to have a potent effect on suicidality. "Visitors to and residents of major gaming communities experience significantly elevated suicide levels. . . . The findings do not seem to result merely because gaming settings attract suicidal individuals" (Phillips, Welty, & Smith, 1997, p. 373). It might be noted that use of alcohol and/or other mind-altering drugs is often associated with suicide within a great variety of settings, and such use is common in Las Vegas, Atlantic City, and other "gaming" communities. (What a splendid word, "gaming"—much more palatable than "gambling," isn't it?)

It is not unusual, then, for the human mind to transform the once-dread prospect of death into the escape hatch for whatever might be disturbing us, whether this be as formidable as a progressive illness or as transient as frustration and embarrassment. Adults who presumably have a mature cognitive model of death may nevertheless seek death as a solution both to the anxieties of life and the uncertainties of dying and death.

REGRET AND DENIAL: TWO ELITE STRATEGIES FOR THINKING ABOUT DEATH

We have already seen that the standard adult cognitive model of death may provide a useful foundation, but falls far short of describing, let alone explaining, how we think about death throughout our lives. Let us visit and revisit two of the more elite strategies. ("Elite" here refers to its root-meaning of "that which is chosen," an approach favored over most others.)

Regret Theory

Some theorists have been taking a fresh look at a state of mind with which most of us have become familiar: regret. Several aspects of regret are clearly evident. It is an unpleasant preoccupation with something in the past, something that we wish had not happened or not happened in that particular way. We see at once that regret can be closely related to grief and guilt. Theorists have given regret a new twist, however. Landman (1993) and others emphasize the role of regret in making decisions that will have consequence for the future. The implicit question is: "Will I be sorry later that I made this decision now?"

For our purposes both the past and future dimensions of regret can be considered within the same framework. Here in the present moment we can scan both the past and future, perhaps to learn from mistakes we would not want to make again.

The earliest theories of regret embodied the minimax principle, that is, we make the choice that seems to hold greatest promise of gain *and* the least threat of loss. People may not necessarily select the most attractive proposition, then, because the downside could also be the most disastrous. We negotiate among the choices, if only in our own minds. Perhaps I want something so much that I will risk everything for the chance. Perhaps, though, I want to be alive, well, and not flat-broke, so will settle for something that offers less but also is less likely to prove harmful. Current theories are more complicated because our lives are more complicated than pictured in the earlier model. We usually have several choices to make within a particular situation. The situation itself may be fairly placid or extremely urgent. If we are not to regret our choice later, we must somehow take into account the *relative* value of each option.

Translated into the concerns of this book, we may go through a series of thoughts such as these:

- "The easiest thing is to ignore this pain in my chest. This has the great advantage of convenience, and also helps to convince myself that nothing really bad is happening."
- "The smartest thing is to call 911. That could save my life if it is a heart attack."
- "Or I could take something for indigestion. That would show that I'm taking a corrective action, and it won't make me look foolish if indigestion is all that it is."
- "Or I could just mention this—discomfort—in my chest. That would make it their responsibility. If they don't make the right suggestion or do the right thing, then whatever happens won't be my fault."

Eventually (but perhaps too late), we might reach a decision that has the apparent advantage of reducing our future regrets, assuming that we do have a future. Our decision, then, might not be based on clear, straightforward self-preservational logic. Instead of giving highest priority to saving our lives (or the life of another person), we might devote our efforts to negotiating among the perceived pluses and minuses of the alternatives. The motive to make a decision we are least likely to regret later can take precedence over life-protecting actions. We may be fully cognizant of death's finality, then, but consider this fact to be less important than avoiding the stigma of making a decision that could turn out to have been mistaken.

To put it another way: we don't have to be crazy to do crazy things about our lives and deaths. We only have to employ thought strategies that submerge the will to live within a convoluted psycho-logic.

What We Call "Denial"

The most often cited strategy for dealing with death-related phenomena is what we call denial. This term is sometimes used so loosely, however, that it covers an assortment of techniques for coping with the threat of death. "In denial" has become a pop culture buzz phrase that has further diluted the core meaning of this term. Psychiatry has long defined denial as the rejection of or inability to accept a significant facet of reality. Our chances of avoiding harm are sharply reduced when we cannot acknowledge reality, so authentic denial usually is found either with people suffering from psychosis or, in a transient form, people who are suddenly overwhelmed by catastrophic events. Many of us have had moments of denial when faced with traumatic events or messages. These moments soon pass, though, and we start to deal with the daunting reality.

Many communications and behaviors that are called "denial of death" actually represent some other kind of avoidance and control strategy. This is a good thing, because the other strategies are generally less extreme and more adaptive. These other strategies include selective attention, selective response, compartmentalizing, deception, and resistance (Kastenbaum, 1998). In all these circumstances, the individual is manipulating information and communication to reduce stress (including the anxiety of the other person). The hasty judgment that a person is "in denial" tends to be premature, closing off further inquiry. Often, all that we have to work on when we say that a person is denying is the belief that this person should be aware of something that we think *we* know—and should be expressing that knowledge in a way that we can understand. Those skilled in reading body language, for example, sometimes do understand that the person is communicating awareness of dying and death effectively, though wordlessly.

Authentic denial and all its less extreme variants have important cognitive dimensions. Information is managed very carefully and may be either expressed or withheld depending on the total momentary situation. Thus, a bedridden patient offers selective responses to a family visitor, responses that imply she is feeling better and will be around for a while. When a favorite nurse comes by, though, she may sigh, pat her hand, and thank her for all she has done—this accompanied by a meaningful and well understood look of farewell. These strategies are intended to counteract the forces of destabilization. For the terminally ill person, exhaustion may be a more powerful force than pain or anxiety. Concern about upsetting visitors because one looks so ill may be an even more powerful source of destabilization: "I don't want to hurt this person. . . . I don't want to lose this relationship."

We might be well advised to put "denial" back on the shelf except when this strategy of desperation has been positively established by competent psychological or psychiatric observation. We would then replace this overworked term with appreciation for the variety of adaptive strategies that people use when death has intruded upon their thoughts. We might also improve our ability to distinguish what might be called *normative denial* from traumatic or psychopathological denial.

Here is a vivid example of normative denial:

One of the videos on file with the Portland Coast Guard—shown as often as possible to local fishermen—was shot from the wheelhouse of a commercial boat during a really bad blow. It shows the bow rising and falling . . . over mammoth, white-streaked seas. At one point the captain says, a little smugly, "Yep, this is where you wannna be, right in your own wheelhouse, your own little domain . . . " At that moment a wall of water the size of a house fills the screen. It's no bigger than the rest of the waves but it's solid and foaming and absolutely vertical.

It engulfs the bow, the foredeck, the wheelhouse, and then blows all the windows out. The last thing the camera sees is whitewater coming at it like a big wet fist. (Junger, 1997, p. 121)

Denial? I guess so. But the captain was not psychotic and, at that moment, not overwhelmed by circumstances. Instead, he was enacting the role of the brave skipper, just as so many of us enact so many other roles that sometimes require us to appear a little more of something than we really are. In his own way, reporter Ben Hecht was also the brave skipper playing his role: he was there to write about other people's tragic losses, each story secretly insulating him from awareness of his own mortality. Even touches of authentic denial are lodged within society's communication network and, therefore, following rules that are nonetheless compelling for being unspoken. And even those who are in deepest denial must know something— otherwise how would they know what to deny?

MIND AND MYSTERY

Our conceptions of death obviously are influenced by the ways our minds work. But how *do* our minds work? Neuroscientists have been providing not only a lot of new information about brain and mind, but also coming up with new theoretical models (e.g., Hobson, 1994; LeDoux, 1996; Pinker, 1998). If their ideas are only half-right, most of us will still have to change our minds about our minds. The part of honesty and caution would be to admit that our "mature" ideas about life and death are products of an amazing biosystem that we use *every* day without quite understanding.

Which brings us to mystery and nothing. Psychology, along with its many companion fields of inquiry, assumes that we can continue to know more than we have ever known before, given diligent research and clear thinking. Developmental psychology adds the further assumption that we know more as adults than we did as children. These articles of faith have taken us a long way. There is perhaps no basis for assuming, however, that we can know everything, even about our own thoughts, feelings, identities, and relationships. There is even less basis for assuming that the evolved and educated mind can ever understand the mysteries of life and death, at least not in the same sense that we understand phenomena through customary empirical and logical operations. We are doing well, I suspect, if we are just capable of recognizing mysteries when we bump up against them.

Perhaps the biggest bump of all is the one that isn't there. Nothing (or, as many like to say, "nothingness") is the most elusive object of thought. The mere activity of thought makes something of nothing. Some of us can think of very little (like a nanosecond or a quark). Nothing is quite a different story, though, and we have the most exquisite difficulty in telling or listening to this story without inadvertently falsifying it. It is as though nothing is a semantic vacuum which we must stuff with attributions and define with imagined dimensions. We are just too gifted in making something of nothing to hold it in clear and steady cognition.

We come closest, I think, in our penchant for metaphorical thought. One of the most promising such metaphors is empty or, if you insist, emptiness. We might say, for example, "There is nothing in this box." Theoretical physicist Henning Genz has recently made systematic attempts to explore the meaning of *Nothingness* (Genz, 1999). His subtitle resonates with our discussion: "The Science of Empty Space." He examines such general concepts as empty space and vacuum, as well as black holes and other astonishing phenomena that are the continuing subjects of scientific inquiry. What is of most interest here is a conclusion that Genz offers after a critical review of the state of knowledge about the universe since Einstein. Any summary of his proposition about the nature of the universe is likely to appear strange in a book on the psychology of death, but we can at least try:

Everything adds up to nothing! ✓

Genz does not put it quite that way. Instead he tells us that "there must be a comprehensive symmetry principle that constrains all contributing terms *{i. e., energies}* to add up precisely to zero" (op. cit. p. 303). In other words, there may seem to be something here and there, but, considered as a whole, the universe adds up to zero. Or in other other words: *the box is empty and there is no box.*

I have invited Genz to testify here not because his theory can be applied directly to the issue of adult cognitions of death, but simply to illustrate how the problem of nothing continues both to allure and perplex. May I suggest that we step back a little from the assumption that we understand death so well that we can evaluate other people's cognitive models and the ways in which they make strategic use of these models. We know a lot about a lot of things, but we know nothing about nothing. We will continue to observe people whose views of death seem unrealistic, even to the point of denial. However, perhaps we will be a little more at peace with our lack of knowledge *of* death. Much has been learned about conditions associated with the passage from life to death, but this does not necessarily tell us anything about death per se. Yes, there are people who are absolutely certain that they know all about death, and some of them may even be right, though many would also have to be wrong. In our heart of hearts we may have an image of death that we feel to be true. We might be going well beyond the bounds of disciplined observation and thought, however, if we claim that science is on our side and attempt to impose our images on others.

REFERENCES

Anthony, S. (1972). *The discovery of death in childhood and after.* New York: Basic Books.

Dickstein, L., & Blatt, S. (1966). Death concern, futurity, and anticipation. *Journal of Counseling Psychology, 31,* 11–17.

Genz, H. (1999). *Nothingness.* Reading, MA: Perseus Books.

Heatherington, T. F., & Weinberger, J. L. (Eds.). (1994). *Can personality change?* Washington, DC: American Psychological Association.

Hecht, B. (1970). *A child of the century.* New York: Ballantine Books. (Original work published 1954)

Heckler, R. A. (1994). *Waking up, alive.* New York: Ballantine Books.

Hobson, J. A. (1994). *The chemistry of conscious states.* Boston: Little, Brown

Junger, S. (1998). *The perfect storm.* New York: HarperCollins.

Kaplan, K. J., Lachenmeier, F., O'Dell, J. C., & Uziel, O. (in press). Psychosocial versus biomedical risk factors in Kevorkian's first 47 "suicides." *Omega, Journal of Death and Dying.*

Kastenbaum, R. (1959). Time and death in adolescence. In H. Feifel (Ed.), *The meaning of death* (pp. 99–113). New York: McGraw-Hill.

Kastenbaum, R. (1961). The dimensions of future time perspective: An experimental analysis. *Journal of Genetic Psychology, 65,* 203–218.

Kastenbaum, R. (1986). Death in the world of adolescence. In C. A. Carr & J. N. McNeill (Eds.), *Adolescence and death* (pp. 4–15). New York: Springer Publishing Co.

Kastenbaum, R. (1996). A world without death? first and second thoughts. *Mortality, 1,* 111–122.

Kastenbaum, R. (1998). *Death, society, and human experience* (6th ed.). Boston: Allyn & Bacon.

Landman, J. (1993). *Regret.* New York: Oxford University Press.

LeDoux, J. (1996). *The emotional brain.* New York: Simon & Schuster.

McLaughlin, N., & Kastenbaum, R. (1966). *Engrossment in personal past, future, and death.* Paper presented at the meeting of the American Psychological Association, New York.

Noppe, L. D., & Noppe, I. C. (1996). Ambiguity in adolescent understandings of death. In C. A. Corr & D. E. Balk (Eds.), *Handbook of adolescent death and bereavement* (pp. 25–41). New York: Springer Publishing Co.

Phillips, D. R., Welty, W. R., & Smith, M. (1997). Elevated suicide levels associated with legalized gambling. *Suicide and Life-Threatening Behavior, 27,* 373–378.

Piaget, J. (1972). Intellectual evolution from adolescence to adulthood. *Human Development, 15,* 1–12.

Piaget, J., & Inhelder, B. (1959). *The growth of logical thinking from childhood to adolescence.* New York: Basic Books.

Pinker, S. (1997). *How the mind works.* New York: W. W. Norton.

Schaie, K. W. (1995). Intelligence. In G. L. Maddox (Ed.), *The encyclopedia of aging* (pp. 513–514) (2nd ed.). New York: Springer Publishing Co.

Sternberg, R. J. (1988). *The triarchic mind. A new theory of human intelligence.* New York: Viking.

4

Death in the Midst of Life

The doctor said I was just having anxiety attacks. *Just* anxiety attacks! What would she say if I really died? That I was *just* dead, nothing to worry about?

—A young woman's conversation during a baseball game.

One of Tom's friends from school, Chad, was killed over the weekend. You know, one of those accidents you hear about and think, "too bad," and go on with whatever you are doing. Except Chad was somebody we knew, and his parents. I went a little crazy inside. I think all the mothers did. It could have been Tom; it could have been anybody's child. Every time he leaves the house now—well, you know. I get this terrible feeling I may never see him again.

—Woman in a seminar on death and dying

I know it could happen and it could happen to me or any member of my family. But I don't, well I don't think about it, because if, like the way I see it is, like, death comes whether you want it to or not, and so, like, what's the point of thinking about it and making yourself all depressed? You know? Well, I probably deny it. Like if I, the way I see it, I'm going to live, like, forever

—High school student responding to an interviewer

Our fear of death is essential fear . . . so involuntary . . . and so deeply programmed. . . . The more one starts to relate to death, the more one starts to relate to fear itself, and then it becomes not just my fear, but *the* fear. We take our fear so personally—we judge it; we get angry at it; we try to manipulate it; we try to change it—we never let it simply float in our heart.

—Stephen Levine, responding to an interviewer

If only death were some place else—and stayed there! I could go about my business and pleasure without that twinge of fear, that shadow of concern. Yes, I know eventually there would be encounters

with death, but not here, not now, and not while I'm still the person
I am at this moment. Death can have it's time and place, as long as
It stays away from mine

—Most of us, most of the time

This chapter is about death anxiety, but also about other thoughts
and feelings that we experience when awareness of mortality
breaks into our daily lives. Many of us find death "interesting"
when it occurs in "interesting" ways to people who are not close to
us: the continuing popularity of violence in television and movies is
one testament to the fascination that some deaths hold for some
people. Few of us, though, relish thinking about death when it is up
close and personal. As we will see, there are divergent theories and
somewhat discordant findings, but general agreement that most of us
prefer to minimize even our cognitive encounters with death.

It is possible that our impression of one's everyday orientation
toward death is overly influenced by sociocultural context. Most death-
anxiety research has involved psychologists and respondents in the
United States. There have been a smattering of useful studies from
other parts of the world, but we are not yet in a position to differentiate
what might be characteristic of death anxiety in general, and what is
peculiar to the United States. Even Canada, so similar to the United
States in many ways, may have different psychological "deathways,"
if this term may be permitted. For example, Canadians are much less
likely to tote and use guns than their U. S. counterparts, with a
correspondingly lower murder rate. Furthermore, the very fact that U.
S. psychologists have been especially active in death-anxiety research
might also be telling us something. Although our approach here is
primarily psychological, we will also need to remember that our attitudes toward death, dying, and grief are subject to sociocultural
influences.

With one exception, the quoted passages that opened this chapter
reveal the common thread of distancing ourselves from death: a physician who did not convey empathy and concern for a woman who
was experiencing death-related terror; a mother experiencing an upsurge of anxiety when an accidental death punctured her psychological
insulation against loss in her own family, a high school student who
has decided there's no point in thinking about it. The one exception

is Levine's observation that fear of death is "deeply programmed"—the fear of fears that we never seem to accept for what it is.

There is reason to think that our desire to maintain a death-free zone of comfort has influenced the way we organize our lives—not only now, but throughout history. Baudrillard (1993) tells us that the separation of the dead from the living was one of the most consequential maneuvers in human history. In his analysis, the segregation of the dead became the template for all future divisions within society. Although this point seems to have been shuffled aside in current psychological research, we might remind ourselves that fear of the dead was at the top of the phobia list for most ancient and many tribal peoples, if the anthropologists have their facts and surmises correct. The carefully boundaried burial place—along with rituals intended to pacify the dead—was the geographical model for the living regardless of national origin, race, socioeconomic status, and other criteria.

The "dead ghetto" has not proven sufficient, though, to assuage our fears. We have made many efforts to keep a distance from the living who have been touched by death. Neighbors and colleagues often avoid substantive contact with people who have been recently bereaved. The social isolation of people with life-threatening or terminal illness eventually became so notorious that it prompted the development of hospice care and the death-awareness movement. Paradoxically perhaps, those who excel in not dying have also been shunned: the aged remind us too much of our own mortal limits.

I had a first-hand opportunity to experience this attempt to wall off death from our everyday lives as a clinical and research psychologist in a large geriatric facility in the 1960s. The community was grateful to have a place that could meet at least the basic needs of frail and multiply impaired elders. However, there was also a sense of relief that the nonthriving aged had been put away. The large and pleasant campus, studded with ugly "temporary" buildings, even had a fence all around to symbolize the boundary between the hale and the frail. I often heard people in the community express their discomfort at the prospect of having to see their elders in a deteriorated condition and then to, well, you know what.

This careful separation of the living from the death-infected continued within the hospital itself. The residents were expected to live on some wards and die on others. Anxiety would spread like wildfire when somebody did not obey this rule. I saw remarkable charades in which a corpse would be treated as though still alive, and could not help but observe how a code of silence was enforced by the staff in the aftermath of a misplaced or mistimed death. The wrong kind of death aroused anxiety, which distorted communication, which, in turn, intensified anxiety. The right kind of death occurred following transfer to one of two special care wards, and the very best kind occurred when there had been enough time for staff to do all they thought they could or should do, after which they moved the patient to a corner and drew the curtains.

I was as naive as can be as a young psychologist in the days before hospice care and books, journals, and courses dealing with death. Nevertheless I could not miss the irony that community and professional staff experienced so much stress and engaged in so many evasive maneuvers while most of the aged men and women themselves were quite aware of their mortality. "They're keeping secrets from us," Mr. Brewer, a stately man in his 94th year confided. "Secrets? Like what?" "Go on—you know what I'm talking about. They don't want us old guys to know that people die." "Why do they do that?" "How the hell should I know? Probably too scared of death themselves." "You?" "I never thought I'd live this long, not nearly. I've been ready for years." Not surprisingly, there were episodes in which hospital staff anxiety increased to the point of panic when a patient died in the wrong place or at the wrong time. Later I would learn that similar reactions could be seen in most if not all medical settings when a patient's death deviated from the implicit rules.

We are often resourceful in devising ways to insulate ourselves from upsurges of death-related anxiety, whether in our homes, our workplaces, or medical care situations. Is this a good thing? Probably: We would not want to suffer distracting and perhaps disabling anxiety in our everyday lives. Probably not: We may protect ourselves so efficiently that we are unable to respond to the distress of others or to our own perils. An exploration of death anxiety, then, requires attention to its functional and dysfunctional characteristics. A more fundamental question must also be addressed, however: just what *is* death anxiety? A host of other questions and problems also arise, as we will see.

In this chapter we focus on anxiety and other responses to death throughout the broad range of daily life. How people think and feel when death is a near prospect is a compelling topic that is explored elsewhere (chapters 6 and 7). Much of our attention focuses on the questions raised, methods employed, and findings obtained by those who have studied "death anxiety" or "fear of death" in adults who were not at obvious risk at the time of their participation. We will prepare ourselves for the data by reviewing some of the more influential and interesting theories that bear on death anxiety.

Two points might be noted at the outset:

1.   The research literature seldom differentiates between fear and anxiety. It is easier to present this literature by using the terms that are favored by the contributing researchers and writers. There really is a useful difference, though. As Rollo May (1979) points out, fears are specific and identifiable, while anxiety is a more global state of apprehension in which the danger might come in any shape from any source in any time. There are additional nontrivial definitional questions about anxiety that we cannot deal with here.

2.   Empirical research on death anxiety has been atheoretical for the most part, although not without untested assumptions. Fortunately, there has been more attention to theory recently, enabling us to take a fresh look at what has been learned and what might yet be learned.

The Classic Theories of Death Anxiety

We begin with a brief examination of the Big Theories, those that may be said to have achieved classic status.

"Never Say Die?"

The best-hated Big Theory in this area is the one attributed to Sigmund Freud. He is generally considered to have dismissed death anxiety as an authentic problem. To the question: "How should we contemplate death?" Freud would be expected to respond, "Never say die!" What Freud actually did suggest is a little more complicated. He was well aware that people had many concerns about death. It was not unusual to find death fears prominent in an anxiety reaction, or expressed through dream reports. Freud even shared some of his own death-associated fears.

Nevertheless, Freud demonstrated once again his unwillingness to draw the most obvious conclusion. Just because an anxious person spoke of death did not necessarily mean that death was at the root of the problem. All that display of concern about death was some kind of cover story, disguising the real problem. Thanatophobia (fear of death) was likely the symbolic expression for some unresolved conflict on a deeper psychic layer.

In one of his most influential passages, Freud wrote:

> Our own death is indeed quite unimaginable, and whenever we make the attempt to imagine it we can perceive that we really survive as spectators. Hence the psychoanalytic school could venture on the assertion that at bottom nobody believes in his own death, or to put the same thing in a different way, in the unconscious every one of us is convinced of his own immortality. (Freud, 1913/1953, pp. 304–305)

There is a fundamental basis for the inability to comprehend our own mortality:

> What we call our "unconscious" (the deepest strata of our minds, made up of instinctual impulses) knows nothing whatever of negatives or of denials—contradictions coincide in it—and so it knows nothing whatever of our own death, for to that we can give only a negative purport. It follows that no instinct we possess is ready for a belief in death. (Freud, 1913/1953, p. 305)

This view is consistent with Freud's overall conception of the "unconscious system" in which there is "no negation, no dubiety, no varying degree of certainty." Unconscious processes are not responsive to the passage of time, "in fact, bear no relation to time at all." By inference, then, death as the end-point of personal time would have no meaning to the unconscious.

There is still another Freudian argument against thanatophobia as a deep and authentic orientation: we have not experienced death—so how can we fear it? We must be projecting some other anxiety to the blank screen known as death. Following this logic, death-related fears must be formulated at the more superficial levels of mental functioning. The terror actually arises from instinctual conflicts that are well within our experience, and which are then cloaked in death imagery. Castration anxiety, for example, was thought by Freud to present a normative challenge in childhood development. The adult who is beset by death fears may be representing unresolved castration anxiety by this subterfuge. (Obviously, this inference shows considerable strain when applied to women, although it was so applied.)

This is not the place to attempt an evaluation of the "never say die!" conception. It is the place, however, to comment on the implications of this view, and its place in Freud's general conception of the human condition. The most obvious implication is that *we should not yield to fears of death. The presence of these fears is a signal that we are having difficulties with our basic instinctual life. It is not "wrong" or "bad" to have such fears, but they point to hidden problems that should receive therapeutic attention.*

Freud was clear enough about the inability of the unconscious to believe in its own death. Nevertheless, this is but one facet of his overall view of mortality and the human condition. Proponents and critics alike have tended to overlook the underlying purpose of the essay, *Thoughts for Times on War and Death*, in which Freud (1913/ 1953) presented the "never say die" theory. This essay was Freud's powerful response to World War I and its aftermath. It is a death-haunted quest to examine "a world grown strange," a world in which civilized peoples had attacked each other with brutal violence. War had stripped the trappings of civilization from us, revealing the primal being in all its blood-red emotions. If civilization—if humankind—were to survive, we would have to face some hard truths about ourselves. In particular, we must recognize our unstable mixture of loving and hating tendencies, our potential for evil and destruction, and our own vulnerability. "Would it not be better to give death the place in actuality and in our thoughts which properly belongs to it . . . ?"

Freud's view is more complex and poignant than many advocates and critics have acknowledged. He did come to take death very seriously indeed. Yes, superficial fears of death are hints of deeper instinctual conflicts, and our unconscious in its stubborn, magnificent, and childish way cannot be persuaded to conceive of its own demise. But, no, this does not mean that we would be wise to put death out of our minds. In fact, the central challenge for humankind is overcoming our appetite for killing with our potential for love (Einstein & Freud, 1932). The wise person will indeed contemplate death in the midst of life—and live in a more enlightened and responsible manner for doing so.

It is a mixed message that Freud has given us, and he may be faulted for not troubling to reconcile the two strands of thought more satisfactorily. Many of us may also be faulted, however, for fastening upon the "never say die" aspect, and neglecting the survival warning that was at the heart of his message.

We Cannot Help But Fear Death

The fear of death is not to be explained away as a superficial and disguised representation of a "deeper" conflict. Quite the opposite! Anxiety—*all* anxiety—is rooted in the awareness of our mortality. The consequences are enormous, and reveal themselves in virtually every aspect of individual and cultural life. Ernest Becker (1973) was a leading proponent of this view. It is the terror of death that drives both the schizophrenic and the person suffering from a psychotic depression to their extremes of escape.

Becker recalls William James' observation that psychosis was the most realistic response to the horrors of life on this planet. "Normal" people buffer themselves in many ways from the acute realization of helplessness, hopelessness, and death. Some people, however, are naked against this threat. In particular, the schizophrenic lacks the insulation provided by the ability to identify with or lose one's self in the activities and relationships of everyday life. "He cannot make available to himself the natural organismic expansion that others use to buffer and absorb the fear of life and death" (Becker, 1973, p. 219). Poorly integrated into the supportive cultural structure, the schizophrenic must face death alone. "He relies instead on a hyper-magnification of mental processes to try to be a hero almost entirely ideationally, from within a bad body-seating, and in a very personal way." *The sad, contrived, and failed heroism of the schizophrenic reveals in its distinctive way the strenuous efforts of the "normal" person to combat what is at root the same sense of impending loss by death.*

Ordinary life in today's society is marked by heavy repression of death-related anxiety (which is to say, all anxiety), according to Becker. This effort takes a toll on us. It is no happenstance that many of us become conformists. We seek the security by tying into a system that will meet our dependency needs and help us deny our intrinsic vulnerability. Individuals and society enter into collusion—and the dynamics of death anxiety and its denial keep this collusion going. Traumatic experiences can disrupt this "let's pretend" system, however. We are then faced with the challenge of either restoring the tenuous system of mutual (and mostly illusionary) support or with confronting death as an aware and vulnerable individual.

What does Becker's position imply for what we *should* do with our death anxiety? We could draw two different inferences. Guardians of the status quo would probably assert that fear of death is a negative, an asocial attitude that bespeaks a weak personality or undeveloped mind. A flourishing society requires active participants who work, breed, interact, and believe in shared values. Fear of death intensifies self-preoccupation and reduces the attention and energies necessary for group endeavors. If too many people become preoccupied and dysfunctional because of their indulgence in death anxiety, then the viability of the society itself may become imperiled.

A focus on individual development, however, might encourage a very different position. We "should" acknowledge our anxieties and contemplate death if we intend to live as an enlightened and self-actualized person. The repression of death-related thoughts and feelings requires too much effort, drains too much energy. *We cannot be complete and mature adults unless we live with the full realization of our mortality.* Interestingly, this interpretation is as much at home in Freud's conception as it is in Becker's. One asserted that, fundamentally, we cannot belief in our own death and that thanatophobia represents other, more basic conflicts. The other asserted that the terror of death motivates much of individual and social functioning. And yet both urge that we give death its due. Becker argues that we must retain a keen sense of death-threat in order to protect ourselves from threats to our lives. We should also work this realization into our philosophy of life in order promote our individual development. The trick is to keep the awareness of mortality from overwhelming us with anxiety and despair. Freud, even more strenuously than Becker, argues that the fate of civilization as well as the maturation of the individual requires a greater willingness to contemplate death (the reluctant unconscious, notwithstanding).

Welcome Dread Death

Perhaps theology should not be included in an examination of psychological theories. It is obvious, however, that the thoughts, feelings, and actions of a great many people have been influenced by religious doctrines. There have also been many treatises on the influence of psychological factors on the development, spread, and utilization of religious doctrines. We will limit attention here to the core Christian conception as it is related to death anxiety and invite others to explore a broader range of religious traditions.

The fact that death concern is at the core of Christian doctrine is not in doubt. Believers hold that the tormented death of Jesus holds the promise of salvation and eternal life. What does this imply for the way that Christians should orient themselves to death? One vital tradition urges the believer to think of death with wonder and gratitude. This corrupt and imperfect life is exchanged for everlasting bliss. There is little reason, then, for either fear or sorrow.

> Our aged father is now conveyed
> To his long home in silence laid
> Hast burst his cage and winged his way
> To realms of bliss in endless day.

This "endless bliss" more than compensates for the pains and disappointments of earthly life as well as the ordeal of "passing on." The believer loses only the shell, not the substance of being:

> Under the sod
> Under these trees
> Lies the body of Jonathan Pease
> He is not here
> But only his pod
> He has shelled out his peas
> And gone to his God.

And yet Christian doctrine has often been presented in a much more fearsome guise. Death is a punishment. "In Adam's fall, we sinned all." The believer faces judgment, rejection, and torment for personal shortcomings as well as original sin. "Hell and brimstone" sermons once were commonplace. How could the believer not fear "the wages of sin"? And how could the individual undergoing a crisis of faith not fear that failure to believe wholeheartedly could result in eternal damnation?

Should the Christian believer, then, live in dread of judgment, damnation, and punishment? Or contemplate death with serenity—even with longing and impatience—because the best is yet to come? Every believer must somehow reconcile these two aspects of Christian tradition, as well as personal thoughts and experiences with death. It is possible that both anxiety and serenity are intensified by Christian doctrine. Particular individuals might develop a naturalistic, matter-of-fact attitude, but the doctrine as such encourages the extremes of anxiety and serenity/joy/transcendence.

Unfortunately, empirical research seems to have neglected the complex ways in which individuals and families come to terms with both the "dread" and the "welcome" of Christian death. What are the key psychological and social factors through which the Christian message either increases or decreases death anxiety? Simply tabulating the self-report death-anxiety levels of Christians and others will not answer this question.

Learn Not to Fear . . . Too Much

This position has not been promulgated as extensively as the others. It has been suggested, however, that death-related concerns develop as part of the general interaction between the individual's level of maturation and his or her distinctive life experiences (Kastenbaum, 1987). One does not require special assumptions such as an "unconscious" that cannot deal in negations, a primary terror that must be restrained by all the resources of the individual and society, or the sacrificial death of the Son of God. Instead, one can study the development and function of death-related concerns as part of the total course of human growth. This approach does not negate any of the others; it simply limits itself to what can be studied through available empirical methods.

Because this approach lends itself more directly to controlled observation, the "should" question could be converted into a set of specific contingencies. In other words, we could learn (a) under what circumstances (b) what type and (c) what level of death concern is related to (d) what outcomes. Lacking the appeal of grand theories, this is nevertheless an alternative approach that may be more congruent with our ever-expanding but still limited inquiry skills.

Several new theoretical paths have been opened recently. These will be considered in the course of our review of the research literature.

We are now ready to consider some of methodological considerations that influence the type of findings obtained and the type of conclusions reached by empirical studies.

Death-Anxiety Research Methodology: Some Limits and Flaws

We begin with problems associated with the sources of information, and then consider specific difficulties that have characterized much of the available empirical research.

Sources of Information

There are several ways in which we might learn how people contemplate death in the midst of life. Each approach has its advantages and limitations.

Self-Report: Structured

We might ask people to express their orientations toward death through a direct and highly structured technique. The most common example is the fixed-choice questionnaire.

Among the advantages:

1. Easy for the researcher to administer, score, and analyze.
2. Requires little time from respondent and does not require a deep "opening up."
3. Makes it possible to build up a standardized data base to compare populations, examine time trends, and so on.

Among the disadvantages:

1. Qualitative and individual facets of death orientations are not given the opportunity to express themselves.
2. The fixed response format also constricts what can be learned about the processes involved in trying to cope with death. Limited to a "T" (true) or "F" (false) response alternative, participants can tell us very little about the thoughts and experiences that have led to the response, and nothing at all in their own words.
3. A direct and highly structured format is subject to falsification and evasion. This would be less a problem—in fact, could even become a source of useful information—if it were possible to distinguish between forthright and less forthright responses. There is no way to do so with the most frequently used self-report death-anxiety questionnaires.

The structured self-report fills the bill for the psychologist who would prefer to focus on quantifiable dimensions rather than encounter wild, hairy, uncompromising death on its own turf. There is no risk of discovering something one really did not want to know. Furthermore, this type of research is self-perpetuating, at least until everybody grows tired of it: exclusive reliance on fixed-choice death-anxiety scales will never find evidence for any psychological response to death other than anxiety!

Self-Report: Freely Structured

We might provide respondents with more natural, flexible, and spontaneous ways of sharing their death orientations. A variety of techniques could be employed. The possibilities include, for example, diaries and semistructured or even unstructured interviews. Each technique has its own particular values and limitations. As a set, however, the more freely structured procedures have methodological characteristics such as the following.

Among the advantages:

1. Respondents can use their own words and express their own feelings and views without being confined by preset categories.
2. There is more opportunity to learn about the thought processes used, as well as the feelings and ideas that have emerged.
3. There is more opportunity to discover nuances, contradictions, conflicts, leading themes, and the overall texture of the respondents' ways of contemplating death.

Among the disadvantages:

1. These techniques require more time and effort from the researcher in all phases of investigation.
2. Respondents also are asked to give more time and thought, and take the risk of opening themselves to an inquisitive stranger.
3. It is more difficult to accumulate comparable and easily reducible data.

Indirect and In-Depth Methods

Orientations toward death might be explored through dreams, fantasies, and projective techniques (such as the Thematic Apperception Test).

Among the advantages:

1. The respondent is given an opportunity to express thoughts and feelings beyond those that can be neatly packaged in response to direct questions.
2. Death-related fantasies and conflicts may come to the fore.
3. Individual patterns of thought and feeling are more likely to be expressed than with more structured techniques.
4. Counseling, psychotherapy, and other possible interventions might be guided by the responses.

Among the disadvantages:

1. The scoring, reliability, and interpretation of these responses may be subject to question.
2. The relationship between fantasy-projection responses and actual behavior may be tenuous, ambiguous, and obscure.
3. This is also an approach that is time intensive for both the respondent and the investigator.

Behavioral Observations

Instead of limiting our information to what the respondent tells us, we might focus on what he or she actually does. Behavioral observations have contributed significantly to many areas of psychological research. Documenting how people actually behave in death-related situations might also be productive.

Among the advantages:

1. Behavior in a situation could be regarded as the most appropriate outcome measure for the various theories regarding death attitudes—without actual behavioral observations the theories might always remain just that.
2. Behavioral observations can lend themselves to objective assessment and quantification.
3. Prevention and intervention efforts might best be guided by observing behavior, rather than relying completely on verbal statements.

Among the disadvantages:

1. Observations of behavior in "real life" situations pose many difficulties (such as the role and influence of the observer), and these intensify in sensitive and emotionally charged circumstances.
2. Questions can be raised about the unit and level of measurement, such as, "micro-units" of individual response or "macro-units" of complex interpersonal actions.
3. Generalizing across situations (as well as establishing "reliability" within the same type of situation) can be as difficult as drawing conclusions from studies of verbal behavior.

Psychophysiological Methods

The state of being to which we give the name "anxiety" is marked by physical as well as psychological distress. It is hardly a stretch to conceive of elevated anxiety as the phenomenological side of an organismic stress reaction. A few pioneering studies of death anxiety did include measures of psychophysiological activity (e.g., Alexander, Colley, & Adlerstein, 1957). Contrary to what might have been expected though, the study of the physical side of death anxiety rarely has been undertaken since. With today's technology it is easier than ever to measure such variables as respiration, heart rate, blood pressure, and electrical conductivity of the skin. With a bit more determination the spectrum of measures could be expanded to include brain activity while processing death-related and non-death-related messages. A resourceful research team could go far beyond verbal self-report. But—maybe it's just too much work! With few exceptions, death-anxiety research has remained on the verbal surface of things.

Among the advantages:

1. Psychophysiological measures provide a data source that does not depend on verbal self-report.
2. Sophisticated psychophysiological measures can help to differentiate the "ripples" of death anxiety at multiple levels.
3. Some psychophysiological measures are quite responsive to situational variables, thereby providing useful opportunities to examine outcomes and changes.
4. The incorporation of psychophysiological measures could help to establish connections between the somewhat isolated area

of death-anxiety research and such other domains of inquiry as stress reaction, sleep and dreams, and interpersonal resonances.

Among the disadvantages:

1. This line of research requires specialized skills that are not necessarily in the repertoire of those who rely on survey and questionnaire methodology.
2. Psychophysiological research usually involves one participant at a time, therefore it is not as quick and inexpensive as the most popular "round up the usual suspects" (generally college students) techniques.
3. The meaning of particular psychophysiological patterns is not necessarily self-evident. Interpretation can also be complicated by coexisting state variables such as use of medications, and by situational influences that may be difficult to detect or weigh.

Experimentation

The experimental method has been responsible for many breakthroughs in science. Few investigators would limit themselves to descriptive studies if they could find a way to subject their material to experimental manipulation. Despite years of research, we still know very little about orientations toward death because we have neither made extensive in-situation behavioral observations or identified and manipulated the relevant variables within a thoroughly controlled research design.

Among the advantages:

1. There is probably still no better way to test a hypothesis than to manipulate the relevant variables in a controlled experiment—and there is no reason to exclude the realm of death orientations from this generalization.
2. Experimentation tends to demand a higher quality of thought and effort on the part of the investigators, so even the planning process may advance the field.
3. Prevention and intervention efforts—on both a personal and sociocultural level—might be developed and tested most effectively through a true experimental approach.

Among the disadvantages:

1. The sensitive nature and complexity of many death-related situations makes experimental manipulation a risky, problematic, and, at times, ethically questionable enterprise.
2. Experimental simulations reduce (but do not necessarily solve) the problem noted above, but one is still left with the question of generalizing from the simulation to the real life situation.
3. Good experiments in this area are difficult both to design and to complete, subject to failure at many points.

The Available Research: Characteristics and Limitations

Self-report questionnaires remain the most popular technique for studying orientations toward death. Durlak and Kass (1981–1982) reviewed 15 such procedures, and others have since been introduced. The Death Anxiety Scale (DAS) developed by Donald Templer (1970) and his colleagues continues to be the most frequently employed instrument, a 15-item inventory with true-false options. A growing number of researchers prefer Kelly and Corriveau's (1995) revised version in which a Likert-type scale replaces the more limited true-false options, or Thorson and Powell's (1994) Revised Death Anxiety Scale, whose 25 items include some imported from Boyar's (1964) scale. The DAS still has a distinctive status as the first self-report questionnaire to have gone through the mill of psychometric evaluation, and, correspondingly, the instrument with the broadest database. Because so much of the available information has come from the DAS and somewhat comparable procedures, it is important to note the overall limitations of this approach (Kastenbaum, 1987–1988).

The typical study restricts its attention to "anxiety." This means that other kinds of response have no opportunity to reveal themselves. An individual's total orientation toward death might include sorrow and rage, for example. These feelings could contaminate and inflate the anxiety score. The other-than-anxiety attitudes might not show up at all. (Fortunately a new instrument and several recent studies have marked a movement away from this restriction, as we will see.)

Even more strikingly, there is no opportunity for respondents to express more positive orientations. Even a person with some "live anxiety" about death might also have such other attitudes as relief or transcendence. The death-anxiety concept tends to perpetuate itself and to command almost all of the attention because the typical study does not identify and assess other responses.

The typical study also has many other limitations. For example, usually the respondents are studied on only one occasion. Such snapshot approaches are commonplace in psychology and not without value. We learn nothing about the dynamic features and contextual moorings of death anxiety, however, when we rely so heavily on a single point of measurement. Furthermore, the respondents are often selected on the basis of easy availability. Captive populations such as college students are drawn upon with numbing frequency. There is some value in utilizing opportunistic samples—these are real people, too, of course—but this convenience tends to gain precedence over gathering data from a broader, more representative spectrum of the population. Noncollegiate, Non-Anglo, and ethnically diverse populations have received relatively little attention.

The problem often is intensified by lack of theoretical direction. College students and other captive populations are on hand, and so is a simple self-report measure—hey, let's do a study! The reader is invited to scan through several dozen studies with the questions in mind: "What is this study really about? What issues are at stake? What could it possibly illuminate or prove?" There are exceptions, to be sure, but the typical study has been pretty much an exercise in raw empiricism, animated by the availability of an instrument and a docile sample.

Other limitations? Few studies employ experimental or quasi-experimental procedures. Even fewer studies attempt to relate death-anxiety scores to behavior and decision making. This failing has contributed to a great divide between the accumulation of death-anxiety scores and behavior either in everyday life or extreme situations. It is also typical to ignore the respondent's overall attitude structure and belief system. The population samples are usually described in minimal fashion. And, curiously, studies often fail to report the basic data they have obtained. This is most likely to happen when the investigator justifies the existence of the study by testing for possible differences in death-anxiety level between two samples.

Robert A. Neimeyer's (1997–1998) review of death-anxiety research has identified still another problem: the overreliance on a single tool of statistical analysis: the simple test of correlation between two variables. He notes that there are many other types of statistical analysis that are more likely to discern complex patterns within the data. Neimeyer's point is well taken. When we begin with a fixed-choice instrument and then just skim the surface of the data we are not likely to add much knowledge—or even a smidget of understanding—to the far from simple topic of death anxiety.

A fictitious example will serve the purpose and yet protect the "innocent." Dudley Deathnik has access to a population of sales representatives for a widget dealership and also to summer students in a remedial backgammon course. Both groups complete a self-report instrument. The computer obligingly performs a correlational analysis. The printout reveals that there is not a significant difference between widgeters and backgammonites. The author's brief report (not published in my journal, *Omega*!) offers a paragraph of discussion that suggests there may be "real" differences in death anxiety between the groups, despite the lack of clear-cut statistical findings. The most popular way of sliding past such a nonfinding is to assert that one of the samples indulged in *denial*. The widgeters, let us say, are the chief suspects. They are really more anxious about death than the backgammonites, and this is shown by their artificially lowered scores. Please understand that I am not spinning a fantasy here; only the particular samples have been invented. You will find a recurrent effort to explain lower-than-anticipated scores as manifestations of denial, thereby implying much higher "real death anxiety."

These gratuitous interpretations are the more repellant because the studies involved have not bothered to include a measure of "denial." At the same time, the reports fail to describe the actual death-anxiety scores obtained by each group, focusing only on the (non)differences. After reading such studies we do not know anything more about the actual self-reported level of death anxiety among widgeters and backgammonites than we did before—nor do we know what meaningful hypotheses might have been at stake when the researchers decided to compare these samples in the first place.

Enough! It should be clear by now that studies too often have contributed their own inadequacies to the intrinsic limitations of death-anxiety scales. Fortunately, there are exceptions, and these positive exceptions are now becoming more numerous. The DAS and other self-report scales can be useful when combined with additional sources of data, and when used in more sophisticated research designs. Moreover, several other instruments have appeared that have some of the advantages of the usual death-anxiety scale, yet provide different kinds of information.

The following survey of research findings will include descriptions of some studies that have gone beyond the usual "cookie cutter" format. When no methodological comments are offered, however, the reader can safely assume that we are dealing with self-report questionnaires.

What's Been Learned from Studies of Death Anxiety?

Something *has* been learned about something! One cannot always be sure that we are learning about "death anxiety" as a relatively pure cognitive, affective, or organismic state, but there are some findings worth attention after more than three decades of research in this domain. We will see some promising signs of more innovative and incisive approaches in recent studies.

We begin with questions and topics that have attracted the most research attention or which harbor the core assumptions in the field.

How Much Do We Fear Death?

There are really two questions nesting here: (a) What is the level of death anxiety we characteristically experience in everyday life? and (b) Do we fear death too much—or perhaps not enough? We might expect research to provide a firm and direct answer to the first question and useful contextual information on the latter. We will focus first on where research has focused: the characteristic level of death anxiety, mostly as represented by scores on a self-report instrument. For the moment we will accept the usual assumption that "death anxiety" is what these instruments actually do measure.

The DAS continues to offer the best opportunity to assess the characteristic level of death anxiety in the general adult population because it has been employed in more studies than any other single measure.

How much, then, do we fear death? Not so very much at all. A respondent's score will appear in a DAS scale range from 0 to 15.

Scores above 8 would tilt in the direction of higher anxiety. Most normal respondent samples have produced mean scores that are slightly below the scale midpoint, as previous literature reviews have also found (Kastenbaum, 1992; Kastenbaum & Costa, 1977; Lester, 1967). It is more common to find samples with mean scores that are below rather than above the theoretical midpoint (e.g., Schell & Zinger, 1984). The general population—at least as sampled—reports a moderately low level of death anxiety. The four samples studied by Templer and Ruff (1971) in their norm-building research all had means within the range of 4.85 to 6.84. If the scale scores do reflect something of the individual's "true" death anxiety, then we probably should conclude that most normal adults experience only low to moderate levels. Furthermore, there is no compelling reason to believe that the DAS midpoint (or its equivalent on other instruments) represents the "real" midpoint of death anxiety in the population: no firm external criteria have been established and validated.

These are the same conclusions when I reviewed the literature for the previous edition of this book, and no data have come forth to alter them. As already noted, some researchers do not even report level of death anxiety in their samples because they are interested only in possible differences or correlations. Strange though it may be, the basic question as to how much death anxiety we characteristically experience (or report) has been abandoned by most researchers.

Perhaps we have abandoned this question too soon. *And why in the world don't we ask people to what extent death anxiety actually disturbs their daily lives?* Although the responses would be subject to the usual limits of self-report measures, we would at least start to learn something relevant to the "should" question: How much or what kind of death anxiety is most conducive to a hardy and rewarding lifestyle? (I have started to pilot test such an instrument, but it would be premature to describe and report results here.)

Several interpretations of the available data compete for our affection. Perhaps the direct self-report technique encourages people to understate their "real" anxiety. The normal person, then, could be seen as "well defended" against death anxiety. With this interpretation one could continue to favor the assumption that we are all fighting death anxiety and succeeding in keeping it under conscious control. It is consistent both with the "We cannot help but fear death" position, and with the view that industrialized technosocieties such as the United States are dedicated to the denial of death (e.g., Wahl, 1959).

A simpler alternative is that most people really do not concern themselves much about death. To be sure, this inference has a subversive ring to it. Much discourse about death has assumed a high level of death anxiety in the population. Nevertheless, this conclusion has the advantage of sticking closely to the facts and invoking no additional assumptions. It has the disadvantage of failing to please any theoretical camp and of calling into question one of the principal tenets of the death awareness movement. Is all this death education, all this preaching, all this advocacy necessary? Perhaps most people have come to reasonable terms with death and don't need to be enlightened, uplifted, desensitized, or therapized!

Both these interpretations might be rejected, however, if one takes a more critical perspective. Perhaps these self-report instruments have very little to do with death anxiety at all. We can draw no conclusions about the level of death anxiety in the general population from these measures. One might arrive at this view either by finding debilitating flaws in the particular instruments that are most often employed, or by maintaining that death anxiety cannot be realistically assessed by *any* psychometric technique. Whatever the scale scores represent, it's not that wrenching organismic and existential experience that deserves the sobriquet of death anxiety. On this view, psychometric techniques will never get the job done, but we keep using them because they're so darned handy!

Here is an even more skeptical interpretation. Perhaps these studies fail to assess death anxiety adequately because they are pursuing a chimera. "Death anxiety" is not a solid and distinctive entity. At best, it is a loose designation that has some value in calling attention to death-related themes that might occur in association with emotional arousal. Conduct a thorough examination of anxiety and stress responses across a broad spectrum of respondents and situations. Include psychophysiological and environmental, as well as cognitive and affective dimensions. What do we learn? Perhaps we learn that anxiety does not come in several different flavors. Perhaps the anxious state of being is fundamentally the same, although it may appear in a variety of contexts and be cued off by a variety of threats. One might hold out for a distinction between "normal" and "neurotic" anxiety (May, 1979), but both involve the same phenomena, although differently patterned. Not everybody will agree with the position I have just described. Nevertheless, one must at least consider the possibility that death anxiety is a seriously flawed conception that has been invoked by naive investigators employing dubious measures.

Are There Gender Differences in Death Anxiety?

This has been one of the most popular research questions, and it has yielded a fairly consistent pattern of results. Testing for possible gender differences is one of the most obvious and convenient types of analysis to perform if one has several hundred sets of test scores and no theory-driven hypotheses. Nevertheless, an interesting interpretive dialogue has developed as the results emerged.

In general, women answer more self-report items in the "death anxious" direction. The first adequate study in this area was conducted by Templer, Ruff, and Franks (1971), an important contribution because it provided a beginning set of normative data on the DAS. Subsequent reviews of the literature by Pollak (1979–1980) and Lonetto and Templer (1986) noted that higher death-anxiety scores for women were also turning up in a number of further studies. More recent reviews and studies continue to report this differential (e.g., Neimeyer & Moore, 1994). The limited data from other nations and cultures also suggest the same pattern, though it would be prudent to suspend conclusions until more such studies are reported. In lieu of impressive data to the contrary, it seems reasonable to conclude that the higher self-reported death anxiety for women is a robust finding.

But why? That is the question that is most of interest today. The most direct interpretation is that women are more anxious about death than men. This would be a consequential interpretation: if women are "too anxious" about death, then we should find out why and do something about it—right? This approach would play into traditional assumptions about "the weaker sex" and take us, willing or not, into the gender politics battlefield. However, one notices immediately that the opposite conclusion might also be drawn from the differential responses. *Perhaps men are not anxious enough!* Perhaps women are closer to their feelings or less inhibited about sharing them honestly. Taking this tack, we might encourage men to become more aware of their own feelings—or even dedicate ourselves to making men *more* anxious about death.

The fact that such conflicting conclusions can be drawn with equal ease from the same data should caution us against indulging too quickly in either adventure. We must have more adequate answers to several questions. One of the most relevant questions has already been touched upon: what do these scores really mean? The available data do not license us to conclude either that women are too anxious or men not anxious enough. Not only do we lack sufficient external (validating) evidence on "how high is high," but there is also much to learn about the sociobehavioral consequences of a particular level of anxiety.

Nevertheless, I suggest that one of these interpretations is more likely to hold true than the other. Consider, if you will, one of the most obvious facts about care for the dying and the bereaved. Who are the caregivers? Who are the people most likely to provide intimate, hands-on, every day, help? Women! Whether one steps into a "death education" course, by the bedside of a hospice patient, or the home of a recently bereaved spouse, one is much more likely to see a woman seeking knowledge or providing a personal service. The higher level of self-reported death anxiety, then, is also somehow associated with sensitivity to the needs of others and a willingness to provide care and comfort. John Wayne and Rambo are seldom on the scene.

A study by Da Silva and Schork (1984–1985) supports the interpretation that the relatively low expressed death anxiety among men has something to do with the macho effect. The researchers drew items from a questionnaire developed for *Psychology Today* by Shneidman (1970). The respondents were graduate students in public health at a midwestern university. The investigators state:

> The typical male respondent . . . recalls that death was not only not talked about openly in his family during his childhood, but when it was mentioned it was with some sense of discomfort. Although he thinks occasionally of his own death, he would be quite comfortable avoiding such thoughts and thinking about death not more than once a year. . . . He does not believe that religion had a very significant role in the development of his attitude to death. Possibly as a consequence he tends to doubt life after death and would rather believe in death as the end. . . . He feels motivated to achieve more in life when he thinks of his own mortality. (DaSilva & Schork, 1984–1985, p. 83)

The profile of the typical female respondent is quite different:

> She recalls that death was talked about openly in her family during her childhood. Presently, she thinks occasionally about her own death, but

quite a bit more frequently than her male counterparts. . . . She believes that religion played a very significant role in the development of her attitude to death. Possibly as a consequence, she strongly believes in life after death. . . . Her reaction when she thinks of her own death is a feeling of pleasure at being alive. (DaSilva & Schork, 1984–1985, p. 83)

These provocative findings well merit further attention. It is particularly interesting to learn that women take from death "a sense of pleasure at being alive," even though most studies find that women also have the higher level of death anxiety. The study also suggests powerful differences between boys and girls in early development and socialization within the family, differences that might be linked with adult attitudes toward death. The women in the Da Silva and Schork study appeared more likely to think and speak about death. Is it possible that the mere willingness to include the topic of death in our mental life has been misinterpreted as an infallible sign of anxiety? And are women perhaps more able to express themselves across the total spectrum of emotions? Dattel and Neimeyer (1990) did not find gender differences in the experience and expression of death concern, but Holcomb, Neimeyer, and Moore (1993) found that men tended to think about death in more abstract and distant terms, which seems consistent with relatively lower death-anxiety scores.

Here, as elsewhere, it would be useful to conduct death-anxiety research within a variety of well-defined contexts. A recent example from Sweden illustrates the possibilities. Sanner (1997) studied the responses of medical students to their first experiences with a cadaver. She observed that the men were more likely to have "very weak" reactions to their autopsy and dissection activities, that is, they regarded these cadaver contacts as interesting learning experiences rather than as emotional encounters with a dead person. Nevertheless, in some respects men and women responded with more similarities than differences. We would be wise to acknowledge but not to exaggerate the importance of sex differences in encountering potentially anxiety-provoking situations.

Is Death Anxiety Related to Age?

All studies bear on age, if only by inadvertence. Administer a self-report instrument to a few samples and one has at least age and sex to toy with as variables. The investigator who is reluctant or unable to come up with hypotheses can find something to report simply by examining the relationship between age and anxiety score. We might pause, however, to ask ourselves what relationship *should* be expected, and why. Two opposing hypotheses will immediately press their claims.

1. People become more anxious with advanced age because of the decreased distance from death.
2. People become less anxious because (a) death does not threaten as many of our values, and/or (b) there is a continued developmental process through which we "come to terms" with mortality.

The first of these hypotheses has an objectivistic and reductionistic slant: psychological response is regarded as an effect of "time" and "age." The individual's life history and personality make-up are negligible factors. The aged person's heightened death anxiety is largely an epiphenomenon, the product of intrinsic biochemical alterations and the implacable slipping of sand through the hourglass. By contrast, the second hypotheses meshes well with a number of life-span developmental theories, such as Erik Erikson's (1979), and with Robert Butler's (1963) concept of the life review. Life's last task is to accept the life we have lead, including the death by which it is concluded. The "successful maturer" might therefore be expected to experience less death anxiety as the turbulence of youth and identity-seeking gives way to a mature sense of fulfillment and acceptance. Therefore, death is not the same catastrophic threat that it was when so much of what one valued existed only in the realm of expectation and hope.

Standing apart from these competing hypotheses is the possibility that:

3. Age per se does *not* have a strong and predictable influence on our psychological orientation toward death.

Gerontological research across a wide variety of topics has shown that chronological age (within the adult spectrum) is not the all-powerful predictor that one might suppose. Marked individual differences occur at the same echelon—in physiological as well as sociobehavioral functioning. Furthermore, current life circumstances can also exert a powerful influence over thoughts, actions, and health status. Perhaps age is but a general index that conceals as much as it reveals. Age might be a valuable piece of information, but only one piece in a larger pattern. If I learned anything from my early clinical experience with geriatric patients, it was that one person's view of life and death was likely to be contradicted by the next person I met. It would be simplistic, then, to expect a strong and universal relationship between adult age and orientation toward death.

So much for the lovely theories. The data are rather more homely. The first thing to notice is that all the studies are cross-sectional. (Unfortunately this statement has remained true over the years: the few major longitudinal studies do not delve much into the individual's experiences and views of the world.) Data obtained from cross-sectional studies do not tell us how the same person regarded death at different ages. The available data only allow us to compare merely the death orientations of younger and older people—who differ by cohort experiences as well as by age. Between today's 20-year-old and today's 80-year-old there is more than a difference of six decades. There is a difference in the actual person, in the historical period during which each entered the world, and in the sociocultural circumstances and events with which they contend at every age level. Furthermore, the 80-year-old has clearly demonstrated that he or she is a survivor; this may or may not be true of the 20-year-old whose attitudes toward death were assessed on the same day. Our sample of older adults is always biased by the (fortunate) fact of their success in surviving earlier perils—and the odds of survival continue to change with each generation.

What conclusions can be drawn from the available data, then, taking into account this major methodological limitation? First, it is clear that *older people in general do not report higher levels of death anxiety.* Virtually no support can be found for the proposition that elderly adults live with an elevated sense of fear, anxiety, or distress centering on the prospect of their mortality. An early study by Jeffers, Nichols, and Eisdorfer (1961) of community-dwelling adults in North Carolina found that many more (35%) reported a lack of death fear, as compared with the relatively few (10%) who admitted to such fear. Corey

(1960) was among the first to compare young and old within the same study, finding no significant differences in death fears on the basis of a "homemade" projective technique.

Outstanding among the pioneering studies was the sophisticated investigation conducted in the Netherlands by J. M. A. Munnichs (1966). One hundred elderly respondents were encouraged to spin out the stories of their lives. More specific questions were then asked about their death-related thoughts and feelings. Several of his results are of particular relevance here. First, clear and important individual differences were observed. As his case histories demonstrate, it would be erroneous to draw up a single profile of the older person's orientation toward death. Several basic orientations or strategies were found. Most frequent was *acceptance*, which, along with *acquiescence*, constituted the most common orientation. About two thirds of the sample expressed a predominately positive conception of dying and preparation for death. Nevertheless, it was not unusual to find *evasion* or *escape* as the dominating strategy. Together with the persistent attempt to ignore death, this set of responses characterized about one person in three. As Munnichs' report makes clear, there were interesting variations within as well as between each general type of death orientation.

Another useful finding was an apparent difference between the "young old" and the "old old." Men and women in their seventies often were still confronting their finitude. Although they differed in the particular ways in which they contemplated personal mortality, there was an active cognitive process at work, as though asking themselves: "What should death mean to me at this time in my life?" By contrast, the very old often seemed to have taken their "final stand" and were no longer interested in altering their views. It is unfortunate that this finding by Munnichs has been almost entirely overlooked. Gerontologists have documented important differences between "young-old" and "old-old" in many domains. Munnichs' study suggests that differences may also be found in the contemplation of life and death as people continue to age. Munnichs "most important conclusion is that only a small category of old people (7 of 100) were in fear of the end. For the greater part (55) their experience of finitude was of a well-known, a familiar phenomenon" (p. 124).

Marked individual differences were also found in a psychological autopsy series (retrospective case histories reviewed from multiple perspectives) conducted in a geriatric hospital (Kastenbaum & Weisman, 1972; Weisman & Kastenbaum, 1968). The 120 elders were almost equally divided between those who continued to be active as long as possible during their final illness, and those who took to their beds and withdrew from others to await death. Again, individual personality seems more important than age as a long life approaches its end.

Most studies in recent years have relied on fixed-choice self-report measures, such as the DAS. Templer et al. (1971) found no significant differences in level of death anxiety among adults in the 19 to 85 age range. Subsequent studies have either confirmed this "no difference" or have found a lower anxiety level for senior adults. Pollak's (1979–1980) literature review concluded that there is no evidence for an increase in death anxiety with increasing adult age, and this conclusion continues to hold true (e.g., Thorson & Powell, 1994). Correlations between death anxiety and age are sometimes weak, sometimes weaker.

Is age an unimportant or irrelevant variable, then? Not necessarily. The pattern of findings indicates that simply knowing a person's age does not provide a satisfactory basis for predicting his or her self-reported level of death anxiety. Nevertheless, age may be a useful variable as part of a more complex and realistic approach to understand how and why people contemplate death. Two studies well illustrate this possibility. Three samples of normal adults (a total of 258) were asked by Stricherz and Cunnington (1981–1982) to express their death concerns: high school students, employed adults (mean age: 42), and retirees. This investigation gave respondents the opportunity to indicate the particular type of concerns they had, not just their overall level of anxiety.

Each age echelon had a somewhat different pattern of concerns. The students were most apprehensive about the possible loss of loved ones, death as a punishment, and the finality of death. The working adults expressed their greatest concerns about fear of pain in dying, as well as the possibility of premature death. These midlife people showed the relatively least concern about the possible impact of their deaths upon other people. The major concerns of the older adults centered around the fear of becoming helpless and dependent on others—the process of dying, rather than the outcome.

A particular fear was of being kept alive in an undignified, semivegetative state. They preferred a quick death at the right time to a long, slow deterioration. The senior adults also were concerned about the impact of their dying and death upon their loved ones. It should be kept in mind that this study, like the others, compared different people at different ages. Nevertheless, the results urge us to go beyond level of anxiety in order to discover the specific concerns of an individual or group. In this study, for example, we could probably find an adolescent, a working adult, and a retired adult with the same overall anxiety score—but each might have a very different priority of concerns, and these differences could be decisive in any prevention or intervention effort.

Another informative study was conducted by Kalish and Reynolds (1977), who interviewed more than 400 adults (from age 20 through 60+) in the Los Angeles area. Unlike almost all other studies, these investigators included substantial samples of African American, Japanese American, and Mexican American respondents, as well as Anglos. Across these diverse samples, the younger adults were most likely to report "having had the unexplainable feeling that they were going to die." The oldest respondents reported dreaming less often about death, and were "more likely to accept death peacefully." Another age difference was found in response to the question: "How would you like to spend the last 6 months of your life?"

The oldest group preferred contemplation and prayer, while the midlifers would not alter their existing life style, and the young were concerned about the effect of their death upon others. It should be noted, however, that many questions were answered in a similar way by all age groups.

We will touch on age again when attention is given to the general pattern of death-anxiety correlations. First, however, let us return briefly to the starting hypotheses.

One hypothesis can be rejected for lack of support, based on available data. There is little empirical support for the view that "People become more anxious with advanced age because of the decreased distance from death." The wind that blows away this hypothesis leaves us with several benefits. *When a particular elderly person does show elevated death anxiety, this should be regarded as a warning signal.* It is not an automatic or natural correlate of growing old—something else must be happening. In other words, the data encourage an activist orientation, not the passive response that "of course, he or she's anxious, that's just what should be expected." Another benefit is the call for a truly psychological approach. Neither chronological age nor the objective (probabilistic) distance from death are as useful as the individual's own thoughts and feelings.

The third hypothesis receives qualified support. A number of studies have shown no adult age differences in death anxiety and concerns in death anxiety. The richer studies have also obtained patterns of findings in which there are both similarities and differences in type of death concern. Age has not disappeared as a variable, but it offers only a weak basis for prediction and understanding. It is a mistake to attribute cause-and-effect power to chronological age in general, and here the empirical findings underline this proposition. A more useful approach is to wonder: "What is it about being 20, 40, or 80 that might contribute to an individual's overall way of looking at death?" The answers will be more complex but also more useful than those milled out by a simplistic age-causation model.

The second hypothesis has been saved for this later point in the discussion. Do we become less anxious with advanced age and, if so, does this result from a mixture of reduced threat and matured perspective?

Studies have often found that a substantial number of elderly respondents express an orientation toward death that is "something other than anxiety." A case can be made for the reduced anxiety hypothesis. A clear example can be found in the Kalish and Reynolds study which, along with an interview, made use of a helpful technique devised by Diggory and Rothman (1961) that asks respondents to indicate their relative concern about several aspects of death. One of the items is: "I could no longer care for my dependents." It is not surprising to learn that the oldest respondents considered this to be a lesser concern as compared with the youngest adults in the sample. In other words, the prospect of death was not as strong a threat in at least one respect: the elderly men and women had already discharged most of their responsibilities as parents and caregivers.

I have recruited this as an example to support the reduced anxiety hypothesis. Some concerns might decrease substantially with age. Other concerns, however, do not diminish, and some increase, such as fear of outliving one's financial resources and becoming a burden on others. Individual differences also remain important. Furthermore, these patterns may change with time and circumstance. For example, the octogenarian who supervises the outreach activities of a church or civic group could be more concerned about "who will take my place and provide care?" than some younger people who operate on a self-absorbed basis.

What of the other facet of this hypothesis—that we "come to terms with mortality" in a more seasoned and matured manner with advancing age, a "final task" for psychosocial development? This is one of the more difficult hypotheses to evaluate fairly. We may be predisposed to accept this hypothesis because it has been endorsed by influential theorists—and because we might like to believe it true. A useful way to gain perspective on this attractive hypothesis is to challenge it with a far less appealing alternative. Here, again, we will draw upon the data base.

"Don't think about it. Doesn't worry me." This type of response was noted by Munnichs among some of his elderly respondents. Ignoring, evading, and escaping death-related topics were more common strategies than out-and-out anxiety. Is it possible, then, that what might pass as serenity should be understood instead as denial? As Munnichs observes, it is not always easy to distinguish between a strongly motivated aversion to thinking about death and the attitude of being "absorbed in the present without worrying about the future." Along with denial is the possibility that "To attach a philosophical significance to the 'end' would be in fact premature." An elderly individual may not be ready to make death his or her number one concern.

The apparently "nonanxious" orientation toward death might reflect, then: (a) *denial*, in which a critical zone of reality has been screened off; (b) *unreadiness*, in which psychological preparations have not yet reached the point of confronting an acknowledged but unattractive aspect of reality; and (c) *acceptance*, in which death has been integrated within a mature life perspective. Many of the available studies provide such limited types of data that one cannot distinguish among these alternatives. Low self-reported anxiety could signify denial, unreadiness, or acceptance—and perhaps other states of mind as well.

There are other reasons to be wary of the hypothesis that maturity naturally brings a reduction in death anxiety. This view assumes that maturity takes essentially the same form and displays the same characteristics in everybody. I find this assumption questionable, and not well supported (or even examined) by life-span developmental research.

There may be truth to the assertion that reduced death anxiety is a key component or outcome of the later phases of adult development.

We race far ahead of the facts if we assume this to be true, however. We also perhaps rush to embrace a pleasing idea without sufficient pause for inquiry. There is still much to learn about the general nature of later development and the specific processes through which we come to terms with personal mortality. The denial hypothesis remains an alternative that cannot be ignored at the present time (not that we understand denial that well, either).

CORRELATES OF HIGH AND LOW DEATH ANXIETY

One person has a relatively high level of death anxiety, another has a relatively low level. In what other ways are these people likely to differ? Age and sex have already been examined. Some studies have attempted to expand the scope of variables that might be associated with differences in death anxiety. We will look at the general pattern of findings that has emerged and give particular attention to recent studies and theories. First, it might be useful to think for a moment about what we might expect to discover. Although many studies are atheoretical, an obvious hypothesis does come to mind:

> H1 *Relatively high death anxiety should be associated with an overall pattern of psychological and perhaps social and physiological distress.*

This hypotheses would be consistent with the view that relatively high death anxiety is a mark of psychopathology or immaturity. For an alternative hypothesis we might consider:

> H2 *Relatively high death anxiety is a distinctive response to a distinctive set of circumstances; therefore, the pattern of correlates will not be characteristic of ordinary psychopathology.*

In other words, there is something special about death anxiety, and we must learn precisely what individual and situational factors are associated with extreme levels of response (high or low).

An additional hypothesis comes to mind when we study the lives of creative people and emergent situations:

> H3 Relatively high death awareness will be associated with
> a keener appreciation of life, heightened creativity, and
> with periods of individual and cultural transition and
> growth.

Perhaps our awareness of death is enhanced during risky situations. This could be a survival-oriented phenomenon. The businessperson contemplating a major new venture, the teen-age couple running off together, the cult trekking off to start its own utopian community—in circumstances such as these one may experience an excitement born of both opportunity and risk. The "deathness" of the anxiety might reflect varying components of both symbolic and literal risk. "I will just die if I don't make it!" is not an unknown feeling, while transition and growth situations may alter the actual risk of death in various ways. Creative people often contribute to producing their own crises as they attempt to turn their visions into reality and may feel as though they are hovering between life and death during these vicissitudes.

Now to the data—

Demographics of Death Anxiety

There are some weak indications that people in favorable socioeconomic circumstances report relatively lower levels of death anxiety. Demographic differences were often reported in a set of studies reviewed by Lonetto and Templer (1986). Being highly educated and enjoying a good income were characteristics usually associated with a relatively low score on the DAS. The actual differences were rather small, however, and not all studies did find differences. Education and affluence, then, might be regarded as buffers against high death anxiety, if not very powerful buffers. However, an unpublished study by Farley (1971) that did not come to the reviewers' attention showed a contradictory finding: among college men, those of higher socioeconomic status also had the higher level of self-reported death anxiety.

The demographic profile of a relatively "low death anxious" person also includes coming from an intact family. Case studies of suicidal people (e.g., Heckler, 1994) frequently reveal backgrounds of major family dysfunction that contribute to episodes of extreme anxiety and depression. These observations suggest that growing up in a secure interpersonal environment offers some protection against death anxiety. There are also hints in the Lonetto and Templer review that higher levels of (test-measured) intelligence also insulate against death anxiety, but these correlations are neither very strong nor entirely consistent. Death educators and counselors frequently come into contact with bright, affluent people from intact families who also are experiencing an uncomfortably high level of death anxiety.

Surprisingly, not much attention has been given to marital status, although this information is routinely obtained in demographic studies. Marital status is related to longevity and causes of death in a number of ways. Married people, for example, generally are at a lower risk for suicide, but this risk increases significantly in the immediate aftermath of a spouse's death. Two early studies (Cole, 1978–1979; Morrison & Cometa, 1982) came up with discordant results. There well may be many caches of death anxiety lying about in which marital status information has been obtained but not analyzed and reported. At present the relationship between marital status and death anxiety remains speculative.

There is more to family dynamics than marital status, of course. A recent study (Reimer & Templer, 1995–1996) finds a "family resemblance" in death anxiety between parents and their adolescent children; this was true both with Filipino and U.S. samples. Perhaps specialists in family relationships would find it useful to include death-anxiety measures in their studies to broaden our knowledge of the interpersonal side of this phenomenon.

Ethnic and Cultural Correlates

Does ethnic-cultural group membership have any consistent relationship with death anxiety? Most studies have been conducted with primarily Anglo populations in the United States and Canada. There have been a scattering of studies with more diverse populations, however. Kalish and Reynolds (1977) found many differences in attitudes toward death among their four Los Angeles samples (Black, Japanese American, Mexican American, Anglo). These differences seem to have reflected socioeconomic status as well as the particular lifestyles favored by each group. This was an indepth study that is worth reading in its entirety. One useful lesson from the Kalish and Reynolds findings should be mentioned here, however. The Mexican American response to death tended to be highly emotional (from an Anglo perspective)—but the Anglo response tended to be "unduly cold and cruel" from the Mexican American perspective! In other words, ethnic and cultural styles can have a marked influence on the frameworks we employ to observe and evaluate death anxiety. The same type and level of response can be seen as either "too anxious" or "not anxious and caring enough," depending upon cultural norms. How much has our overall view of death anxiety been distorted by overreliance on mainstream Anglo norms? We do not have a firm answer to this question.

Two studies have found that Egyptians report levels of death anxiety that are slightly higher than those of Canadian and United States citizens (Abdel-Khalek, 1986; Beshai & Templer, 1978). As the latter investigator notes, however, "the Egyptian and American death anxiety similarities overshadow the differences" (Abdel-Khalek, p. 483). Beshai and Templer prefer to emphasize the differences, though, and suggest that "A developing society such as Egypt is more likely than a society such as the U. S. to find itself in the throes of compounded threats to human life." A study conducted in Hong Kong (Ho & Shiu, 1995) took note of the extremely high level of anxiety about cancer within that culture. Interestingly, the DAS scores of cancer patients were neither higher than a comparison group of patients with hand injuries, nor than the usual norms for a general population. However, the authors observed a different pattern of communicating about dying and death among those cancer patients who did have high DAS scores. These patients used passive aggression more frequently which

> can be understood by the fact that the Chinese seldom express their anger openly and tend to avoid direct confrontation in dealing with conflicts. Rather they would use . . . indirect language, middlemen, face-saving ploys, and so on to resolve conflicts. This is especially so in dealing with mystical things like death. Hence, it is likely that Chinese cancer patients with very strong fear toward death tend to use an indirect way to express their anxiety and anger. (Ho & Schiu, p. 64)

Ho and Schiu's use of behavioral observation and cultural insight along with a standard death-anxiety measure provides more valuable information than studies relying entirely on scales. Our understanding of culture-relevant ways of experiencing and coping with death anxiety would be advanced by more studies of this type.

If death anxiety is closely related to the objective or perceived threat of death, then we might expect Blacks in the United States to express more concern than Anglo's because of their less favorable life expectation. A study utilizing responses to a national Lewis Harris poll failed to support this hypothesis (Marks, 1986–1987). Because of methodological limitations noted by the author, this study can be considered only as an exploration. It is possible, for example, that a person in good health may consider questions about advanced age and death as topics too remote to take seriously.

Religious Affiliation and Belief

Religion could be seen as either a buffer against death anxiety, or a source of special concern (e.g., fear of damnation), (salvation and immortality). It would be naive, however, to expect any simple relationship to emerge. Religious belief and practice can differ appreciably within the same faith, and the link with emotional response can also be an idiosyncratic matter. In clinical work with aged men and women, I have known a number of people who maintained an unquestioned belief that they would awaken after death to find themselves in heaven. And yet, some were experiencing an anxiety state, and others were serene. Religious faith was certainly important to all these people, but did not of itself adequately predict or explain what they were experiencing as death approached.

Templer and Dotson (1970) found no significant relationship between a variety of religious variables and death anxiety in an undergraduate sample. A variety of subsequent studies have come up with almost every kind of finding imaginable—no differences, positive relationships, and negative relationships! There is some indication that "faith" may be associated with a lower level of death anxiety, while a "good works" orientation toward religion has little or no bearing. Substantially higher death-anxiety scores have been found for Catholics as compared with Protestants in a sample of about 400 California high school students and their parents (Reimer & Templer, 1995–1996). Nevertheless, possible differences among various denominations remain unclear, and we still know even less about the relationship between religious belief and practice and the individual's personal orientation toward death. Even studies limited to a few quantifiable variables tend to come up with inconclusive or perplexing results (e.g., Thorson & Powell, 1994). It is probable that religion enters into our death orientations in a complex manner that requires understanding of cultural history, situational context, and individual psychology.

Is the "death anxious" person more anxious in general? And does religion serve mostly to insulate or to elevate death anxiety? These are questions we still cannot answer on the basis of solid data. Enterprising researchers might find it fruitful to look beyond the usual indices of church affiliation and activity. Many people have religious motivations and experiences that are not bounded by traditional religious institutions. These alternative approaches to religious experience encompass a broad spectrum of beliefs and practices, some of which feature conceptions of reincarnation that are not included in the core Judeo-Christian tradition. Furthermore, near-death experiences often have a mystical dimension, and it has been widely reported that a reduction in death anxiety occurs in consequence of such experiences. Alternative religious practices and responses to near-death experiences are among the potentially instructive new area for death-anxiety inquiry. Further use of the Death Threat Index (TI) could also be helpful. This measure (Neimeyer, Dingemans, & Epting, 1977; Neimeyer, Epting, & Rigdon, 1984) is more sophisticated and theoretically grounded than the death-anxiety scales that still dominate the field. At present the TI findings on religiosity do not adhere into a coherent pattern, but show enough promise to be worth continued investigation.

Personality and Lifestyle Correlates

Are certain personality or lifestyle characteristics differentially associated with death anxiety? One major lifestyle characteristic is sexual affinity. In their norm-building study, Templer and Ruff (1971) included 260 homosexuals (165 males, 95 females) with an age range extending from 17 to 87. The overall level of self-reported death anxiety fell in the midrange for normal (nonclinical) populations. There was no particular reason to expect any basic differences in death anxiety on the basis of sexual preference (although the male to female discrepancy usually found in heterosexual populations did not show up here).

AIDS has radically affected the lives of many people since the Templer and Ruff study, with homosexual males among those at particularly high risk. Furthermore, continuing developments in medical management of AIDS might be expected to have continuing influences on death anxiety both among those with HIV/AIDS and those in fear of contracting the illness. In the early years of the epidemic it was generally believed that HIV would always convert to AIDS sooner or later, and that AIDS would invariably prove fatal. This "death sentence" assumption has now given way to a more complex set of experiences and attitudes as more people live longer and in better health though afflicted with HIV. The improved outlook for people with AIDS does not guarantee a substantial reduction in death anxiety, however. When uncertainty replaces despair there may well be an upsurge of anxiety: it is difficult to keep both hope and dread in balance.

Research on the relationship between AIDS and death anxiety is just starting to be reported. Hintze, Templer, Cappelletty, and Frederick (1994) found that death anxiety was higher among those HIV-infected males with a more impaired medical status. This would seem to be a common-sense finding, but actually it deviates from previous studies, which have *not* found a strong positive relationship between severity of physical illness and death anxiety. There was another unexpected finding that might affect our understanding of health communication if substantiated by additional studies: *death anxiety was higher for those men whose diagnosis was known by family and partners.* Most counselors have been acting on the assumption that it is helpful to develop an open communication context to encourage mutual support and understanding. The present findings suggest that there may be important exceptions to this principle and therefore deserve further investigation.

Several studies have sought to test the general hypothesis that death anxiety will be associated with other indices of disturbance or ineffective coping techniques. There is some support for this hypothesis, but the differences are often small, and some studies find none at all. This mixed picture was well summarized a few years ago by Pollak (1979–1980). College students who reported a relatively higher sense of competence, for example, tended to report lower levels of death anxiety (Farley, 1971; Nogas, Schweitzer, & Grumet, 1974). Although statistically significant, these differences would have little value in any practical circumstance.

A set of pioneering studies showed some support for the hypothesis that people with a clear sense of purpose in their lives and/or high self esteem have less death anxiety than those lack purpose or "meaning" (e.g., Davis, Martin, Wilee, & Voorhees, 1978; Durlak, 1972). Viswanatham's (1996) recent questionnaire study of physicians adds new dimensions to this line of inquiry. He found that physicians who felt they had a strong purpose in life had a lower level of self-reported death anxiety. Having a sense of being in control of one's life also was related to lower death anxiety. These findings held true across gender and medical specialty (although, as usual, death-anxiety scores were higher for the female physicians).

Viswanatham broadened his inquiry to include the physician's preferred way of communicating with next of kin when a patient is critically ill or has died. We might expect that physicians with high death anxiety would prefer indirect notification (telephone instead of direct contact). And so it was! This finding illustrates one simple but effective technique for exploring links between death anxiety and behavior. It also builds up the credibility of the hypothesis that having one's own life under control both keeps death anxiety within bounds and makes it possible to interact with people who are encountering death-related problems.

A recent Canadian study further supports a connection between personality, anxiety, and behavior in death-related situations. Taking an innovative approach, Lefcourt and Shepherd (1995) hypothesized that people with humorless authoritarian personalities would have relatively higher fear of death and would therefore avoid dealing with the question of organ donation. This hypothesis was borne out: The humorless authoritarians in their sample were the ones most likely to leave blank the organ donation forms attached to their driver's licenses. Lefcourt and Shepherd suggest that people with authoritarian type personalities would also be especially resistant to facing their mortality in a wider spectrum of situations.

Earlier studies reported that people with relatively high death anxiety tend to be more open, sensitive, and vulnerable than those with low self-reported death anxiety (e.g., Neufeldt & Holmes, 1979; Thorson, 1977). These are also people who seem more capable of empathy and less invested in aggressive, exhibitionistic, and achievement-oriented activities. This configuration is found among both sexes, but seems to occur most often in women—who, as already noted—comprise the larger proportion of people who select person-oriented and caregiving professions.

The more "armored" orientation of those with lower self-reported death anxiety makes it difficult to evaluate one type of person as better adjusted than the other. Is vulnerability, sensitivity, and empathy a positive configuration if accompanied also by higher death anxiety? Is lower death anxiety a positive characteristic if accompanied by a more self-seeking and emotionally defensive orientation? Or are these but alternative lifestyles, each with their advantages and each with their emotional cost?

It should be kept in mind that we are still dealing here with studies of normal or nonclinical populations. The high death-anxiety respondents do not appear to be incapacitated by their concerns, nor are the low anxiety respondents necessarily displaying a pathological degree of evasion or denial. The student of social work with a relatively high level of death anxiety and the student in the college of business with a lower level probably have many other differences in the way they approach life, and it would seem inappropriate to categorize one as "healthy" or "mature," and the other in pejorative terms. Conceivably, society is well served by having people with varied orientations toward death—including the steadfast denier who will take risks that others shun.

Terror Management Theory and the Anxiety-Buffer Hypothesis

A theoretical approach with some promise has recently been introduced into the study of death anxiety. Terror management theory draws on the writings of Becker (1962, 1973, 1975) who, as already noted, argued that fear of death is at the root of all our other fears. Becker believed that much of what we call civilization consists of a desperate attempt to keep our death anxiety under control. We are mortal. We are vulnerable. We cannot really eliminate all threats to our security. What *can* we do, then? As a society we can construct and preserve a worldview that gives us the sense of coherence and stability. As individuals we can buy into this worldview. If I am successful in being the kind of person who is approved by my society, then I am protected from mortal anxieties both by my personal self-esteem and the sense of belonging to a powerful entity greater than myself. The prospect of symbolic immortality through our enduring social institutions helps to insulate the individual from the fear of personal annihilation.

Terror management theory was introduced into the dying and death literature by Tomer (1994) as he identified possible theoretical directions that might stimulate more useful research. Tomer observed that several studies had already found a negative correlation between self-esteem and death anxiety. A therapeutic possibility was also noted: People with high death anxiety might find relief by interventions that increased their self-esteem.

This approach is already stimulating interesting research. Harmon-Jones et al. (1997) attempted to test both the self-esteem hypothesis and the implicit *anxiety-buffer hypothesis*:

> If a psychological structure (worldview faith or self-esteem) provides protection against anxiety, then strengthening that structure should make one less prone to exhibit anxiety or anxiety-related threats, and weakening that structure should make one more prone to exhibit anxiety or anxiety-related behavior in response to threats. (Harmon-Jones et al., p. 24)

Instead of relying on the usual correlational approaches, this research team conducted three experiments which attempted to manipulate the participants' sense of self-esteem and determine the effect on their worldviews. The results of all three experiments supported the hypotheses. Heightened self-esteem seemed to "fortify a frontline, direct defense against death-related concern" (pp. 33–34). Participants with higher self-esteem also had less need to protecting themselves against death anxiety by increasing their reliance on a worldview defense. In other words, we can defend ourselves against the breakthrough of death anxiety either by increasing our self-esteem or making a greater psychological investment in reassuring sociocultural constructions of life and death. Either or both of these self-protective strategies may come into play when we encounter "mortality salient" situations.

This study is encouraging not only for its findings but its methodology. It is one of the few death-anxiety researches that has employed an experimental method to test theory-driven hypotheses. It is true that the experimental manipulations were of the classroom variety and the participants were the usual convenience sample of college students, but it nevertheless represents an advance over most previous studies.

Terror Without Management?

What should we expect to happen if this type of experiment were reversed—lowering self-esteem or undermining the worldview defense? Would death anxiety than leap out of the bushes like a hungry tiger? And, if so, how would we respond to this menace if our most effective defensive strategies were disabled? There are ethical reasons to hesitate before designing such a study. We might instead look at situations that occur as part of the disappointments and risks of everyday life in a changing society. Our methodology might first include the identification of situations in which people suffer a major or precipitous loss of self-esteem: a lover rejected, an employee "downsized," a person "dissed" by his or her peer group. If the results of the Harmon-Jones et al. study can be read in reverse, we would expect a heightened vulnerability to anxiety when one encounters a death-related situation (perhaps even as indirect as something seen on television). But the effect might be even more powerful. Perhaps ordinary situations would start to look and feel dangerous. Having lost faith in one's self, the person may feel more at risk in everyday life. Here we are going beyond the assumption that some situations are "mortality salient" while others are not. Almost any situation could be perceived as death related if one felt exposed and helpless.

Becker and the terror management theorists would probably suggest at this point that the person suffering from low self-esteem would seek rescue by embracing a comforting worldview. In all likelihood this worldview would be one that is already well established and dominant. One might become more religious, for example, or more patriotic, or both. The intensity of one's need to keep death anxiety under control might contribute to such a zealous advocacy of a worldview that much else is neglected. At the extreme we would have the fanatic. Many others might stop short of fanaticism but go through life with their energies absorbed by the need to maintain a worldview that offers protection from mortal anxiety.

But what if reassuring worldviews were not so readily available? What if neither individual self-esteem nor cultural belief systems were up to the task of defending us against death anxiety? Our methodology might then expand to include behavioral outcomes on the one hand and the broad panoply of sociotechnical change that has become known as postmodernism. For example, what if the individual finds it both more difficult to believe in traditional religious faiths and to embrace an uncritical patriotism. And what if the weakening of traditional social institutions occurs at the same time that family structure is also under increasing stress? And—if you can pardon one more "what if"—suppose that the mad violence of war has also made a powerful impact on society? in other words: suppose we have had Korea and Viet Nam as well as a constant stream of both foreign and domestic violence flowing to us through media if not through personal experience?

In theoretical terms, it would seem that mortality salience has penetrated our society's defenses through war and terrorism while traditional societal institutions have seemed to falter (or even to have taken the side of destruction). Self-esteem may be even more difficult to develop for children reared in families under multiple pressures who then face the rigors of a highly competitive society. The individual therefore may be exposed to mortality salient situations without the resources of a firm developmental basis for self-esteem or a secure worldview. How, then, are death terrors to be avoided? How about suicide? How about murder, becoming the instrument of death oneself? How about alcohol? How about drugs? These are by no means the only possible responses to the fear of fear. Nevertheless, we might give increased attention to possible links between terror management and some of the major problems in our society today.

Anxiety or Depression?

Many of the people I have known during the last phase of their lives did have fears as well as a general sense of anxiety. The fears were usually realistic: perhaps they would not receive adequate medication if they experienced severe pain; perhaps they would not be able to guide their children through their own difficult situations. The anxiety often hovered around uncertainties in the situation, such as, when would they lose their remaining physical and mental functions? Nevertheless, most of these people were not overwhelmed with anxiety. They had various feelings at various times, including a sense of relief, even eagerness to have it all over and done with, as well as positive feelings related to the good lives they had experienced and the good things they had accomplished. But, day in and day out, they often felt sad. I should say they were depressed. I think, though, that "sadness" more accurately conveys their feelings about leaving all they have known of life.

As previously noted, research has focused on anxiety to the near exclusion of other feelings and attitudes. Fortunately, the range of inquiry is broadening. One study has already found empirical differences between death-related depression and anxiety (Triplett et al., 1995). Some people were more likely to report feelings that life is bleak, meaningless, and unhappy, while others reported fear and dread. Abdel-Khalek (1997) has also found differences between anxiety and depression with an Egyptian sample. These findings will not surprise experienced clinicians, but they do suggest that we may learn more if our inquiry methods give depression and anxiety a chance to sort themselves out.

Personifications, Imagery, Fantasy, and Dreams

Many of the studies already consulted have relied on direct self-report measures. We now sample some of the studies that have explored imagery and fantasy life.

The tendency to visualize Death as a person has been demonstrated throughout history. Personifications had appeared in art, literature, drama, and mythology long before Death starred as a sardonic chess player in Ingmar Bergman's masterful film, *The Seventh Seal*. Awareness of this tradition enabled McClelland (1963) and Greenberger (1965) to include personifications in personality theory and research. Nagy (1959) also found spontaneous personifications in her studies with children. We will concentrate here upon studies of death personification in adults.

Our own early research on death personification was summarized in the original *Psychology of Death* (Kastenbaum & Aisenberg, 1972). In the first study, a set of open-end questions was posed to 240 adults;

another sample of 421 responded to a multiple choice version. Most of the respondents in both samples were college students.

The open-end version included the following questions:

> If death were a person, what sort of a person would Death be? Think of this question until an image of death-as-a-human being forms in your mind. Then describe Death physically, what Death would look like. . . . Now, what would Death be like? What kind of personality would Death have?

The age and sex imagined for Death was obtained by follow-up questions, if not clear from the first response. Additionally, respondents were asked to indicate their sources for their images of death and the degree of difficulty the task had held.

The multiple choice version was established after analyzing data from the open-end version:

1. In stories, plays and movies, Death is sometimes treated as though a human being. If you were writing a story in which one character would represent Death, would you represent Death as (a) a young man, (b) an old man, (c) a young woman, (d) an old woman? If other, please specify.
2. Would Death be (a) a cold, remote sort of person, (b) a gentle, well-meaning sort of person, (c) a grim, terrifying sort of person?

Four clear types of personification emerged from these studies. These were labeled The Macabre, The Gentle Comforter, The Gay Deceiver, and The Automaton.

The Macabre was characterized as a powerful, overwhelming, and repulsive figure. The image often was of an emaciated or decaying human, or of a monster with only faint resemblance to human form. Sometimes there was the specific image of a death-like death, in which Death is portrayed as himself in the process of being consumed. Macabre personifications also tended to be emotionally close to their creators. One young man, for example, reported that "a shivering and nausea overwhelms me" when he thinks about the image he has produced. A young woman pictured death as a "gigantic being of superhuman strength. A body to which one would relinquish all hopes of resistance. He would be cold and dark, in such a way that one glance would reveal his mission. He would be always dressed in black and would wear a hat which he wore tightly over his head . . . self-confident with an abundance of ego. He would naturally be callous and would enjoy his occupation. He would get a greater thrill when the person whom he was claiming was enjoying life to a great degree." The Macabre personification often was presented in the form of a hideous old man.

The Gentle Comforter is embued with the theme of soothing welcome. It could be seen as an adult of any age. When presented as an old man, Father Time received much credit as a source. The Gentle Comforter was an image that came readily to many respondents. The idea of a powerful force quietly employed in a kindly way is perhaps at the core of this personification. The respondents often felt they were emotionally close to their Gentle Comforter image, but not in a threatened manner. One woman's response well typifies this type of personification:

> A fairly old man with long white hair and a long beard. A man who would resemble a biblical figure with a long robe which is clean but shabby. He would have very strong features and despite his age would appear to have strength. His eyes would be very penetrating and his hands would be large. Death would be calm, soothing, and comforting. His voice would be of an alluring nature and, although kind, would hold the tone of the mysterious. Therefore, in general, he would be kind and understanding and yet be very firm and sure of his actions and attitudes.

The Gay Deceiver was pictured as an attractive and sensuous person of either sex, often elegant and worldly. Poised and sophisticated, the Gay Deceiver entices its victim, a knowing companion one might seek out for amusement, adventure, or excitement. Those who depict this type of personification often state explicitly that the Gay Deceiver tempts and lures us on, and "Then you would learn who he really is, and it would be too late." That "who he really is" might be a modern dress version of the devil is a possibility, and there are occasional direct references, such as, "He is a little on the slim side though looks fairly powerful. He has a very dark goatee coming to a point . . . wearing a dark suit. . . . I see death right now almost in the same way as the devil." Another respondent:

> Death is either a man and/or a woman. This death person is young to middle-aged and very good looking. The man is about 35 or 40

with dark hair, graying at the sides. The woman is tall, beautiful with dark hair and about 30. . . . Both have very subtle and interesting personalities. They're suave, charming, but deceitful, cruel, and cold. . . . Both are really sharp. You like them and they lead you on.

The Gay Deceiver seems to embody characteristics of both an ego ideal (for some people), and a con man. Perhaps on one level, the Gay Deceiver is a character who has stepped out of a morality play—one of the temptations from Everyman, or Sportin' Life in Porgy and Bess. The explosive rise in use of illicit drugs in recent years (mostly since this study was done) also suggests a connection between the Gay Deceiver and the pusher.

The AIDS epidemic may be an even more potent intensifier of the Gay Deceiver image. "Come with me—what a time we will have!" is not only The Gay Deceiver's lure, but also resonates with the facts of AIDS transmission through sexual intercourse as well as drug injections with contaminated needles. The biological fact is that heterosexual as well as homosexual intercourse can transmit the AIDS virus. The sociohistorical fact, however, is that the first wave of AIDS in the United States was associated with promiscuous homosexual activity in several major cities. Among our various personifications of death, The Gay Deceiver is the image most suited to the AIDS epidemic, at least in its early phase. (It should be noted that the term "Gay Deceiver" had no association with homosexuality when it was introduced.)

Perhaps on another level, however, the Gay Deceiver represents the respondents' own efforts to divert themselves from the prospect of death. In effect, one declares: "By immersing myself in all the pleasures that life has to offer, I will have neither the time nor the inclination to admit dark thoughts. The very fact that I revel in sophisticated enjoyments suggests that death cannot really be catastrophic—Am I kidding myself? Of course! But that's the solution I prefer."

The Automaton may be in a class by itself: the image of death as an objective, unfeeling instrument in human guise. The Automaton looks like a normal person but lacks human qualities. Unlike the other personifications, he (usually a male) does not establish a human relationship of any kind. He advances with neither diabolical pleasure nor gentle compassion, but as an automatic—soulless—apparatus. Two examples from respondents:

He is sort of a blank in human form. I don't know what he looks like. . . . Probably he is not very short or very tall or very good-looking or very ugly. He is just somebody you would never notice because he just goes his own way. He looks angry or sullen, but he really doesn't feel anything. I guess he is more like a machine than anything else. You would probably never have anything in common with a guy like that. Death, we will not call him Mr., is not the frightening person one would imagine, but he is not a jolly sort of person either.

Physically he is above average height with dark hair and clear brown eyes . . . dressed in a dark suit with a conservative tie. His walk is almost military, as if he were a man who is formal in most of his dealings. . . . Psychologically, he has no feeling of emotion about his job—either positive or negative. He simply does his job. He doesn't think about what he is doing, and there is no way to reason with him. There is no way to stop him or change his mind. When you look into his eyes you do not see a person. You see only death.

A special problem is posed by The Automaton: What are the victims to do with their own feelings? The macabre personifications might terrify, but terror is at least a human condition: one can respond to the terrifying with terror. Even such grotesque personages as the vampire and the werewolf have the reputation of establishing some kind of relationship with their victims. By contrast, one can express nothing to a "blank in human form."

Perhaps The Automaton is a creature of our own times, representing the indifferent, machined termination of a failed apparatus (the human body), rather than a death that holds a spiritual meaning of some kind.

This pair of studies also found that death was most often represented as a male, and as a person of middle or advanced adult years. The Gentle Comforter type of image was the most frequently given—suggesting that "death anxiety" may be alleviated rather than intensified through this fantasy modality for most people. For what it might be worth, funeral directors and students of mortuary sciences were the subsamples with by far the highest percentage of "no personifications," encountering some type of inner resistance to a task most others did not find very difficult. Among less frequent types of personification, the depiction of Death as a shapeless void was noted.

Richard Lonetto (1982) subsequently found that women who depicted Death as female had the highest levels of self-reported death anxiety. Men who saw Death as a male were particularly concerned with the sight of a dead body, with the prospect of another world war, and with the shortness of life. The Lonetto series confirmed the existence of the types of personification found in our studies, but also found some differences and examined the components in more detail. The Gay Deceiver type of imagery proved the most common, perhaps reflecting some changes in our views of life and death over the decade between the two sets of studies

One unusual contribution of the Lonetto studies was to examine highly specific aspects of the personification imagery, such as the hands and feet of Death, how Death walks, what Death is doing, and so forth. Although the Macabre image remained less frequent than the others, these elements seem to be important to the respondents as ways of humanizing and communicating with Death. In addition to the common features, each individual's distinctive way of portraying death could provide specific clues to fantasy life and concerns. For example, people whose concerns focused on the swift passage of time and the brevity of life were less likely to depict Death as the Gentle Comforter. It is from this group, in fact, that the Macabre image is most likely to come. One might, then, explore the possible link between "time anxiety" and death concern with individuals who seem to live with their eyes on the clock and the calendar. Another provocative finding appears worth pursuing: " . . . lowered death anxiety was achieved by men and women who did not see death in sexual terms but rather as a spiritual light, a feeling, a great openness, or as a vivid pattern of colors." This finding resonates with the lowered death anxiety reported by some people who have had near-death experiences that included visions of brilliant light (e.g., Greyson, 1994).

McDonald and Hilgendorf (1986) confirmed some of the general findings already reported: Death usually seen as a male, and seldom as a young person, as well as the basic categories of personification type. However, it was also found that students who elected to enroll in a thanatology course had "more positive images of death and were less fearful of the dying of others" than were students in an introductory psychology class. Additionally, those who created more positive images of Death had lower DAS death-anxiety scores. McDonald and Hilgendorf suggest that understanding the individual's distinctive death imagery could be a valuable tool in psychological assessment and therapy because it seems to represent a highly personal aspect of thought and feeling.

We returned to death personifications recently to see if there had been any changes since the original study (Kastenbaum & Herman, 1997). There was a sharp increase in the number of female personifications from female respondents, although death was still pictured as a male by both men and women. The type of personality attributed to death also seems to have shifted. Death is still usually the gentle comforter for women, but men now are more likely to describe death as a "cold and remote person," and also more likely than women to see death as "grim and terrifying." There is still a tendency to see the gentle comforter as an aged person, but the association with advanced age has been reduced in the other types of personification.

From the beginning of the personification studies there has always been an interest in the origin or inspiration for the reported images of death. This time we paid special attention to the possibility that Dr. Jack Kevorkian might have influenced some of the personifications. During the period of this research, Kevorkian's photograph appeared on the cover of national magazines and he was frequently seen on television in connection with his advocacy for physician-assisted suicide. Nobody—not a single respondent—mentioned Kevorkian as the source or even an influence on the death personification. After the personification procedure was completed we found that almost all the respondents knew of Kevorkian, but even his massive media exposure as "Doctor Death" had not influenced their views. Perhaps our death personifications come from earlier experiences and/or deeper levels of consciousness.

The possibility of sociocultural differences in death imagery has been explored in a Swedish study (Tamm, 1996). Death was most often personified as an old man in dark clothing, rather similar to the gentle comforter, although somewhat impersonal. She found a similar pattern of responses with respect to gender: about a fourth of the women but only one man saw death as a female. Women were also more likely to think of death as a person who takes care of people "not frightening, only benevolent and caring" (p. 14). Tamm interprets her data as suggesting that death imagery arises from an archetypical level of consciousness, in keeping with the theories of Jung (1959) and Neumann (1974).

Death-related fantasies and images may appear either by invitation or unbidden dreams. A variety of methods are available to the investigator, such as analysis of conversations, daydreams, essays, poems, and drawings, and responses to projective techniques. There is an abundance of such material already available that could be explored.

For example, I remember being shown a drawing made by a 77-year-old woman who resided in a geriatric facility. She had been asked to make a set of drawings—a map of where she had lived and her own place in it. The request did not seem to have anything to do with death. M. G. chatted as she made the drawings. After sketching the outside of the hospital and her ward area, M. G. started on the drawing in question. Her monologue became more focused and intense: "The Boss is calling me. He wants me in his office. I will go up there real soon. See? Home sweet home!"

On the surface, it appeared that she was sketching the office of the hospital's superintendent, situated on the only second floor in the facility. But I could not resist the thought that she was telling us of her impending death and of being called to an even higher authority. The clinical record and the ward staff both indicated that she was not in any obvious jeopardy; Mrs. M. G. was one of many frail elderly people who had been admitted to the institution for their general safety and well-being, rather than a pressing medical condition. Nevertheless, she died suddenly 3 days after drawing "Home Sweet Home." Was this an artful communication of impending death that perhaps could not have been better expressed in any other way? Or a coincidence? This question cannot be answered decisively. It does remind us, however, that "death content" can be implicit as well as explicit, and that information from more than one modality (e.g., visual representation and verbal comment) might contribute to our understanding.

Dreams of Death

What about the dream? In folklore, dreams of death—or of the dead—have often been considered to be especially important. Perhaps the most common interpretation has been that such dreams predict a death to come. With the advent first of psychoanalysis and then of modern sleep and dream research, there have been many more hypotheses advanced about the "meaning" of dreams. Unfortunately, very little has been firmly established about the functions and consequences of death dreams in healthy, normal adults. Studies of dream imagery and fantasy have seemed less attractive to many researchers since the influence of psychoanalysis has declined and the prestige of neural research risen. Accordingly, we do not know much more about the dreams-death connection than the little we did some years ago.

An exploratory study identified the nightmare sufferers among a sample of more than 1300 undergraduates (Feldman & Herson, 1967). Biographical information was then collected. A significant relationship was found between nightmare frequency and self-reported concern about death. This relationship held true for both sexes, although in the total sample women were the more likely to have reported frequent nightmares with recurrent themes. Those who reported frequent nightmares were also more likely to think often of their own death, to imagine themselves as dying or dead, to think about being killed in an accident—and to have dreams of dying or death. Interestingly, actual death experiences were so few in this undergraduate population that the investigators could not examine the possible relationship between exposure to death and nightmares. The results do suggest, however, that fearful dreams with a death theme do not necessarily depend on actual exposure to death-related situations. A later report by Herson (1971) also found a positive relationship between nightmares, death anxiety, and the particular type of dream memories that could be recalled. However, another study with college students, employing a different instrument and somewhat different research procedures, did not find a significant relationship between death anxiety and reported frequency of nightmares (Lester, 1968). These discordant findings have yet to be sorted out and tested again.

It might be surprising to learn that dreams of death and dying often have a pleasant rather than a terrifying quality. This phenomenon had come to my attention through the unsystematic collection of dreams from people with whom I have been in contact over the years. For example, a faculty colleague shared this dream with me

> While it's still fresh. I was wearing my new beige suit. You haven't seen it because I actually haven't worn it yet. I looked great, except I was dying. There were sea gulls flapping around outside the window, and they were more interesting to me than the committee meeting— imagine, wasting a dream that way! Bad enough I have to go to them

when I'm awake. Anyhow, so there I was dying and sort of smiling at the sea gulls, letting them know it was all right, I was ready. Other people get angels—I get gulls! Finally somebody noticed. A guy with a big stack of, I guess, personnel folders. He said, "There goes Elaine," and went back to the folders. I didn't mind. I was happy; I was blissful. Lightheaded all over. So that's how I died last night. Tell me, what does it mean? No—don't tell me!

Abraham Lincoln's dream of his impending assassination is a famous example from American history. It should be noted, however, that he had already escaped the bullets of at least one assassin and knew that his death was being sought by a number of dissidents. We do not have to make extraordinary assumptions to consider the possibility that there is an elastic give-and-take between the waking and sleeping mind.

A study by Barrett (1988–1989) has provided more systematic information on dreams of death. Studying healthy young adults, she found most of them to have a pleasant affective tone. One example:

I find myself standing in my bedroom at home in New York . . . something has awakened me from my sleep. I look out through the bedroom window. Suddenly I am overcome with intense feelings of fear and at that instant there is a white flash from outside my window. Slowly I begin to fall to the floor, realizing that I have just been killed. *The sensation of dying is very pleasant and I begin to enjoy the experience.* The dream ends.

The similarity between the "very pleasant" experience of dying in this dream and reports of near-death experiences may be worth further consideration.

Barrett worked with almost 1200 dreams compiled from "dream diaries" kept by her students. These were rated independently by two readers for content and emotional tone. In a second study she worked with a smaller sample of students who reported having had dreams of their own deaths. Dreams of dying were reported by 3% of the total sample, with a tendency for the same person to have more than one such occurrence. Dreams of dying were usually rated as pleasant (86%). Perhaps even more striking is the fact that those not rated as pleasant were considered to be neutral. Barrett reports that "Not one dream of actually dying was rated as predominately unpleasant." And yet—those who dreamed of "almost dying" were very like to have had an unpleasant, unsettling experience (94%). Nobody reported a "nearly dying" dream as being a pleasant experience. We have a new puzzle to consider, then: Why should dream-dying be such a pleasant experience, while dream-nearly dying is quite the opposite? Furthermore, "near-death experiences" seem more like the "actually dying" than the "nearly dying dreams."

Barrett's study also found two major types of dream-dying (both with positive affect). The slightly more common type involves dying and then going on into some type of postdeath experience. An excerpt from one such dream:

> The clock hands both pointed to 12 and I suddenly had a dizzying, thrilling rush. My mother and I turned into pure energy, pure light. We could go anywhere, free of our bodies. I see my father far below us, drinking his drink. My usual anger at him was diffused by compassion for his fearful, small existence. We soared up to the windows at the top of the ceiling and looked out. Then I incarnated and was walking in the dirt road down below. I knew that I was still dead, but wanted to take a look around at my old self . . . I knew that death was freeing.

The other type of dream-dying is one in which death comes and concludes the episode: "I feel my life gradually slipping away and it feels a bit like fainting only very peaceful and I just let go myself and let myself die."

The explicit death dreams analyzed by Barrett could also be regarded as symbolic of other concerns and processes—as she notes, a Jungian interpretation might well be invoked. This would emphasize the death dream as a symbol of other types of transformation, such as the struggle to become a more mature and individuated person (Jung, 1958; Herzog, 1969).

In opening ourselves to the study of dreams, then, we enter a rich, ambiguous, and complex realm that is far removed from the study of death anxiety by fixed-choice self-report measures. It is much too soon to attempt to draw conclusions, indeed, the more urgent challenge is to improve our methods and gather more information. However, it is also obvious that there is much to learn by considering the dream and other types of mental imagery and fantasy if we really care to know about the human response to death.

Death Anxiety in Theory and Practice: A Few Suggestions

We have explored some of the hypotheses, methods, and findings that have become associated with the concept of death anxiety. For the most part our attention has focused on normal adults who do not appear to be in particular jeopardy for their lives nor beset with clinically significant psychopathology. Several criticisms of this overall enterprise have been noted along the way and need not be repeated.

An additional caution should be mentioned, however. We cannot be sure that the responses given by normal adults in relatively safe situations represent their deepest or most acute thoughts and feelings about death. Perhaps an element of real danger or the need for urgent decision making is required before we can know our own minds well. It is remarkable how well "unexpected turbulence" at 30,000 feet can recruit feelings that may not be available to us when we are completing a self-report questionnaire on *terra firma*.

We are now ready to consider a few implications for theory and practice, including a slightly different orientation toward the concept of death anxiety.

First, we have seen that most adults report a low-to-moderate "walking around" level of death concern. If we are spinning around in a whirlpool of death anxiety, most of us don't seem to know it. There are appreciable individual differences, as with practically every aspect of human behavior and experience. There is also a fairly consistent gender-related differential, with women reporting a relatively higher level of death anxiety.

What we have not seen is any clear basis for determining how high is too high and how low is too low. This question has been mentioned with respect to the gender differential: should we conclude that women are too anxious, or men not anxious enough? It also arises in many other contexts. For example, some death educators take anxiety reduction as one of their primary objectives, an objective that assumes students come in with "too much" anxiety. Although there has been continued progress in improving the psychometric features of assessment measures, much less has been done to determine the function of death anxiety in naturally occurring behavioral settings. Part of the problem here is methodological: it is hard work to devise and carry out effective studies in real life settings. Much of the problem remains in the conceptual sphere, however. How *should* people feel and act in death-related situations? How can we distinguish between situations in which anxiety is disabling and situations in which it is "healthy" to be anxious to adapt to risk or come to the aid of others? There is so much stigma attached to "looking anxious" or "acting emotional" in professional circles that the positive function of anxiety may have been underestimated and underresearched.

Beyond generalities, we need more attention to how particular individuals function in particular situations. For example, who is most and least likely to respond to a sudden crisis in which another person's life is in jeopardy? Is a little more than "normal" death anxiety a positive trait in a person who often has responsibility for other people's lives? What situational characteristics arouse, anesthetize, or mask death anxiety? I have observed, for example, that people caught up in immediate life-threatening situations have very different types of response depending on the opportunity to engage in some kind of instrumental action (Kastenbaum, 1998). It is possible that many of us experience anxiety surges when we cannot find a way of making an immediate adaptational response to a dangerous situation—and that the anxiety, perhaps having achieved its purpose, dissipates when we do become active.

The *anxiety surge* phenomenon is not detected by self-report instruments. Instead, anxiety is regarded as a point on a scale, rather like a fuel or motor oil level. The existing theories also have a somewhat static quality. We cannot fear death, so that's that (early Freud), or we are always trying to avoid drowning in our fear of death (Becker). Terror management theory has introduced some dynamics with the inference that we become more anxious when encountering a "mortality salient" situation and respond by calling upon our repertoire of individual (self-esteem) or societal (worldview) buffering strategies. This is a useful step forward, although the subtle interactive ways in which we construct "mortality salient" situations has not yet been considered.

I would suggest that we take still another step toward recognizing the process and functional dimensions of our psychological relationship with death. We might call this an *edge theory* of death anxiety. The following observations would be germane:

1.   Assume that people usually are reporting their thoughts and feelings as accurately as they can when responding to a typical death-

anxiety measure. We have no firm evidence to the contrary. As already noted, their responses most often fall within the low-to-moderate range on the particular measure.

2.   Recognize that this moderate level of death anxiety is at odds with existential theoreticians such as Becker and with the findings of the few multilevel empirical studies (e.g., Alexander et al., 1957; Feifel & Branscomb, 1973). The findings are in accord with Becker's contention that we are scared to death inside even though we may say otherwise. Somehow our defenses filter out or neutralize many death-related prompts.

3.   Reach out a little and touch another source of psychological stress that many of us have experienced: test anxiety. (This experience actually has a lot in common with any other form of anxiety; it earns its name not so much from the particularities of the feeling-state as from the sociobehavioral context of being required to perform under pressure.) Test college students on test anxiety and we will often find either cool unconcern or disturbance and apprehension. The difference resides chiefly in whether or not the student has a test to face on the near temporal horizon. In the first instance the student neither admits nor demonstrates anxiety because the "panic button" is in the off position. Anxiety is not being repressed or denied in any meaningful sense of these terms. No danger, no anxiety. In the second instance anxiety does not break through the defenses. The surge of uneasy alertness is occasioned by the prospect of having to meet a performance challenge that is so close one can feel its hot breath.

4.   What we call death anxiety has much in common: a time of reckoning on which all that a person is or wants to be is laid on the line. The danger, though, has many more lurking places, and cannot be confined to an academic schedule, nor can one be sure of precisely what will be on the "final." Similarly, people are not necessarily concealing death anxiety when they are asked to deal with this topic in the midst of their daily lives. Their potential for anxious alertness has not been activated. From the edge theory perspective, then, typically we are not "in denial." Rather, we do not feel ourselves to be at significant risk at the moment—and usually this is a reasonable assessment.

5.   Remind Freud that he recognized the difference between two patterns of anxiety: (a) a neurotic form that overgeneralizes and persists

across people and situations, and (b) a normal form in which we become alert to dangers and thereby improve our ability to survive them. Death concerns can take either form. Perhaps thanatophobia can be demoted to a secondary fear, as Freud once asserted. Adaptation and survival, however, are realistic concerns. This means that Freud has missed something in contending that we cannot fear death because we have not experienced this condition, nor can our "unconscious mind" believe in its own nonexistence. The important point is that, like our fellow creatures on earth, we *do* face risks to life and we *are* equipped to scan for at least some of the dangers. Furthermore, we' are also sensitized by all the losses and injuries we have either experienced or witnessed. Vigilance to safeguard our own lives and the lives of others is not an inexplicable phenomenon—it's what has helped the human race to survive this long.

6.   Think of "death anxiety," then, as the psychological, self-aware side of a complex organismic response to danger, to feeling ourselves to be at the edge of what is known, familiar, and safe. One step further and there may be destruction. We become more alert and focused when we interpret our external and internal cues as indicating that we have come upon the edge of existence. This is anxiety but, more importantly, it is preparation.

7.   Consider that we live in a world of symbols, meanings, and relationships as well as a world of physical objects and forces. Within these nesting worlds it is often difficult to discern and evaluate potential dangers. We make this challenge harder for each other by exaggerating some dangers and concealing or trivializing others to suit various purposes. It is not surprising, then, that some people become locked into persistent or hair-trigger anxiety states while others have given up the arduous task of detecting and evaluating dangers.

Edge theory emphasizes our ability to detect sources of potential harm both through built-in biomechanisms (such as the alarm response) and through the development of high level cognitive, affective, and instrumental skills. Perhaps our attention should focus on helping people to keep their danger-scanning abilities as well-honed as possible to be just anxious enough when an actual risk appears, yet wise enough to call off the emergency footing when we discover a false alarm. The ability to live with some anxiety from time to time could be one of our most useful resources just to keep living.

REFERENCES

Abdel-Khalek, A. M. (1986). Death anxiety in Egyptian samples. *Personality & Individual Differences, 7,* 479–483.

Abdel-Khalek, A. M. (1997). Death, anxiety, and depression. *Omega, Journal of Death & Dying, 35,* 219–230.

Alexander, I. E., Colley, R. S., & Adlerstein, A. M. (1957). Is death a matter of indifference? *Journal of Psychology, 43,* 277–283.

Barrett, D. (1988–1989). Dreams of death. *Omega, Journal of Death and Dying, 1,* 95–103.

Baudrillard, J. (1993). *Symbolic exchange and death.* London: Sage.

Becker, E. (1962). *The birth and death of meaning.* New York: Free Press.

Becker, E. (1973). *The denial of death.* New York: Free Press.

Becker, E. (1975). *Escape from evil.* New York: Free Press.

Beshai, J. A., & Templer, D. I. (1978). American and Egyptian attitudes toward death. *Essence, 3,* 155–158.

Boyar, J. I. (1964). The construction and partial validation of a scale for the measurement of the fear of death. *Dissertation Abstracts International, 25,* 20–21.

Butler, R. N. (1963). The life review: An interpretation of reminiscence in the aged. *Psychiatry, 26,* 65–70.

Cole, M. A. (1978–1979). Sex and marital status differences in death anxiety. *Omega, Journal of Death and Dying, 9,* 139–147.

Corey, L. G. (1960). An analogue of resistance to death awareness. *Journal of Gerontology, 16,* 59–60.

DaSilva, A., & Schork, M. A. (1984–1985). Gender differences in attitudes to death among a group of public health students. *Omega, Journal of Death and Dying, 15,* 77–84.

Dattel, A. R., & Neimeyer, R. A. (1990). Sex differences in death anxiety: Testing the emotional expressiveness hypothesis. *Death Studies, 14,* 1–11.

Davis, S. F., Martin, D. A., Wilee, C. T., & Voorhees, J. W. (1978). Relationship of fear of death and loss of self esteem in college students. *Psychological Reports, 42,* 419–422.

Diggory, J. C., & Rothman, D. Z. (1961). Values destroyed by death. *Journal of Abnormal & Social Psychology, 63,* 205–210.

Durlak, J. (1972). Relationship between various measures of death concern and fear of death. *Journal of Consulting & Clinical Psychology, 38,* 463.

Durlak, J. A., & Kass, C. A. (1981–1982). Clarifying the measurement of death attitudes: A factor analytic evaluation of fifteen self-report death scales. *Omega, Journal of Death and Dying, 12,* 129–141.

Einstein, A., & Freud, S. (1932). *Why war?* Chicago: Chicago Institute for Psychoanalysis.

Erikson, E. H. (1979). Reflections on Dr. Borg's life cycle. In D. D. Van Tassel (Ed.), *Aging, death and the completion of being* (pp. 29–68). Philadelphia: University of Pennsylvania Press.

Farley, G. (1971). An investigation of death and the sense of competence. *Dissertation Abstracts international, 31*, p. 7595.

Feifel, H., & Branscomb, A. B. (1973). Who's afraid of death? *Journal of Abnormal Psychology, 81,* 282–288.

Feldman, M. J., & Herson, M. (1967). Attitudes toward death in nightmare subjects. *Journal of Abnormal Psychology, 72,* 421–425.

Freud, S. (1953/1913). Thoughts for the times on war and death. In *Collected works* (Vol. IV, pp. 288–317). London: Hogarth Press.

Greenberger, E. (1965). Fantasies of women confronting death. *Journal of Consulting Psychology, 29,* 252–260.

Greyson, B. (1994). Reduced death threat in near-death experiences. In R. A. Neimeyer (Ed.), *Death anxiety handbook* (pp. 169–180). Washington, DC: Taylor & Francis.

Harmon-Jones, E., Simon, L., Greenberg, J., Pyszczynski, T., Solomon, S., & McGregor, H. (1997). Terror management theory and self-esteem: Evidence that increased self-esteem reduces mortality salience effects. *Journal of Personality & Social Psychology, 72,* 24–36.

Heckler, R. A. (1994). *Waking up, alive.* New York: Ballantine Books.

Herson, M. (1971). Personality characteristics of nightmare subjects. *Journal of Nervous and Mental Disease, 53,* 27–31.

Herzog, E. (1969). *Psyche and death.* New York: Putnam's Sons.

Hintze, J., Templer, D. I., Cappelletty, G. G., & Frederick, W. (1994). Death depression and death anxiety in HIV-infected males. In R. A. Neimeyer (Ed.), *Death anxiety handbook* (pp. 193–200). Washington, DC: Taylor & Francis.

Ho, S. M. Y., & Shiu, W. C. T. (1995). Death anxiety and coping mechanisms of Chinese cancer patients. *Omega, Journal of Death and Dying, 31,* 59–66.

Holcomb, L. E., Neimeyer, R. A., & Moore, M. K. (1993). Personal meanings of death: A content analysis of free-response narratives. *Death Studies, 17,* 299–318.

Jeffers, F. C., Nichols, C. R., & Eisdorfer, C. (1961). Attitudes of older persons toward death. A preliminary review. *Journal of Gerontology, 16,* 53–56.

Jung, C. G. (1958). *Psyche and symbol.* Garden City, NY: Doubleday.

Jung, C. G. (1959). *Four archetypes.* Princeton, NJ: Princeton University Press.

Kalish, R. A., & Reynolds, D. (1977). *Death and ethnicity: A psychocultural study.* Los Angeles: University of Southern California Press.

Kastenbaum, R. (1987). Death-related anxiety. In L. Michelson & L. M. Ascher (Eds.), *Anxiety and stress disorders* (pp. 425–44). New York: Guilford Press.

Kastenbaum, R. (1987–1988). Theory, research and application: Some critical issues for thanatology. *Omega, Journal of Death & Dying, 18,* 397–410.

Kastenbaum, R. (1992). *The psychology of death* (rev. ed.). New York: Springer Publishing Co.

Kastenbaum, R. (1998). *Death, society, and human experience* (6th ed.). Boston: Allyn & Bacon.

Kastenbaum, R., & Aisenberg, R. B. (1972). *The psychology of death.* New York: Springer Publishing Co.

Kastenbaum, R., & Costa, P. T., Jr. (1977). Psychological perspectives on death. In *Annual review of psychology* (Vol. 28, pp. 225–249). Palo Alto: Annual Review Press.

Kastenbaum, R., & Herman, C. (1997). Death personification in the Kevorkian era. *Death Studies, 21,* 115–130.

Kastenbaum, R., & Weisman, A.D. (1972). The psychological autopsy as a research procedure in gerontology. In D. P. Kent, S. Sherwood, & R. Kastenbaum (Eds.), *Research, planning, and action for the elderly* (pp. 210–217). New York: Behavioral Publications.

Kelly, M. N., & Corriveau, D. P. (1995). The Corriveau–Kelly Death Anxiety Scale. *Omega, Journal of Death & Dying, 31,* 311–316.

Lefcourt, H. M., & Shepherd, R. S. (1995). Organ donation, authoritarianism, and perspective-taking humor. *Journal of Research in Personality, 29,* 121–138.

Lester, D. (1967). Experimental and correlational studies of the fear of death. *Psychological Bulletin, 67,* 27–36.

Lester, D. (1968). The fear of death in those who have nightmares. *Journal of Psychology, 69,* 245–247.

Lonetto, R. (1982). Personifications of death and death anxiety. *Journal of Personality Assessment, 46,* 404–408.

Lonetto, R., & Templer, D. I. (1986). *Death anxiety.* New York: Hemisphere.

Marks, A. (1986–1987). Race and sex differences and fear of dying: A test of two hypotheses—high risk or social loss? *Omega, Journal of Death and Dying, 17,* 229–236.

May, R. (1979). *The meaning of anxiety.* New York: McGraw-Hill.

McClelland, D. (1963). The harlequin complex. In R. White (Ed.), *The study of lives* (pp. 94–119). New York: Atherton Press.

McDonald, R. T., & Hilgendorf, W. A. (1986). Death imagery and death anxiety. *Journal of Clinical Psychology, 42,* 87–91.

Morrison, J. K., & Cometa, M. C. (1982). Variations in developing construct systems: The experience corollary. In J. C. Mancuso & J. R. Adams-Webber (Eds.), *The construing person* (pp. 152–169). New York: Praeger.

Munnichs, J. M. A. (1966). *Old age and finitude: A contribution to psycho-gerontology*. Basel: S. Karger.

Nagy, M. H. (1959). The child's theories concerning death. In H. Feifel (Ed.), *The meaning of death* (pp. 79–98). New York: McGraw-Hill.

Neimeyer, R. A. (1997–1998). Death-anxiety research: The state of the art. *Omega, Journal of Death and Dying, 36,* 97–120.

Neimeyer, R. A., Dingemans, P. M. A. J., & Epting, F. R. (1977). Convergent validity, situational stability and meaningfulness of the Threat Index. *Omega, Journal of Death & Dying, 8,* 251–265.

Neimeyer, R. A., & Moore, M. K. (1994). Validity and reliability of the Multidimensional Fear of Death Scale. In R. A. Neimeyer (Ed.), *Death anxiety handbook* (pp. 103–120). Washington, DC: Taylor & Francis.

Neimeyer, R. A., Epting, F. R., & Rigdon, M. A. (1984). A procedure manual for the threat index. In F. R. Epting & R. A. Neimeyer (Eds.), *Personal meaning of death* (pp. 213–234). Washington, DC: Hemisphere.

Neufeldt, D. E., & Holmes, C. B. (1979). Relationship between personality traits and fear of death. *Psychological Reports, 45,* 907–910.

Neumann, E. (1974). *The Great Mother: Analysis of the archetype.* Princeton, NJ: Princeton University Press.

Nogas, C., Schweitzer, K., & Grumet, J. C. (1974). An investigation of death anxiety, sense of competence, and need for achievement. *Omega, Journal of Death and Dying, 5,* 245–255.

Pollak, J. M. (1979–1980). Correlates of death anxiety: A review of empirical studies. *Omega, Journal of Death and Dying, 10,* 97–122.

Reimer, W., & Templer, D. I. (1995–1996). Death anxiety, death depression, death distress, and death discomfort differential: Adolescent-parental correlations in Filipino and American populations. *Omega, Journal of Death & Dying, 32,* 319–330.

Sanner, M. A. (1997). Encountering the dead body: Experiences of medical students in their anatomy and pathology training. *Omega, Journal of Death & Dying, 35,* 173–192.

Schell, B. H., & Zinger, A. T. (1984). Death anxiety scale means and standard deviations for Ontario undergraduates and funeral directors. *Psychological Reports, 54,* 439–446.

Shneidman, E. S. (1970, August). Death questionnaire. *Psychology Today,* pp. 67–72.

Stricherz, M., & Cunnington, L. (1981–1982). Death concerns of students, employed persons, and retired persons. *Omega, Journal of Death and Dying, 12,* 373–380.

Tamm, M. E. (1996). Personification of life and death among Swedish health care professionals. *Death Studies, 20,* 1–22.

Templer, D. I. (1970). The construction and validation of a Death Anxiety Scale. *Journal of General Psychology, 72,* 165–166.

Templer, D. I., & Dotson, E. (1970). Religious correlates of death anxiety. *Psychological Reports, 26,* 895–897.

Templer, D. I., & Ruff, C. F. (1971). Death anxiety scale means, standard deviations, and embeddings. *Psychological Reports, 29,* 173–174.

Templer, D. I., Ruff, C. F., & Franks, C. M. (1971). Death anxiety: Age, sex, and parental resemblance in diverse populations. *Developmental Psychology, 4,* 108.

Thorson, J. A. (1977). Variation in death anxiety related to college students' sex, major field of study, and certain personality traits. *Psychological Reports, 40,* 857–858.

Thorson, J. A., & Powell, F. C. (1994). A revised death anxiety scale. In R. A. Neimeyer (Ed.), *Death anxiety handbook* (pp. 31–44). Washington, DC: Taylor & Francis.

Tomer, A. (1994). Death anxiety in adult life—Theoretical perspectives. In R. A. Neimeyer (Ed.), *Death anxiety handbook* (pp. 3–30). Washington, DC: Taylor & Francis.

Triplett, G., Cohen, D., Reimer, W., Rinaldi, S., Hill, C., Roshdieh, S., Stanczak, E. M., Sisco, K., & Templer, D. I. (1995). Death discomfort differential. *Omega, Journal of Death & Dying, 31,* 295–304.

Viswanatham, R. (1996). Death anxiety, locus of control, and purpose in life of physicians. *Psychosomatics, 37,* 339–345.

Wahl, C. F. (1959). The fear of death. In H. Feifel (Ed.), *The meaning of death* (pp. 16–28). New York: McGraw-Hill.

Weisman, A. D., & Kastenbaum, R. (1968). *The psychological autopsy: A study of the terminal phase of life.* New York: Behavioral Publications.

5

A Will to Live and
an Instinct to Die?

Knowing that it is our fate to die—and, what is worse, that it is our fate to know that we will die—makes us furious at nature.
—Evan Eisenberg, *The Ecology of Eden*

After flinging the corpse from the bridge, the enraged crowd peered over the edge to see the victim lying at the bottom of the river, with his ghastly face still exhibiting his fearful death agony. Now "wild and madly excited," the mob, which had spent its only live abolitionist, turned its fury on those in the street who were dead. "Curses were freely uttered against them, and kicks and blows inflicted upon them," reported a Maryland newsman.
—Thomas Goodrich, *War to the Knife*

I was hanging all right, but I wasn't dead. That's why I had the axe in my hand. Just in case. I chopped (my neck) best I could, but it wasn't good enough. I'll do better next time.
—Elderly woman describing her suicide attempt to the author

People are sometimes very determined to kill themselves or somebody else. Furthermore many societies, including our own, have made determined assaults on the natural environment. More subtle inclinations toward death can also be observed. There is:

- The uncooperative patient who chooses not to follow a medical regime that might prolong life
- The risk-taking youth who experiences a high in challenging death

- The teen who cannot get enough of video games in which icons of living creatures are destroyed in bursts of graphic violence
- The skinhead adorned with symbols of menace and violence who, like some of his Nazi predecessors, presents himself as an instrument of death
- The quiet, almost invisible person who cannot stay away from funerals and cemeteries
- The bruised and discouraged person whose suicidal reveries serve as an escape hatch that could be used should life become completely unpalatable
- The person who is coming around to the belief that his or her life has run its course and therefore is thinking of leaving the night light on for Death

In this chapter we examine a controversial theory that offers an explanation for all these diverse behaviors and more. One is tempted to say that it is the "most failed" theory of a failed theory-spinner. Sigmund Freud's influence has declined among mental health experts over the past several decades, although many of his ideas continue to flourish in the popular and literary-dramatic spheres. Currently there is a revival of interest in the man and his work, as illustrated by major retrospectives in Russia as well as the Library of Congress. It is possible that Freud's reputation will rise again, following a familiar pattern for the postmortem career of people who achieved distinction in life.

Nevertheless, Freud's theories and key observations have been subjected to powerful critiques (e.g., Crews, 1998). The basic assumptions of psychoanalytic theory are regarded as unsupported if not completely mistaken by some articulate critics, and claims for the therapeutic efficacy of the treatment method have been repeatedly challenged. In the continuing assault on Freudian psychology there has not been much attention to one of his most ambitious conceptions. The death instinct hardly seems worth the ammunition to most contemporary critics because it was left for dead years ago.

Nevertheless, there is something about Freud's death-instinct theory that refuses to lie quiet in its grave. The phenomena his theory addresses remain ubiquitous. For an instinct that does not exist, *thanatos* seems to be alive and well across a broad spectrum of behavior from international terrorism to domestic violence. Furthermore, there are resonations with biological, psychological, and cultural phenomena that deserve another look. And so, as unfashionable as it might be, we will once again raise the lid of the coffin for another postmortem dialogue with the corpse of death-instinct theory.

HISTORICAL CONTEXT

Freud's Vienna was a cauldron of creative activity in science, learning, and the arts. The young Freud was enthralled by these achievements. He longed to join the ranks of the illustrious. He had some success as a neuroscientist, but a career in that field did not seem promising. At that time many good minds were thinking psychologically, although psychology itself was just emerging as an independent field of inquiry and practice. Freud was in position to make significant contributions because he could draw upon his experience with medical research, his apprenticeship under the celebrated psychiatrist Jean-Martin Charcot, his knowledge of culture and the humanities and, now, the patients who came to his door with perplexing symptoms and seemingly intractable problems. Within a few years he became the first psychoanalyst and the first client. Having conducted what he described as a self-analysis, Freud spent the rest of his long life in developing, revising, advocating, and defending psychoanalytic theory and practice.

Origins of Death-Instinct Theory

Death-instinct theory was a late addition to Freud's explanation of the human condition. There were both technical and socioemotional reasons for introducing this concept. Technically, the new twist helped him to dispense with the "multiplication of instincts" problem. By the 1920s instinct theory had become undisciplined after years of popularity. Competing theoreticians presented ever-expanding lists of instincts that were supposed to provide a root explanation of thought, feeling, and action. Freud did not go so far as to take himself out of the instinct business, but he did engage in an act of simplification. There are really only two primary instincts. *Eros* is oriented toward life, love, and activity. When we spring out of bed in the morning with a song on our lips, ready for the day's adventure, we are a plaything of *Eros*. *Thanatos* draws us toward cessation and death. When we pull the covers over our heads and tell the day to get along without us, we are in the grip of *Thanatos*. These instincts, though oppositional, work in tandem. We are always performing a kind of balancing act between these two fundamental orientations that Freud chose to speak of as instincts. The paired instinct theory was offered by Freud in *Beyond the Pleasure Principle* (1920/1960) and *New Introductory Lectures on Psychoanalysis* (1933/1961).

There was a more compelling reason, however, for Freud's introduction of death-instinct theory at this time: World War I and its aftermath. Death, grief, and despair had become central facts of life in Austria and Germany (nor were the victorious nations spared heartbreak). Himself aging, ailing, grieving, and disillusioned, Freud could no longer dismiss death concern as a secondary neurotic symptom. It was time for psychoanalytic theory to give death its due. Furthermore, the worst might be yet to come. How could civilized nations engage in such mass, sustained brutality? What did this horrifying surge of violence portend for the future?

The idea of a death instinct was not original with Freud, but drew attention because of its author's reputation and its audacious scope. The new theory received a mixed response. This response gradually shifted over to the negative in succeeding years. This rejection was in part a reflection of the growing disillusionment with instinct theories in general, but also because many psychoanalysts found it difficult to apply the theory in clinical situations. Those with a strong interest in suicide prevention tended to give the death-instinct theory a longer trial, but its appeal in this sphere also faded. It would be about a half century before the clear emergence of the death awareness movement and hospice care. By this time a new generation of clinicians and researchers had come of age, focused more on the pragmatic problems in front of them than on grand theories of the human condition. If my experiences are any guide, few people on the front line of prevention-intervention-postvention have had any familiarity with Freud's death-instinct theory. What, if anything, have they been missing?

Here, then, are the essentials of Freud's death-instinct theory. In later sections we will identify some of the applications and critiques of the theory and, finally, see what might be learned from the whole endeavor.

THE CORE THEORY

Freud first ventured death-instinct theory in a lecture. He was anxious about its reception, so displayed the touch of a wry humorist. Freud inoculated his audience with the admission that this is "A queer instinct, indeed, dedicated to the destruction of its own organic home!" Teasingly, he slipped in the fact that the mucous membrane of the stomach has a tendency to dissolve itself—but did not claim this as evidence of an underlying self-destructive tendency. Already condemned by some for luring sex out of the closet, Freud was not eager to be targeted as the inventor of death as well.

The theory he proposed is built upon eight basic assumptions:

1. *All* instincts are conservative. They aim to repeat or restore some earlier state of affairs. Freud cites as examples the tendency of many organisms to regenerate lost body parts and of migratory birds to follow the same seasonal routes.

2. This "compulsion to repeat" (Freud's term) rules both our mental and vegetative functioning. It is one of the basic operations built into the logic of our system, to invite the computer analogy. We cannot hope to understand this compulsion by focusing only on the mental or the organic sphere to the exclusion of the other.

3. The compulsion to repeat or restore an earlier condition can take precedence over the usual forms of gratification. Instead of acting so as to experience pleasure, one may actually seek pain and loss in order to appease the repetition compulsion.

4. "But how can the conservative characteristic of instincts help us to understand our self-destructiveness? What earlier state of things does an instinct such as this want to restore?" Freud offers a bold answer to his own question: "If it is true that—at some immeasurably remote time and in a manner we cannot conceive—life once proceeded out of inorganic matter, then . . . an instinct must have arisen which sought to do away with life once more and to re-establish the inorganic state" (Freud, 1933, p. 107).

5. The death instinct (more accurately although less frequently translated as death-drive, *Todestrieb*) operates "in every vital process." All living organisms at all phases of their functioning exhibit a tendency toward self-destruction.

6.   A strong countervailing force also exists in all living organisms. This force (*Eros*) seeks "to combine more and more living substances into ever greater unities." Eros is dedicated to pleasure, the stimulation of growth and the promotion of survival.

7.   Eros and Thanatos are mingled throughout life, each jousting with the other in an attempt to achieve its own aims. We are never wholly oriented toward survival and development, and only in the most extreme conditions, if ever, does the death instinct reign without challenge.

8.   Death is one of life's most fundamental aims. We live with the intention to die. However, life is also an aim of life. Both aims are built into the very nature of the living organism, from processes occurring in every cell of our bodies to the powerful tendencies at work in our (largely unconscious) mental operations.

This is the core of Freud's dramatic theory of the death instinct and its faithful companion, Eros. We consider now some of the more specific problems that Freud hoped to address with his new conception.

A Pain- and Death-Obsessed Society

Human motivation is founded upon the tendency to seek pleasure and avoid pain. Or is it? This commonsense notion had long been familiar; indeed, it was enshrined in the philosophical position known as hedonism. It was also taken for granted by the forerunners of contemporary behaviorism. A positive or pleasant experience will act to reinforce the behavior that produced or became associated with it; a negative or unpleasant experience would have the opposite outcome.

It had become evident to Freud, however, that people sometimes acted as though they were seeking pain rather than pleasure. He was not referring to simple miscalculations—pleasure sought, pain found. Instead, Freud perceived a quality of compulsion in these enigmatic behaviors. People "had to do it," even though a painful experience was almost guaranteed. Historian Peter Gay (1993, p. 509) would later write that "One did not have to be an obsessive neurotic to be a nineteenth-century bourgeois, but it helped." What Freud detected repeatedly not only in his consulting room but throughout the land were people who repeatedly sought painful experiences.

Freud was keen on discovering previously unrecognized relationships among diverse phenomena. This skill now came into play again. Some of his own patients showed a stubborn tendency to relive the past—not simply to remember, but to "go through" painful experiences over and again. This seemed to be a departure from the "pleasure principle" that Freud had already integrated into psychoanalytic theory as part of the "primary process" (later symbolized as "The It" or Id).

War neuroses presented an even more disturbing phenomenon. In the safety of their own homes, some veterans experienced terrifying dreams related to their war experiences. These disturbing episodes could also take the form of waking terrors. Years later psychiatrists would establish the diagnostic category of posttraumatic stress disorder, influenced much by the alarming flashbacks associated with service in Viet Nam. Freud knew that anxiety dreams can also occur in the ordinary run of human experience as well. The psychoanalytic contention that even anxiety dreams represent the operation of the pleasure principle no longer seemed entirely convincing.

Another set of unresolved clinical problems pressed on Freud: the dynamics of sadism and masochism. Some people seemed to need self-punishment, and some apparently could not enjoy sexual relations without inflicting pain of some type on others. Again, these phenomena were departures from the pleasure principle. Freud's far-ranging mind located still another type of repetition compulsion—the insistence shown by some children in playing and replaying the same game. All the phenomena mentioned here had in common a "daemonic" quality, in Freud's view. There was an intense inner pressure to repeat or restore a painful situation.

In puzzling over these phenomena, Freud was strongly influenced by the eruption of raw aggression in the recent war and by indications that these dangerous forces had not been laid to rest by the signing of treaties. His theoretical solution to these clinical problems would also need somehow to reflect the reality of destructive forces in modern civilization, forces that must have their root in human nature itself. The possibility that aggression was a fundamental part of human nature had been rejected by Freud in the past, but now he was ready to reconsider. Within a few years he would come to the conclusion that the aggressive component of our nature was a threat to the survival of civilization. From a neuroscientist preoccupied with tracing the development of nerve fibers to a clinician skeptical of death anxieties, Freud became a reluctant prophet of megadeath—although with a possible "out" that would be expressed in his correspondence with Albert Einstein.

The Death Instinct As Explanation

Freud's revised theory of psychosexual development perhaps should be known instead as a theory of psychothanatosexual development (why stop with five syllables when we can have eight?). Developmental progress involves constant interaction between the two instincts. Eros is forever urging us onward and upward, and Thanatos is forever urging the reduction of tension to the inorganic zero point. Death-strivings, then, are not limited to the extremes of terminal illness, advanced age, or acute suicidality. The contest between life and death instincts is played out from the very beginning and does not end until the final breath is exhaled. This position is a major departure from his earlier theory of psychosexual development in which aggression is incidental to the drive for sexual mastery.

What Freud next must explain is how we manage to develop and survive at all, beset as we are by the hypothetical drive toward oblivion. This is accomplished, he tells us, primarily through *fusion* and *redirection*. The two antithetical urges collaborate with each other, if uneasily. The organism's strivings toward development and gratification require vigorous action in and against the world. Eros enlists the aggressive energies of Thanatos for this purpose. It is a double coup when successful. Not only do thanatic-driven energies make it possible for the organism to act aggressively upon barriers and challenges in the world, but this mission also keeps it too busy to turn upon its host. One thinks of impulse-ridden young toughs who have been sent off to engage in combat on foreign turf instead of staying around to harass the peace-loving folk at home.

In "normal" development, then, the intrinsic urge toward self-destruction is transformed into aggressive actions directed toward the outside world—including other people. Children show these dynamics with less disguise. The innocent little boy and girl may alarm and puzzle adults by the enjoyment taken in squashing bugs or tormenting animals. Killing is fun! And the fun comes, at least in part, from indulging the aims and energies of the death instinct without falling victim one's self. Killing is a lot better than getting killed.

Because we have all passed through the vicissitudes of the juvenile death instinct, it is perhaps not surprising that the world is crowded with adults who try to manage their self-destructive urges by deploying them on each other. Had Freud attended a professional boxing match, hockey game, or football contest, he might have nodded in grave satisfaction as players and officials heard the assault of Thanatos from thousands of hoarse voices. A Little League game attended by highly involved parents might have provided an even more impressive demonstration.

The stadium, however, is not actually a psychiatric ward and most fans are responsible citizens. The "collective death instinct," if this phrase might be countenanced, is usually given only limited opportunities for expression. "Normal" people who are also rabid fans temper their destructive impulses with the wisdom and charity of Eros. Only a part of the self wishes to crush and eliminate the foe. Eros eventually reassumes command to add a glow to victory, a consolation to defeat, and, above all, *to keep the game going*. The athletes themselves, given half a chance, often feel impelled to honor and embrace their opponents at the end of the contest. Although Freud did not analyze competitive sports, in this arena the collaboration between Eros and Thanatos is available for all to observe.

Perhaps the most vital point regarding the role of the death instinct in early development is simply that aggressive impulses are real and fundamental. They are not just secondary derivatives. True, the infant and child might show increased aggression upon being frustrated. This, in fact, is one of the clues to the repetition compulsion in children. Denied the gratifications sought, the child may stubbornly re-create the disappointing situation in the hope of "making it right" or restoring the lost object. Nevertheless, in Freud's revised theory he does not see aggression as only and always a response to frustration or deprivation. Aggression is there from the beginning and represents the claims of Thanatos. And from the beginning this aggressive drive threatens the development and survival of the self—and perhaps of society.

Anna Freud, much more experienced than her father in direct work with children, accepted this view: "In very early phases aggressive energy may find outlets on the child's own body, just as sexual energy (libido) may find outlets in autoerotic activities. . . . it is essential for the child's normality that the aggressive urges should be directed away from the child's own body to the animate or inanimate objects in the environment" (A. Freud, 1949, p. 40).

In summary: the infant and young child must quickly find a way of balancing the contradictory claims of Eros and Thanatos. The basic strategy is to turn the aggressive impulses outward—including vigorous use of muscles and energies. This will be a challenge over the entire life-span as well. Eros must somehow manage to give Thanatos its opportunities, yet prevent catastrophe.

Problems that occur during the individual's early development are likely to have prolonged and accumulative consequences. This is a fundamental proposition in psychoanalytic theory. How might it apply to the vicissitudes of aggressivity and the death instinct in childhood? Consider a child who is angry at a parent. This child, in fact, is *very* angry! Fearing retaliation if this anger is expressed directly, the child turns the fierce, murderous rage in upon itself. This maneuver has something of a suicidal thrust to it, although seldom is a lethal instrument involved.

Years later this child, once furious with a parent (almost always the mother, in early psychoanalytic literature) will have strong masochistic urges. Both the mother's aggression and the child's own sadistic impulses have become a permanent thorn in the psyche. Yearnings for intimacy, warmth, and gratification have also gone unfulfilled, further contributing to the build-up of anger. One must be punished, just to survive, just to control the unacceptable rage. (This is a simplification of the actual course of events that would have occurred between child and parent during a critical period.) Other patterns of early aggressive and erotic interactions with parents will result in other patterns of adult neurosis. The key point is that whatever interferes with the young child's ability to turn the death instinct outward is also likely to generate enduring problems—especially those expressed by the compulsion to repeat painful and frustrating experiences.

Once this new psychodynamic key has been turned, perhaps other doors could also be unlocked. The problem of suicide had become of more than clinical interest to Freud. Several of his associates in the psychoanalytic movement killed themselves. This compelled increasing attention to suicide. Perhaps the death instinct could be recruited as an explanation for suicidal actions as well. How? Suppose that Eros had failed in its constant struggle to keep potentially self-destructive forces occupied with other tasks. The death instinct could then slip its chains. If external channels for the expression of aggression and anger are blocked, one becomes one's own target. This view also suggested a different way of looking at murder: we take another person's life as a proxy for our own. "I kill the me in you," it might be phrased.

Perhaps the death instinct operates through many self-destructive modalities, not only those that are traditionally classified as suicide. This approach was taken up by eminent clinicians such as Menninger (1938) and Farberow (1980). One might discern potentially lethal maneuvers of the death instinct even in the absence of obvious suicidality. Both direct suicide and more circuitous paths to self-destruction could be triggered by lapses in ego integrity—such as, a psychotic episode, a drinking binge, an indulgence in illicit drugs. Given the opportunity, the death instinct ever active in all of us may seize its moment.

The concepts of *conflict* and *ambivalence*, already important in psychoanalytic theory and practice, became even more critical with the introduction of the death instinct. Life *is* conflict. The ego is faced every day (and night) with the challenge of mediating between the demands of Eros and Thanatos, as well as between those of external reality and inner drives. Death-instinct theory offers a revised perspective: in a fundamental sense, conflicts are never fully resolved; therefore this is not a feasible aim of therapy. Particular conflicts in the life of a particular individual are linked to the basic Eros versus Thanatos contest common to all people.

The "winner" at last must be death. Therefore, it is the part of wisdom to delay this secular version of the last judgment until one has completed a long and active life. One is reminded of the cynical Stage Manager in Thornton Wilder's classic drama, *Our Town*. He has observed many of the town's inhabitants enact their life stories from the bloom of youth to the cemetery on the hill. The details differ, the ending is the same, and only rarely is the whole story "interesting." Freudian death-instinct theory strongly implies that we (ego and Eros) should give Thanatos a long and eventful contest before joining the others on the hill. In other words, we should keep our life "interesting." It is folly—or suicide—to seek a full "resolution" of the Eros/Thanatos conflict in the midst of life.

Other clinicians and researchers have applied death-instinct theory to so-called "psychosomatic" disorders. (This term has been criticized for its implicit mind–body dualism, but retains a descriptive utility.)

Melitta Sperling (1969), for example, reports that depressed clients with severe migraine headaches actually underwent an "instant somatic discharge of destructive energies." The migraine attacks are said to occur "when there is an acute increase in death instinct and when the inhibitory and defensive functions of the depression no longer suffice in protecting the patient from acute self-destruction." Total organismic distress in infants and children who have been rejected by their parents, ulcerative colitis in adults, and other life-threatening physical problems have been seen by various psychoanalysts as manifestations of the death instinct out on the loose.

Ely Jellife, a pioneer in this field, suggested (1933) that death instinct, taking the form of sadism against the self, has "operated like a castration or partial death of an organ or of certain functions of an organ and thus brought about the disharmony of function." His case examples include an exceptionally broad range of conditions, such as myopia, hyperthyroidism, kidney disfunction, and skin disorders. The implacable drive toward cessation is seen as taking an almost infinite variety of forms by those inclined to accept Freud's dueling instinct theory.

ASSAULT ON THANATOS

Despite the care he took to disarm criticism of death-instinct theory, Freud saw this idea attacked fiercely within the ranks of psychoanalysis as well as from the outside. One cannot help but imagine that the discarnate spirit of Sigmund Freud (perhaps puffing on a discarnate cigar) would characterize this negative reaction as "resistance" that itself is a derivative of the sadistic death instinct. Nevertheless, many of the objections are trenchant.

The objections occur on both attitudinal and empirical levels. "I don't agree with the world-view represented by this theory, and I dislike the theory itself—it's so unpleasant" might summarize the first level of objections. The second level argues that "Death-instinct theory is false, useless, and misleading as either psychological theory or therapeutic guide."

Attitudinal and Philosophical Criticisms of the Death Instinct

Norman O. Brown (1959) charged that Freud has bequeathed complete therapeutic pessimism." The dual instinct theory is "worse than useless for therapists." This sorry state of affairs follows directly from Freud's insistence that biological forces are responsible for the conflicts we experience at the psychic level. Not in a single 50-minute hour nor in years of intensive psychotherapy can one expect to alter the biological imperatives. If Freud is right, then, psychotherapy is a doomed cause. Gloom also clouds the general tidings that psychoanalysis offers to humanity: Fundamentally, we are slaves to our biological make-up. In modern as in ancient times, we struggle with competing instinctual drives. "Progress" is a hollow concept in this view, for the most sophisticated person alive today must still contend with the brute inner forces that drove our remotest ancestors.

Brown argues that Freud has left us with a kind of sick religion. "All organic life is then sick; we humans must abandon hope of cure, but we can take comfort in the conclusion that our sickness is part of some universal sickness in nature . . . it is true religion" (Brown, 1959, p. 82). We are all torn with neurotic conflict. Furthermore, these personal tribulations are also manifestations of a "sick" (conflicted) universe. How can any of us expect to become mature and serene when the spirit of the universe is itself conflicted at every level?

Is the dual instinct theory really so relentlessly pessimistic? Brown recognizes that Freud proposed a more positive option. The ego might call upon the instinctual strength of Eros to unify opposites, to reconcile and harmonize the opposing tendencies that contribute to conflict. Just as Thanatos seeks limitation and cessation, so Eros seeks expansion and gratifying activity. Perhaps, then, it is only when we forget about Eros that Thanatos appears as such an inexorable opponent.

This more optimistic facet of Freud's thinking is not persuasive to Brown. Life and death cannot really be unified. Freud has indulged in a redemption fantasy of the genre that had already been familiar in German philosophy and literature since the turn of the eighteenth century. The dual instinct theory perhaps should be read as a farewell contribution to the romantic movement rather than as a modern psychological thesis. Brown also implies that Freud's is a failed romanticism. There is no possibility of a triumphant ending to the story of our instinctual conflict-ridden lives. Given a choice, then, we would be wise to reject Freud's dual instinct theory and its burden of pessimism.

The pessimistic implications of Thanatos are particularly disagreeable because we seem powerless to improve the situation through our own efforts. This intractable characteristic of the death instinct is part of Freud's overall conception of human nature and its place in the universe. The death instinct operates in a *deterministic* manner. It could hardly do otherwise, for the universe itself is subject to laws that operate in a deterministic mode. Furthermore, scientific study has *reductionism* as its goal. One explains by reducing the complex to the simple. Determinism and reductionism were powerful guiding tenets of nineteenth century science.

Like many other scientists of his day, Freud aimed to reduce the complex to the simple and to identify a chain of causal relationships. Freud subjected both waking and sleeping experience to the grindbox of reductionistic determinism. He felt like a real scientist when he could demonstrate cause-and-effect relationships, especially between events and experiences that were usually thought to be unconnected. Death-instinct theory, then, was an especially impressive triumph of psychoanalysis as science. Suicidal and murderous thoughts and actions could be reduced to instinctual drive.

Freud also transferred to psychology the mode of thought he had applied as a young investigator in the neurophysiological laboratory. One might learn a great deal about the nervous system by tracing structures from their earliest form. The *developmental approach* was relatively new and vigorous at this time. Even fresher was Freud's application of this general method to the human mind. His first traversal led to a theory of psychosexual development that had a major impact on society as well as psychology. Freud's revised formulation also took the developmental approach. Perhaps the most audacious contention in the dual instinct theory was his suggestion that every living creature seeks a return to inorganic status—the (hypothetical) starting point for all development. The vicissitudes of Eros and Thanatos in the development history of individuals are also given prominence.

What can be faulted here? Isn't the developmental approach highly relevant to the understanding of human experience and behavior? And isn't it true that a great many other theoreticians and researchers have cultivated developmental approaches since Freud? It may seem unfair to criticize Freud for a bold and radical application of the developmental approach, while at the same time giving respectful attention to the more circumspect theories that formed in his wake. I must, nevertheless, add a criticism here. *Freud's idea of development emphasizes the power of the past to the near exclusion of other possibilities.* Present thought and behavior is driven by instinctual forces and conflicts. The ego labors to keep these inner pressures and conflicts from overwhelming the total organism, simultaneously attempting to cope with the demands of external reality. Poor, beleaguered ego!

There is an alternative position available. Gordon Allport (1955), Abraham Maslow (1968), and a number of other personality theorists have conceived of a more active and creative self that is influenced by but not held captive to the past. The self-actualization movement inspired largely by Maslow's writings is one of the most obvious examples of this approach. Within the ranks of psychoanalysts there have also been numerous departures from the reductionistic, deterministic developmental approach associated with Freud. Common to these once-maverick views are the following themes: (a) the developing self does organize itself around its basic psychophysiological needs and functions (b) as these interact constantly with the environment (especially the human environment, but (c) the self or ego also has its own resources and agenda that (d) become progressively autonomous as maturation continues, (e) unless held in neurotic bondage to the past. The past-driven determinism that occupies the center of Freud's attention on many occasions can be seen as the outcome of developmental *failure.* Those who have experienced wise, loving, and nontraumatic upbringing are *not* held as hostages to the past, but instead strive toward futures of their own creation.

On this view, one might go so far as to accept the reality of Eros and Thanatos as primitive instinctual forces, but forces that have come under the control of a developed, educated, and competent self-system. Stressful circumstances might stir up the primitive instinctual forces, just as storms might threaten even a well-governed city. Under more benign circumstances, however, Eros and Thanatos lend and blend themselves to the enjoyment of the present and the cultivation of the future. Past-driven determinism rules only for the person under great stress, or the neurotic, or the individual who has suffered exceptional deprivation and trauma in early development. To be sure, enough people exist in these categories to grace every psychoanalytic couch in the world. Theoretically, however, *normal* development is characterized by a progressive liberation from instinctual and past-driven determinism. This, at the very least, is a significant alternative formulation of development that would change in many respects the way in which we would think of the death instinct and other (hypothetical) drives.

Dueling Dualism

Freud's death-instinct theory has also drawn criticism for its *dualistic* conception of human nature. It is not only Life versus Death. It is also Mind (ego) versus Body (id). And it is Man versus Nature. Dualism has a philosophical tradition whose antiquity can be traced beyond Plato and the pre-Socratic thinkers. Those who attempt to construct the mental life of our most remote human ancestors most often conclude that a primitive form of mind-soul/body dualism reigned. Freud could be seen, then, as "repackaging" dualism.

There is certainly merit to the criticism. Freud does seem to assume a fundamental dualism within human nature and between ourselves and nature. He also does not keep a firm distinction between dualism as an idea and specific facts about nature and the mind that should be established through empirical inquiry. It is commonplace for theories to include assumptions that are not subject to validation within that theory. Indeed, the philosophy of science has since reconstructed its views to recognize inherent uncertainties and limits both to logical analysis and to empirical inquiry (e.g., Prigogine, 1996). The problem, I think, is not that Freud hoved to the dualistic tradition, but that his writings did not clearly separate guiding assumptions from established facts—or facts that required further investigation. Over the years, Freud the philosopher tended to take over for Freud the sharp-eared clinician and questing psychologist.

Freud can also be criticized for endorsing an adversary attitude between nature and human nature. The Eros/Thanatos formulation could be seen as a blatant attempt to impose a kind of dueling dualism, a cosmic conflict, on our relationship with the universe.

A. J. Levin presents this criticism rather vividly:

> The elements, according to Freud, mock at all human control; the earth quakes, burying man and his works; floods submerge all things; storms

drive all before them; diseases attack living creatures; and finally there is the "painful riddle of death," for which no remedy at all has yet been found, nor probably ever will. (Levin, 1951, p. 262)

Levin cites many examples from Freud's writings in which nature is perceived as adversary and threat to human life. This attitude, according to Levin, is fundamental to Freud's entire theory as well as his approach to psychotherapy, "the need to protect oneself *against* stimuli, rather than live with nature. This dualism is said to exist in our relationship with society as well. We must defend ourselves against our own kind, even (or especially) in the social order that presumably exists for mutual support and protection.

You against me! Me against me! All of us against nature! This attitudinal component of Freud's dualism certainly deserves critical attention. It is not the only available attitude toward self and nature. The Navajo, for example, have a long-standing tradition of living in harmony with nature, and do not make the sharp distinctions between human nature and the rest of the universe that are embodied in Freud's dualism. In practical terms, many of us may be so immersed in the competitive, aggressive, and individualistic traditions of Western society that we resonate more to Freudian dualism than to the Navajo sense of harmony. Nevertheless, Freud could be accused of perpetuating and intensifying a grim and exaggerated vision of universal conflict.

Nature to Freud's Rescue?

We have seen that Freud's view of our relationship with nature is not only unpleasant, but also subject to criticism as overstating the scope and prevalence of conflict. It may be surprising, then, to discover that nature may be becoming to Freud's rescue. Evan Eisenberg (1998) has explored humankind's relationship to the natural environment from antiquity to the present. In this project he shows no interest in rehabilitating Freud's death-instinct theory, but he does propose a reading of nature that is consistent with Freud's emphasis on perpetual conflict.

Eisenberg demonstrates that the "dream of Eden" has been with us since the beginnings of civilization. This vision of living in harmony with nature has taken many forms. The most dominant image for some time now has been a garden blessed with peace and delight.

However, the most ancient idea of Eden was that of "a wild place at the center of the world from which all blessings flow" (p. 422). Studies in ecology are much more in accord with the wild than with the tame version of Eden. In real gardens, fields, oceans and other settings, real animals—and plants—compete for turf and substinance. Furthermore, microcreatures such as bacteria and fungi exist by virtue of their ability to feed on macrocreatures at the same time that the more powerful are devouring those lower down in the food chain.

Freud is invoked briefly as part of Eisenberg's analysis of our fantasies about nature. He picks up on Freud's (1900/1938) observation that there is a parallel between "the mental realm of phantasy" and the lands we set aside as nature preserves. In both cases we try to preserve the original state of things and do not require these sheltered enclaves to be "useful" in the usual sense of this term.

The problem today, according to Eisenberg, is that we are attempting to shape much of the world according to our collective fantasies about an original harmony with nature that is capable of being reinstated. Nature has never been harmonious, or so Eisenberg argues. What we are trying to impose on the real world is our comforting, rather childish fantasies of a conflict-free zone in which milk and honey flow. In the actual world of nature, blood flows, too. We do violence to nature when we try to eradicate conflict, when we attempt to replace risky, challenging reality with the Disney version.

For Eisenberg, life has always been lived best on the edge. Individuals and species develop and thrive amidst the uncertainties and dangers inherent in what we call nature. It would be folly to mistake our fantasies of harmony for the bracing realities of nature. Eisenberg is perhaps going too far when he asserts that knowledge of our mortality makes us furious at nature. Nevertheless, this thought does suggest that our wish for a "peaceable kingdom" may at root be a wish for a world without death.

Freud also went too far in reading his conflict theory into the cosmos. But his conviction that strong impulses toward creation and destruction, life and death are paramount in the realm of nature may be at least partially redeemed by the rapidly growing knowledge base in ecology.

Freud: A Death-Haunted Man?

The criticisms already considered here portray Freud as a relentless materialist whose death-instinct theory burdens us with a most unattractive load of pessimism, reductionism, past-driven determinism, and dualism, all of which are influenced by the dynamics of failed (neurotic) development. History may eventually view him as one of the last giants in a dying tradition. Freud's Europe was fast disappearing; science was already undergoing major changes in conceptual and methodological approaches. Among other changes in the air was a drawing away from Big Theory in the grand philosophical tradition. Death-instinct theory, then, might have had its greatest impact and best opportunity for acceptance had it been offered to the old world Freud knew when young.

And yet, the philosophical and attitudinal criticisms do not end even at this point. At least two more lines of attack have been waiting their turn. Freud himself is the target of one of these assaults, and Ernest Becker (1973) perhaps his severest critic. Becker sees Freud as a man who was haunted by death anxiety all his life. He examines Freud's life as well as his work to demonstrate that the founder of psychoanalysis carried a "dread of dying" through him from youth to old age. According to Becker, Thanatos represents a not-very-clever effort to conceal Freud's own death anxiety. To support this interpretation Becker identifies some of Freud's least attractive patterns and quirks. This selective portrayal results in a portrait of Freud as an overcontrolling and driven individual. Even those aspects of Freud's personality that some have found admirable are presented as neurotic (the astounding productivity as a writer while also conducting a busy clinical practice, leading the development of psychoanalysis, etc.), or as unremarkable (the courage in living for many years with physical agony).

Becker believes "that we can justifiably fish around for some hints about Freud's special orientation to reality and about a 'problem' unique to him. If we get hints of such a problem, I think we can use it to throw light on the overall structure of his work and its possible limits" (Becker, 1973, p. 102). Essentially, Thanatos is said to be Freud's way of avoiding confrontation with the "terror of death." The death instinct was really intended to control one man's personal anxieties, then, rather than provide a universal law of human thought and experience.

The last criticism to be considered in this section differs markedly from the others, and is one of the most interesting. Freud had suggested that the death instinct is a kind of remembrance of the peaceful inorganic status that existed prior to the emergence of life. We have a fundamental yearning to return to this tension-free state that contrasts so completely with the pressures, strivings, and tumult of impulse-ridden life. It is again Levin who observes that Freud's theory is inconsistent with the knowledge that has been gained about physical matter. There can be no return to what Freud once called the "peace of the inorganic world," not since Einstein "revealed to mankind the tremendous forces locked in 'inert' atoms." The death instinct is, therefore, a fiction.

In the decades since Levin's article there has been a continuing series of revelations about the forces at work in the universe on both the micro and macro levels. Nowhere has been discovered a haven for inorganic matter whose ambition consists of drowsing through eternity. Perhaps, though Freud would have made something of black holes with their propensity for swallowing everything that comes their way, including light. Freud's attribution of "peacefulness" to inorganic existence was open to question from the start. Now it appears to be decisively contradicted by modern physics. What is more, this kind of theory seems to be precisely what Freud himself described when he compared "the mental realm of phantasy" with zones of the physical world that we have set as "preserves" for nature in its supposedly original and harmonious state.

Clinical and Empirical Criticisms of the Death Instinct

The second set of criticisms is also varied, but has in common the contention that Freud's death-instinct theory is either useless or misleading when applied to specific problems.

Freud's introduction of the dual instinct theory into his account of psychosexual development did not convince many of his followers. He left Thanatos in a particularly weak position. In outlining sexual development, Freud referred to such familiar entities as mouth, anus, and genitalia. Nobody doubted the reality of these organs. This grounding in consensual reality made it possible for Freud to propose the sequence from oral to genital sexuality. His readers could make their own observations to confirm or contradict Freud's, and many did agree with some propositions while rejecting others. For example, many rejected his account of female development, while finding some of his other ideas palatable.

His first theory of psychosexual development also included a major construct that helped to track the vicissitudes. Libido—sexual energy—is an idea with some appeal to the imagination while at the same time suggesting an actual substance or process. Again, Freud could build upon the familiar: sexuality is an acknowledged dimension of life. It might therefore be reasonable to consider the possibility that the genitalia are also sources of sexual feeling and energy. The rest of libido theory does make greater demands on credibility, but at least it does begin with plausible statements about observable facts of life.

The death instinct was turned loose by Freud without such advantages. Where is the bodily organ for death, equivalent to the genitalia for sex? And what process or substance is akin to libido? Freud did consider introducing a "something" that would be Thanato's parallel to libido. He could not find this something, however, and dropped the idea. In discussing developmental history, then, Freud could not offer a detailed account of the death instinct's adventures. The new concept was remote and abstract. One could see what Freud meant by libido and psychosexual development—not so with Thanatos. This difficulty in describing the death instinct probably contributed much to the initial cool reception it received. This failure to make the death instinct seem palpable and observable was not subsequently overcome, so the first reaction was not subsequently overcome.

The problem of suicide might have been expected to be one of the primary beneficiaries of death-instinct theory. We kill ourselves when the death instinct becomes all too powerful, or our ego resources all too weak. This would be the simplest and most direct implication. However, the new theory did not seem to make much of a practical contribution to understanding, predicting, or preventing suicide. This failure had much to do with the already noted: the somewhat remote and abstract nature of the death instinct concept. How is one to measure or assess the intensity of a given individual's death instinct? Freud, the neurophysiologist and physician, offered no laboratory tests or clinical examinations for this purpose. The researcher's difficulty was no less severe. How is one to operationalize this concept? What criteria could be used? What objective determinations of initial value or change?

Philosopher and suicide expert Jacque Choron (1972) concluded that Freud did not satisfactorily explain why the death instinct at times is able to overcome our fundamental impulse toward self-preservation. Without a persuasive explanation for the occasional breakthroughs of the death instinct, the concept adds little if anything to the quest for understanding, prediction, and prevention. For example, there is some association between mental illness and acts of self-destruction. One does not need death-instinct theory to support this connection, however, as the statistics speak for themselves. It might be asserted that individuals with a history of mental or emotional disorder are at a higher risk for suicide because their ego strength is less adequate for managing inner tensions. However, this plausible contention would fail to demonstrate the value of death-instinct theory. Not all individuals with psychiatric problems complete or even attempt suicide. The clinician and researcher would seem better advised to examine ego strength—a difficult but not impossible concept to operationalize— than to ponder about the intensity of the invisible Thanatos. In practice, specialists in suicide prevention and research take a great many factors into account, environmental, psychological, and biological. Adding the death instinct to a very long list of identified factors does not appear especially helpful.

Most books on suicide make limited reference (if any) to death-instinct theory. In his cogent description of *The Suicide Syndrome*, for example, Larry Morton Gernsbacher dispenses with Thanatos after a mere three paragraphs in his introductory chapter. This very brief treatment nevertheless adds still another criticism:

> The endorsement of the death instinct theory would automatically inter-pret suicide as resulting from an instinctual drive which must be medi-ated, displaced, or sublimated for survival. But the absence of suicide in all other living creatures would imply that only human beings—the least instinctually motivated of creatures—would possess the death in-stinct. Or it would imply the equally untenable view that other animals have intellectually learned better to resist it. (Gernsbacher, 1985, p. 18)

Edwin S. Shneidman, a pioneer of modern suicidology, does not mention death-instinct theory at all in his *Definition of Suicide* (1985). This is a particularly significant omission, since Shneidman is quite familiar with Freudian theory. Freud is mentioned chiefly for the sug-gestion that suicide is essentially murder turned inwardly. (This hypoth-esis, while consistent with death-instinct theory, does not necessarily depend on it.) One of the many interesting facets of Shneidman's approach is the way in which he has utilized several concepts that have some kinship to death-instinct theory without making the more philosophical assumptions associated with Freud. *Lethality* is perhaps the most relevant concept here. This term has a family resemblance to Thanatos, but is more closely related to practical applications, and does not carry the excess baggage of death-instinct theory. A lethality rating can be made on the basis of behavioral observations, interviews, and other readily available methods. One can even come up with a scaled score for lethality in the particular situation under investigation—a clear difference from the speculative approach usually associated with death-instinct theory. For Shneidman, "any act, deed, or event in the world can be rated on a lethality dimension" (1985, p. 205). This view nearly rivals Freud's for universality, but is more closely tied to observable and verifiable phenomena.

It has often been concluded by clinicians that death-instinct theory introduces an unnecessary and unsatisfactory complication. Symons (1927), for example, judged that Freud's earlier formulations were more useful in understanding the dynamics of sadomasochism and the repetition compulsion. One did not have to invent a new force that opposed the pleasure principle. Years later, Galdston (1955) was even more critical of "Freud's dismal excursion into the realm of death." Galdston contests Freud's interpretation of the metabolic processes involved in the development and survival or organisms. Furthermore, the death instinct cannot serve as an explanation of masochistic behavior because "it cannot be validated in experience." Galdston also rejects Freud's dualistic view of Eros and Thanatos at war with each other throughout life. He does leave room for a revised theory in which the death instinct could be seen as the fulfillment of Eros. The normal, coping adult somehow manages to embrace the painful and threatening side of life, along with the pleasures and gratifications. More recent examinations of suicidal behavior are more likely to ignore death instinct altogether (e.g., Heckler, 1994; Kosky, Eshkevari, Goldney, & Hassan, 1997).

Perhaps enough has been said here to indicate that Freud's death-instinct theory came under serious criticism right from the beginning. Empirical research to test or extend this theory seems to be virtually nonexistent. Clinicians often dismiss the theory as useless or misleading. There is not much point to adding further examples. It is important, however, to acknowledge one of the most powerful and broadly based challenges that have arisen. This challenge was clearly prefigured in Galdston's insightful but nearly forgotten article. His insider's critique centered around his own belief that "Those who fear to die lack the courage to live." This, in effect, became the rallying cry for the existential challenge.

The main thesis of Becker's influential book is captured by its title, *The Denial of Death*. As already noted in connection with his attack on Freud's life and character, Becker sees death-instinct theory as itself a denial of death. Freud was attempting to control his own anxieties by proposing this theory, so this is a powerful reason for rejecting the theory. There is an even more powerful reason, however. The terror of death is central to the human condition. Our "deepest need is to be free of the anxiety of death and annihilation" (Becker, 1973, p. 66). No abstract speculations about inorganic peacefulness and warring instincts can help us to face our personal anxieties. The courage to live must begin with our recognition that we do, indeed, fear to die.

This is not an ordinary criticism of death-instinct theory but, rather, an alternative conception. It is only after this theory has been examined on its own terms (chapter 4) that a useful evaluation and comparison can be made with Freud's view.

EVALUATION OF DEATH-INSTINCT THEORY TODAY

It is time now to see what can be learned both from Freud's effort and the critical response. There has already been some discussion of the criticisms, but further evaluation is needed. This will be followed by an attempt to discover what might yet be learned from Freud's insights.

Critical Review of the Response to Death-Instinct Theory

Death-instinct theory has been portrayed as pessimistic, deterministic, reductionistic, past-oriented, and dualistic. It could hardly seem to be more unappetizing. But would it really be the part of wisdom to spurn the theory on these grounds?

Pessimism was indeed one of Freud's personal traits. If we interacted with him on a daily basis we might feel that we were in the presence of a guarded, watchful, skeptical person who expected the worse of human nature and was seldom disappointed. He was rather a different fellow, however, when he was in what might be called his romantic hero modality. Freud believed we could be better than we were and that his new science of psychoanalysis could show the way. He was also well within the romantic hero tradition in having both severe criticism and doubts about the present human condition and a tempting glimpse of a better world that might be won through vision, courage, and determination. This shifting between pessimism and optimism can be found in many poets and artists of Freud's time and of the entire romantic period.

The question that needs to be answered here is whether or not death-instinct theory is so pessimistic that we are left without any constructive courses of action. Notice first the difference between a nihilistic attitude and a recognition of limits. Freud did not try to discourage us from bringing the death instinct under more effective control. This, in fact, became of the highest priority to him. There was a strategic plan involved in his certification of Thanatos as a fundamental instinctual drive. Yes, one could feel pessimistic about human nature if an aggressive, destructive component has such deep roots within us. Recognition of this challenge, however, is a positive first step. Freud urged us to realize how much was at stake and what forces we would have to overcome, tame, or sublimate to assure the survival of civilization.

Freud's exchange of letters with Einstein clearly expresses both the urgency and prominence he gave to the problem, as well as his guarded optimism for a successful resolution. The correspondence was initiated in 1931 when the League of Nations invited Einstein to contact another intellectual leader of his own choosing for an examination of some topic of great mutual concern. Einstein had already met Freud and read some of his major works. The question he asked Freud: "Why war?"

Interestingly, the distinguished physicist had already arrived at an answer that might have come directly from Freud. "How is it possible that the mass of the people permits itself to become aroused to the point of insanity and eventual self-sacrifice?" asks Einstein, who immediately adds, "The answer can only be: Man has in him the need to hate and to destroy." There was urgency, but not pessimism, certainly not nihilism in Einstein's approach to Freud. He thought it might be possible "to so guide the psychological development of man that it becomes resistant to the psychoses of hate and destruction. . . . "

Freud's (Einstein & Freud, 1932) response deserves close reading by all concerned with the danger of megadeath as well as those specifically interested in the death instinct concept. The most relevant points for us here are the following:

1.   The community (society) can acquire sufficient strength to place the rule of law over the more primitive impulse to exercise raw power and force.

2.   For the "justice of the community" to succeed, however, requires a key psychological achievement: the recognition of common feelings, a strong sense of bonding with others. The effectiveness of society in controlling aggressive and self-destructive impulses, then, is dependent on the mature psychological development of its citizens.

3.   Eros and Thanatos are both real in a sense, but "You recognize that this is basically only the theoretical transfiguration of the universally known contrast of love and hate, which perhaps has an essential relationship to the polarity of attraction and repulsion that plays a part in your field. . . . Each of these drives is just as indispensable as the other; the phenomena of life evolve from their acting together and against each other. . . . "

4.   War—the expression of the death instinct on a broad scale—can be prevented by "anything that creates emotional ties between human beings." This, in turn, occurs when we are able to identify emotionally with others. Eros is the perfect counterbalance to Thanatos.

Freud and Einstein both express keen awareness of the forces that lead to tension and conflict in society and both conclude that the potential for self-destruction is real and not to be uprooted from human nature, at least in any foreseeable future. This, however, is a long way from nihilism or the depths of pessimism. The deadly, disagreeable dual-instinct theory of Old Man Freud takes on a rather different look when he adds, quite simply, that "Psychoanalysis need not be ashamed when it speaks of love, because religion says the same: 'Love thy neighbor as thyself.' " Furthermore, there is a wide avenue available for those willing to take constructive action because "Everything that leads to important shared action creates such common feelings, such identifications" (p. 8).

The critics, then, have neglected the fact that Freud considered Eros to be fully competitive with Thanatos. It is not "sick" to experience conflict. The normal business of life requires the interaction of processes opposite in their individuals aims, but that together contribute to effective development and functioning. Instead of dismissing Thanatos as leading to "complete therapeutic pessimism," Brown might as one-sidedly accused Eros as leading to "complete therapeutic optimism." Love is as real as hate, anabolism as real as catabolism.

The death instinct does eventually triumph—through death itself. This outcome, however, is not proof of Freud's nihilism nor is it any reason for a mature person to creep through life under depression's dark cloud. We did not need Freud to tell us that life ends in death: whatever fear or sorrow might accompany our knowledge of mortality was entrenched in our minds well before a Viennese psychiatrist published his latest book in 1920.

There is also a more specific reason to disentangle "bad feelings about death" from Freud's dual instinct theory. We are capable of living full and productive lives, loving and being loved. This potential is best realized by developing a firm sense of self-worth and social responsibility. Thanatos will then play an important but subsidiary role in our lives. Aggression will be channeled in positive directions, free of hostility toward self or others. A society comprised of such people will raise its children in a coherent and loving manner and will not be susceptible to the primitive temptations of suicide, murder, or—worse of all—war. The person who has lived long and well can face death without terror. (In this belief Freud is in full agreement with subsequent existentialists and self-actualization theorists.) The end does not come violently, nor does it destroy the value of what was already achieved in life, still less does this death inflict harm upon others, other than the inevitable ordeal of normal grief. The actual cessation of life, then, represents as much a victory for Eros as for Thanatos. It was quite a party—now it's time to go!

Admittedly, Freud did not string these thoughts together in quite the way presented here, but this scenario is entirely consistent with his dual instinct theory, and much of his other writings including his letters. The man himself often was pessimistic. This attitude certainly had something to do with his own personality development, but also had much to do with the troubled times through which he lived. Could he have been a thinking man and not have found reason for pessimism and doubt? Nevertheless, Freud's overall emphasis remained on the hope that human nature could progressively gain rational and socially responsible control over the destructive side of its impulses. The correspondence with Einstein makes it clear he still felt humanity had a chance, death instinct and all! Is it realistic to ask for more?

So much for the pessimism. What about the *determinism?* Freud did try to see human nature as but one part of the universe and, therefore, subject to scientific investigation that would eventually yield laws and principles. Determinism involved an act of faith. In Freud's time many scientists adhered to the belief that the world could be completely measured and understood, given sufficient time, effort, and ingenuity on their part. A vocal minority of scientists and many humanists attacked determinism as a reprehensible denial of the vital principle of life, choice, responsibility, and morality. To make things a bit more complicated, some of the most determined determinists also labored to rescue the concepts of individual choice and responsibility in a clockwork universe.

In the end, attitudes toward determinism did not count for as much as the actual results of scientific labors. Either we were able to predict and explain phenomena on the basis of deterministic conceptions, or we were not. When young Freud started his laboratory investigations of the central nervous system, neither he nor any one else knew how far the deterministic credo would take him. When middle aged Freud became simultaneously the first psychoanalyst and the first patient, he again could not have specified the outcome. When old Freud formulated and defended his death-instinct theory, the deterministic credo was once more simply a guide and inspiration. The first of these projects met with modest success; the second (expressed chiefly through *The Interpretation of Dreams*) was a breakthrough; the final effort has been treated generally as a failure. These differential outcomes were in projects carried out by the same person who maintained essentially the same philosophy of science throughout.

Determinism is not a serious "ism" to worry about. The results have never fully justified the deterministic credo in any field of scientific inquiry. Certainly, the psychological and social sciences (not to exclude economics) have remained intractable to all-out determinism, whether of the Freudian or behavioral type. Furthermore, the whole deterministic enterprise has for some time appeared naive and outdated in light of the theory of relativity, the principle of uncertainty, and chaos theory. The mechanical cause-and-effect approach that was still foremost in the nineteenth century no longer entices theory builders.

Were Freud with us today, he would probably have made these new wrinkles his own. The dual instinct theory could be reframed for consistency with current knowledge and assumptions. Just by dropping "instinct," that politically incorrect term, Freud could neutralize a good bit of the criticism. Although stubborn, especially when under attack, Freud did pride himself on the scientist's willingness to revise theories and assumptions on the basis of new information. The critics are right, I think, in faulting Freud for his reliance on determinism. But neither his general theory nor the death instinct in particular are dependent on a thorough-going determinism.

In some of Freud's most important passages he ignored or violated his own roots in determinism. Once the knowing and flexible ego gains control of the instinctual drives, it (we) is no longer caught up like a helpless puppet or slaving machine. If determinism was part of Freud's credo, so was the belief that successful human development enhances our ability to make choices and control our own destiny. The person who is still caught in the toils of a past-driven determinism is not the psychologically robust and vibrant person who is presently engaged in reading *The Psychology of Death*. The individual whose life does reveal a pattern of relentless determinism is the neurotic victim of his or her own past.

The *reductionistic* and *past-driven* aspects of Freudian theory can be considered together. Both are pendants to the belief that knowledge of the past can lead to prediction of the future. This is hardly a radical and barely a controversial idea. If we want to predict whether a registered voter or a laboratory rat will turn either right or left at the next choice-point, it is obviously useful to have a record of the organism's history of choice-point behavior. Furthermore, we might be very interested in discovering an even simpler (i.e., reductionistic) basis for predicting the choice behavior. A person who is philosophically opposed to the deterministic–reductionistic would probably still welcome economic status, age, or gender as a basis for prediction. Most of us do use reductionistic markers from past experience in an attempt to understand, predict, and control future contingencies. This approach is not always successful, of course, but we persist with the effort to discover a strong link between past and future. Freud would have faced even more withering criticism had he abandoned a deterministic-reductionistic approach and asserted instead that what we think, feel, and do tomorrow has no relationship with what we thought, felt, and did yesterday!

The real question is whether or not death-instinct theory is crippled by an unjustifiably extreme form of deterministic reductionism. It is possible to read Freud's theory in this way. He works hard in trying to convince us that we possess—or are possessed by—powerful instinctual drives that are rooted in forces more universal and ancient than our own biographies. Here is an alternative interpretation that I base on Freud's general contributions to psychoanalytic theory and the way he actually uses the Eros/Thanatos formulation, one could propose the following version:

1.   It is really *the person in the immediate situation* who determines how the competing impulses will affect his or her life. The past is only *represented* in the here-and-now.

2.   The particular way in which the past is represented depends much on the individual personality and lifestyle that has formed over time (a thesis that owes much to Alfred Adler, 1956). This personality did not yet exist when Eros and Thanatos first began to stir within the young organism, but now the fantasies, competencies, and experiences of a unique human being have much to say about the further adventures of the instinctual drives.

3.   More enlightened child-rearing practices, psychoanalytic therapy, mental health education, and a society that is not at war with its own impulses can help to produce adults capable both of loving and of acting aggressively upon the world when appropriate. As mature adults, they are no longer driven and determined, but simply *influenced* by the ancient instincts within their organic structure.

4.   When the instinctual drives are *represented* in our own mental dramas, they take on a form that is more appropriate to Psyche, the mistress of distinctively human thought. It is *love* and *hate* that feature in our waking and sleeping fantasies. Primitive organic urges must transform themselves into more re-presentable characters in order to gain admission to the theater of our minds. In this significant sense, then, *the past conforms itself to the present, rather than the reverse.*

In summary, what we do tomorrow *can* be linked to critical events in our personal pasts and the operation of instinctual drives—*but we* are helpless in the grip of these forces only if we have failed to achieve mature selfhood. Interestingly, many other theory-spinners have also described instinct-driven behavior as rigid or mechanical. This is in contrast to the idealized normal person whose intelligence and experience results in a more flexible and creative approach to life, the instincts still active, but serving higher purposes. Much of what Freud said about instincts was also being said by other investigators and theorists. Distinctive to Freud, however, was his assertion that those who grow up neurotic—or who fail to grow up emotionally—are held captives to instinctual drives they should have mastered.

Freud probably did rely too much on the reductionistic-deterministic credo that was so appealing to scientists of his generation. It is an open question, however, as to whether or not the psychologist of our own times can afford the luxury of condescension. Our journals are filled with raw, or at best, half-baked empiricism in which multivariate computer statistical packages take the place of searching and reflective thought. It is as though determinism and reductionism have lost some of their power to inspire our efforts, but have not been replaced by any new principle of comparable vigor.

The critics are accurate but selective in characterizing Freud's theory as *dualistic*. Eros and Thanatos are depicted as instinctual drives with opposite aims. Conflict is inevitable and unremitting. This concept is in keeping with psychoanalytic theory in general, brimming over with steamy pressures and tensions, and demarcated between the dualism of internal and external spheres. Philosopher John Dewey's (1920) scorching attack on dualistic thinking is even more telling than the critiques on Freud in particular. For Dewey, the universe is neither a completely integrated whole, nor a set of rigid dichotomies. Dualistic thinking does untold mischief by allowing us to indulge in glib oversimplifications. Such traditional pairings as "mind" and "body," "means" and "ends," and "good" and "evil" create mental traps that burden society at large, as well as individuals. Dewey would probably have found Freud "guilty" (assuming he could reconcile in his own mind the guilt/innocence dichotomy).

Freud's dualism, however, would not have been possible without an underlying monism! After all, those antagonistic instinctual drives are battling for the same turf, the same resources. It is the same person who either lives or dies, loves or kills (or both). Freud clearly assumes a strong common framework within which conflicting impulses can have at each other. Conflict between instincts would be pointless unless there was something to fight over (i.e., the self). Furthermore, the antagonism itself is subsidiary to collaboration. We could not function without the reciprocal operation of Eros and Thanatos, any more than we could metabolize without both an anabolic and a catabolic process.

Freud did see conflict as a central fact of life. He did enjoy telling us stories in which the dramatic conflict is heightened. As perceptive listeners we can recognize that all this strife between Eros and Thanatos takes place within the unity of the human soul. And if we find it surprising to associate Freud with respect for the "soul," then we have not yet reached Bettelheim's (1983, pp. 9–15) level of understanding.

Two other philosophical-attitudinal criticisms of death-instinct theory were presented earlier. Becker rejects this theory on the basis of Freud's own personal problems and quirks. Believing he had found a connection between Freud's anxieties and the development of death-instinct theory, Becker concluded that the theory could therefore be dismissed. It is ironic but no longer unusual for the psychoanalytic approach to be turned against Freud. One may or may not consider Becker's *ad hominum* arguments to be fair play. More important, however, is the question of inferential logic. Does knowing (or guessing) the mood and motives of a creator provide a sound basis for judging the product? Would Freud have developed a better theory had he been completely free of death-related anxieties? Or did Freud—once again—consult his own inner experiences as he wrestled with a significant theoretical issue? I do not consider it sound procedure to judge the product on the basis of the process that went into its creation. Death-related motivations had major influences on Darwin, Twain, Mahler, and many others whose contributions, like Freud's, ultimately are judged on their intrinsic merits.

Finally, there was Levin's interesting criticism of the physical theory underlying Freud's assumption of "inorganic peace." Freud was wrong about that. The fundamental error was in attributing *any* psychological quality to the cosmos. He was not the first to project human attributes on the heavens; ancient astrologists read personal destinies into the stars, and physicists later spoke of "attractions" and "affinities." Even so, Freud was asking for trouble in building his death-instinct theory on the far-fetched assumption of a primordial inorganic state to which our own instinctual drives owe allegiance. Freud recognized—and perhaps counted on—the likelihood that this theory was unverifiable. Even as he formulated this theory, however, it was being made to look absurd by achievements in physics, astronomy, and related fields.

If we take the "inorganic peace" component seriously, then it stands as a classic example of the Psychologist's Fallacy (first identified by William James, 1896). The fact that we can analyze or read things into the world (or into each other's behavior) doesn't make them true. Nevertheless, there are two ways in which one might attempt to rescue this moribund speculation. The more amusing approach would be to argue that inorganic nature feels perfectly at ease with itself, even though many physicists hold that the universe is racing away from itself at the highest velocity possible. What, though, is velocity, after all, to "matter" that flows in "waves"? The inner life of inorganic nature might be at its most serene under these conditions, for all we know.

Another approach would be to conclude that Freud was just telling us stories again. He could not resist the dramatic impact of making a Big Cosmic Statement—and he did hedge this statement with a variety of disclaimers, including characterizing it has a kind of mythology. Freud might have taken us for very dull folk if we accepted "inorganic peace" as a concrete description of reality when all he wanted to do was to prepare us to look kindly upon his reformulation of our instinctual life. One can imagine him drawing another puff from his forbidden cigar and sighing, "So, they can't take a little joke, can they?"

Central to most of the clinical and empirical critiques has been the difficulty of working with the death instinct in any practical sense. As already noted, the introduction of Thanatos did not provide any "handle" comparable to the sexual instinct's libido, nor could particular organ systems be readily identified as hosts to the death instinct throughout the developmental process. Freud did not offer enough specifics for most clinicians and researchers to find productive use for the death instinct.

There is a predicament here from which we might draw instruction. The hard-headed scientist will not be satisfied until phenomena can be reduced (that word, again) to numbers. Clinicians, however, must deal with inferences. Freud was both the scientist and the clinician. He remained frustrated by his inability to reconcile the goal of quantification with the qualitative and inferential aspects of clinical practice.

He struggled with this problem through a life time of work. A significant example is his treatment of *Inhibitions, Symptoms, and Anxiety* (1925/1959). This is an heuristic contribution to the dynamics of anxiety, with particular emphasis on differences between "normal" and "neurotic" responses to danger. "Differences in intensity" and other concepts that imply quantification are critical to his discussion. Nevertheless, Freud still cannot turn the corner and actually convert the qualitative into the quantitative. This frustration is evident in his presentation of death-instinct theory as well. Freud does want to provide us with a way of assessing the relative strength of Eros and Thanatos, as well as of the ego functions per se. He remains troubled by his inability to do so. We have been led to expect some kind of useful tool, don't receive it, and walk away from the death instinct.

The useful lesson, it seems to me, is that a zone of "best application" exists for most theories and methods. Freud might have continued to employ concepts that imply quantification in his philosophical forays as well as his structural creations in psychology. There is some value, for example, in recognizing that both the forces of repression and the impulses repressed might have variable levels of intensity. This idea might be usefully included even if we never actually measured the forces in any precise way.

It was probably a mistake, though, to build up expectations for measuring the death instinct as though it were a readily observable and palpable phenomenon. Freud would have had to draw back from his grand theoretical project and instruct us instead in the art of clinical inference. "Of course, Thanatos is not like the nose on your face, or the whatever on your whatever," Freud might have lectured. "We *infer* the death instinct from certain patterns of speech, action, and communication. If we are good observers, then we will have improved our sensitivity to the inner struggles experienced by our clients. And if we are *not* competent to observe and infer, or well trained to draw then we should probably be wrapping herring instead!" (Freud told me so himself in a dream visitation: if you revisit his *Wit and Its Relationship to the Unconscious* (1905/1938), you will come across an absurdist jest in which the symbolic relationship between a herring and a bath towel is daringly exposed.)

Had Freud settled for the death instinct as a hypothetical construct (in the jargon of a later psychology), and offered us more clues to the processes of observation and inference, we in turn might have given

Thanatos more serious trial as a guide to clinical practice. Instead, he tried to force "scientific quantification" into an area in which it has seldom been comfortable.

It is also worth keeping in mind that even in a "hard" science such as physics there has been more success in predicting behavior of the "group" (e.g., a large aggregation of molecules in the form gas), than of the "individual" (a single molecule or subatomic unit). Suicidology from Durkheim (1897/1951) to the present day has also had some success in identifying subpopulations who are at relatively high risk and even putting some numbers on the risk factor.

The quantitative approach, however, still leaves much to be desired in prediction of suicidal behavior by a particular individual. A persistent problem in suicide prevention and research is the large number of false positives. Attention must be given to a relatively large pool of people whose general characteristics have been associated with suicidality, instead of being able to focus down on the smaller number who will actually make attempts on their lives. Freud—and everybody else—has had only limited success in identifying suicidal risk in particular individuals by reliance on quantitative methods alone. Competent clinicians, however, especially with additional training in suicide prevention, are often able to assess suicidal potential for particular individuals through a variety of observations. Their estimates can even be expressed in a lethality scale or some other predictive instrument, but what gives these formalized techniques much of their power is the clinician's overall sensitivity and competence, not the numbers per se.

Could, then, death-instinct theory be useful from a clinical standpoint if we proceed as clinicians instead of misplaced number-crunchers? A logical place to start might be Freud's characteristic emphasis on the importance of early development. Identify the child who has turned anger and aggression inwardly as a basic coping style and we may have identified a person at unusual risk for direct or indirect suicide. Such a person might be said to have organized his or her self around Thanatos. It is as though circumstances impelled this person, while still a relatively helpless child, to conclude: "I will be a self-murderer. This is the only way for me to survive."

It would be much more useful to observe such at-risk children in their own natural settings and while they are still children, as compared with reliance on retrospective analysis. This tact has now been taken by a growing number of counselors and researchers whose sensitivities may have been honed by Freud's emphasis on the influence of early experiences. We are learning more about the early life circumstances that seem to set some people on the pathway to destructive thoughts and actions (e.g., Nader, 1996; Range, 1996; Wass, 1995).

AN AFTERLIFE FOR THE DEATH INSTINCT?

One might choose to agree with Becker (1973) that the death instinct "can now securely be relegated to the dust bin of history." Or one might hold a more philosophical and appreciative view of dust:

> Oh, do you know this dust, then? Do you know what it is and what it can do? Learn to know it before you despise it. This matter which now lies there as dust and ashes will soon, dissolved in water, form itself as crystal, will shine as metal, which will then emit electrical sparks, will by means of its galvanic intensity manifest a force which, decomposing the closest combinations, reduces earths to metals; nay, it will, of its own accord, form itself into plants and animals, and from its mysterious womb develop that life for the loss of which you, in your narrowness, are so painfully anxious. Is it, then, absolutely nothing to continue to exist as such matter? . . . Whatever pertains to the will holds good also of matter. (Schopenhauer, 1883/1957, pp. 260–261)

Let us examine briefly the dust that still swirls about from the death of a theory that seems to have few mourners. Perhaps, just perhaps, Freud's death-instinct theory may be more useful in its afterlife than in its original incarnation. I would call your attention to its possible contributions to (a) naming and owning the unnamable, (b) doing death, and (c) killing to stay alive.

Naming and Owning the Unnamable

The dead have—or are—an Otherness that bring us up short, according to the heuristic phenomenologist Edmund Husserl (1973). They do not respond to our communications, nor to their own inner promptings. Contemporary phenomenologist Maxine Sheets-Johnstone (1990) believes that humankind formed its conception of death from a self-discovery linked to the inability to penetrate the Otherness of the dead. No matter how we put it, death is hard to think and talk about. We can grasp that "this person is no longer alive." It is much more difficult, however, to comprehend what it is or might be to no longer be alive.

This perceptual–cognitive barrier to understanding death adds to our emotional aversion. We don't want to think of death, anyhow. It's too depressing, too scary. The literature is replete with examples of our multiform strategies for evading acknowledgements of death. (For example, there was until recently a strong taboo in our society against saying the word "cancer," the name having taken on the symbolic attributes of a condition then presumed to be fatal.) One of the most powerful strategies has been the externalizing of death. Death is out there. We may catch our death of cold by not wearing our sweaters and mittens despite mother's warning, or death may catch us in any number of ways. Constructing death as an external threat has often been found to be a salient characteristic of young children's views on the subject (chapter 2).

Death-instinct theory offers one way of naming the unnamable. It does not presume to divulge the nature of death per se. However, it does provide "identification papers" for what might be construed as our most intimate link to death. Something that answers to the name of death is inside us. Whatever might be its ontological status, death instinct is an identifier and a locator. Death figures into our very being: so much for "Otherness."

What might be the practical consequences of accepting a concept such as death instinct? We might become more attentive to the ways in which our lifestyles are flecked with insinuations of death, for example, the unnecessary risks to which we expose ourselves and our loved ones, or the fatalism that interferes with our capacity to take effective action. We might also become more attentive to the ways in which other people's death-insinuated lifestyles can endanger our own survival.

On the philosophical–attitudinal level, we might be inspired to take a more responsible attitude toward our lives/deaths. "This death is not an imposition from the outside that I can blame on others, and it is not entirely a shapeless void that I am incapable to comprehend. This death of mine is inherent to my being, so it has always spoken to me in its own way, and I am learning how to speak to it."

On the cognitive level, the death instinct might provide the counter-weight essential to dialectical thinking and discourse. For sake of brevity we might focus here on the logical maneuver known as *negation*. Philosophical analyses have demonstrated that negation takes many forms and is subject to linguistic and logical controversies (Horn, 1989). Perhaps negation's simplest form is most appropriate here. "X is alive" is a meaningful proposition because it is possible to frame the negation. An assertion of a positive attribute requires the shadow of a possible negation. Death is negation's omnivorous shadow, drawn up to its full, eclipsing height.

Adding now the poetic–mythic dimension, the death instinct enables us to engage more fully with such concepts as the life force or will to live. Although imprecise from a scientific standpoint, "will to live" is sometimes a viable, even a crucial, concept in situations where a person might or might not be able to pull through. To have a way of speaking about competing will-to-live and will-to-die orientations is to enter into an urgent and consequential dialogue. Furthermore, death instinct may be what is assumed when observers note the importance of acts of destruction in the creative process (as did Nietzsche, 1885/ 1927, in envisioning the transvaluation of values in the modern world).

Do we really have a death instinct in the same way that we have bones, muscles, and red blood cells? This is a question for future research to answer. What we do have with "death instinct" is a way of speaking, a way of representing one key facet of our relationship with mortality. Freud knew that he was often telling us stories in which psychological truths were embedded. In the death instinct story, Freud endowed Thanatos with a self-propelled quality. It was a force, a drive. This was not necessarily a bad idea. Physicists worked productively with "forces" and "attractions" for many years and even today find it useful to speak of such whimsical pseudo-beings as "strange attractors."

A driving, insistent, death-oriented force has resonations with the determined and obsessed behavior that has all too often been observed when members of our species engage in acts of violence. Determination certainly describes the attitude of the woman quoted earlier who, having failed to kill herself by hanging, started hacking at her neck with an axe. It also describes some killers who keep shooting at anything that moves, and then fire again into those who have already fallen victim. This brings us to the threshold of one of the most disturbing propensities of our species: Doing death.

Doing Death

Human actions and interactions often have key roles in ending a life. Usually, though, the death is an outcome, not the culmination of a purpose. Carelessness, neglect, ignorance, and perseverance in a deleterious habit seldom have death as the avowed or acknowledged purpose. Even high-risk activities—sky-diving, for example—do not necessarily signify a powerful wish to die. Instead, one may treasure the excitement or beauty of the risk-taking activity and hope to survive to do it again and again. Furthermore, some suicides and homicides also do not have death as the central purpose. A grieving parent feels she cannot face another day of emotional pain. A criminal panics when a robbery attempt goes awry and shoots a convenience store clerk. Both engaged in actions that proved lethal, but neither had death as the top priority. The grieving woman wanted the pain to stop; the thief wanted to evade arrest.

Here we step aside from what might be called "mainstream killing," deaths that happened in the course of other activities and in the service of other motives (Grossman, 1995). We approach the zone of maximum discomfort for most of us—the zone where people kill for killing, where people volunteer themselves to do death's own work.

There are horrifying episodes in which people kill each other for the satisfaction of killing. Destroying another person is felt as pleasurable, even thrilling. Late-night horror movies and other sadistic entertainments have often portrayed a demented glee in killing. Occasionally thrill killing is featured even in prime time as the media continues to feed what it assumes to be the public's insatiable appetite for violence. But reality also bites. Both individuals and groups have committed lethal atrocities in situations where they were neither threatened nor stood to gain any practical advantage. In fact, some of the most savage and merciless slaughters have been carried out by perpetrators whose belief system and usual code of conduct reflected generally accepted moral principles.

This chapter opened with a description excerpted from the report of one of many episodes of "wild and madly excited" killing that occurred in "bleeding Kansas" prior to the Civil War. The issue of slavery vs. abolition had divided the population and would soon divide the nation. In this climate of tension and conflict it would not have been surprising if there had been occasional episodes of violence. What actually happened, though, went far beyond taking sides and perhaps taking up arms. Some people became enthusiastic killers. They could not kill their neighbors dead enough. Individual passions were intensified and shared moral principles dissolved by the mob mentality. Solid and reasonable people seemed to be enjoying killing more than they had ever enjoyed anything else.

History offers all too many examples in which aggregates of undisciplined people have found keen enjoyment in killing. Lethal atrocities in the United States have included murders in which racism played a dominant role. In fact, one cannot restrict these killings to the past tense, as exemplified by the recent savage and senseless murder of a black man who was dragged behind a car. The evident enjoyment felt by the killers in such episodes tells us that they were killing for pleasure rather than for achieving even a distorted purpose. Other tensions and conflicts have also boiled over into violence whose overreactive and merciless character reveals that thrill killing was the motivating force, rather than the particular problem at issue. Worker–management issues were at times "negotiated" with lethal beatings and bombings. The United States has had at least its share of episodes in which a savage joy in doing death's work has taken over problem situations for which a more rational and measured approach could have been successful.

Perhaps more graphic examples should be presented here to illustrate the merciless and needless violence that people have inflicted on each other in many lands at many points in history. We might, for example, rediscover the horrors inflicted by an invading Japanese army on the people of Nanking in 1937 as detailed by Iris Chang (1997). To view just one photograph would be enough to verify the— one would like to say "inhuman"—violence that some people have enjoyed inflicting on others. One might instead take equally disturbing examples from the actions of the Crusaders whose high purposes did not deter them from slaughtering children, women, and the aged. We might turn in so many directions and collect so many examples of killing as a delirious blood sport that our minds finally escape into numbness. And the Holocaust, in which more than six million people were killed during the Nazi reign, has not even been mentioned up to this point.

Perhaps the reader will excuse me if I do not present a large gallery of atrocities in which the killer's passionate enjoyment played a significant role, whether as a participant in group action or a sole perpetrator. The case makes itself.

What must be added, though, is the disturbing fact that many of those people who have committed lethal atrocities were pretty much "everyday people" both before and after the episodes. There is no shortage of individuals with violent tendencies. Most of the larger massacres and pogroms, however, have been carried out by people who otherwise lived rather conventional and well-ordered lives. Researchers into 20th-century savagery, for example, have often found that the sadistic torturers and merciless killers had resumed their quiet and socially acceptable lives.

Death-instinct theory does not really explain these phenomena. However, it does give us a place to start. The aging Freud judged that the human race had a propensity for violent aggression that threatened not only the occasional outbreak, but the survival of civilization. Take one person's potential for expression of the death instinct. Multiply this potential by the madness of groups that have a slogan to kill by. Provide a situation in which one no longer has to negotiate between loving and destructive impulses and no longer persist with inhibitions. The result could well be the explosion of something like a death instinct.

This view does not assume that we all have a raging death instinct that is being held precariously in check. It is just an invitation to examine those situations in which the deeper layers of our emotional life become both aroused and oversimplified within a social context in which traditional moral guidelines have temporarily lost their sway.

It is also an invitation to think again about the powerful destructive potential that is generated when aggression is fused (as Freud would say) with sexual impulses. Orgiastic killing becomes a possibility.

"Know thyself" was the Delphic Oracle's famous advice to Socrates. Knowing that each of us has the potential for both sexual and aggressive, both creative and destructive actions might be the best approach to deterring us from doing death's work in forms more brutal than usually employed by death himself.

Killing to Stay Alive

Here is a brief and highly speculative possibility to add to our consideration of the afterlife of the death instinct. Psychiatrist Dorothy Otnow Lewis (1998) has been called on to assess the mental state of many killers, including some of the most notorious. Among her observations she notes the high prevalence of paranoid thinking, whether or not the killer is psychotic. Lewis notes that paranoid thinking emerges within a variety of personality structures and disorders, presumably as a kind of stress product. Most relevant here are two of her observations: (a) "Paranoia must have strong survival value" and (b) many killers have some form of brain abnormality.

Paranoia might—just might—be a fundamental response of the organism to what is perceived as a persistent threat to its survival. This response is more likely to be triggered easily in some people than others, but we might all have this potential. Lewis touches on a possible neural basis for the paranoid response:

> We know that our basic aggressive and sexual instincts, and our pleasurable feelings, spring from what we currently call the limbic system—those deep, primitive brain structures . . . that have widespread connections to the rest of the brain. We know that our sense of fear is localized predominately in the amygdala, a nucleous of cells hidden within each temporal lobe. We know that destruction of these nuclei eradicates fear, whereas stimulation . . . can induce it. We cannot do without the amygdala. But fear is often the basis for paranoia. A certain amount of fear is necessary for survival. On the other hand, too much can make us dangerous. (1998, p. 288)

Lewis reminds us that "the primitive urges springing from the limbic system are modulated or controlled by our frontal lobes" (1998, p. 288). Injuries to the frontal lobe impair our ability to control ourselves.

Implications? Some large proportion of individual killers may be functioning with impaired self-control abilities related to brain damage. A persistent state of fear might accompany the realization that one cannot cope with the challenges and stresses of life. A high level of chronic fear, perhaps escalating over time, triggers paranoia. Reality often provides us with an abundance of messages and interactions that could be interpreted as confirming the paranoiac view. Paranoia, then, could be a line of defense in which a neurally impaired and frightened person may kill to avoid being killed. Undifferentiated and undirected sexual and aggressive impulses would further intensify the paranoid response.

Freud's story about biologically based sexual and aggressive drives does not seem quite as wild in the light of current neuroloscience, nor does his urging that we learn as individuals and as a society to integrate and control these impulses through our ego (frontal lobe?) strength. Nothing here proves the validity of the death-instinct theory, but it seems to be enjoying a surprisingly active, if mostly invisible, afterlife.

REFERENCES

Adler, A. (1956). *The individual psychology of Alfred Adler: A systematic presentation in selections from his writings.* New York: Harper & Row.

Allport, G. W. (1955). *Becoming: Basic considerations for a psychology of personality.* New Haven, CT: Yale University Press.

Becker, E. (1973). *The denial of death.* New York: Free Press.

Bettelheim, B. (1983). *Freud and man's soul.* New York: Knopf.

Brown, N. O. (1959). *Life against death.* New York: Viking Press.

Chang, I. (1997). *The rape of Nanking.* New York: Basic Books.

Choron, J. (1972). *Suicide.* New York: Charles Scribner's Sons.

Crews, F. C. (Ed.). (1998). *Unauthorized Freud.* New York: Viking.

Dewey, J. (1920). *Reconstruction in philosophy.* New York: Holt.

Durkheim, E. (1951). *Suicide.* New York: Free Press. (Original work published 1897)

Einstein, A., & Freud, S. (1932). *Why war?* Chicago: Chicago Institute for Pschoanalysis.

Eisenberg, E. (1998). *The ecology of Eden.* New York: Alfred A. Knopf.

Farberow, N. (Ed.). (1980). *The many faces of suicide.* New York: McGraw-Hill.

Freud, A. (1949). Aggression in relation to emotional development: Normal and pathological. *Psychoanalytic Study of the Child, 34,* 37–42.

Freud, S. (1938). *The interpretation of dreams.* New York: Random House. (Original work published 1900)

Freud, S. (1938). *Wit and its relation to the unconscious.* New York: Random House. (Original work published 1905)

Freud, S. (1959). *Inhibitions, symptoms and anxiety.* New York: Norton. (Original work published 1925)

Freud, S. (1960). *Beyond the pleasure principle.* New York: Norton. (Original work published 1920)

Freud, S. (1961). *New introductory lessons on psychoanalysis.* New York: Norton. (Original work published 1933)

Galdston, I. (1955). Eros and Thanatos: A critique and elaboration of Freud's death wish. *American Journal of Psychoanalysis, 15,* 124–134.

Gay, P. (1993). *The cultivation of hatred.* New York: W. W. Norton.

Gernsbacher, L. M. (1985). *The suicide syndrome.* New York: Human Sciences Press.

Goodrich, T. (1998). *War to the knife.* Mechanicsburg, PA: Stackpole Books.

Grossman, D. (1995). *On killing. The psychological cost of learning to kill in war and society.* Boston: Little, Brown.

Heckler, R. A. (1994). *Waking up, alive.* New York: Ballantine.

Horn, L. R. (1989). *A natural history of negation.* Chicago: University of Chicago Press.

Husserl, E. (1973). *Cartesian meditations.* The Hague: Martinus Nijhoff.

James, W. (1896). *The principles of psychology* (Vol. 1). New York: Holt.

Jellife, S. E. (1933). The death instinct in somatic and psychopathology. *Psychoanalytic Review, 20,* 121–132.

Kosky, R. J., Eshkevari, H. S., Goldney, R. D., & Hassan, R. (Eds.). (1997). *Suicide prevention: The global context.* New York: Plenum Press.

Levin, A. J. (1951). The fiction of the death instinct. *Psychiatric Quarterly, 25,* 257–281.

Lewis, D. O. (1998). *Guilty by reason of insanity.* New York: Ballantine.

Maslow, A. H. (1968). *Toward a psychology of being* (2nd ed.). New York: Van Nostrand Reinhold.

Menninger, K. (1938). *Man against himself.* New York: Harcourt, Brace.

Nader, K. O. (1996). Children's exposure to traumatic experiences. In C. A. Corr & D. M. Corr (Eds.), *Handbook of child death and bereavement* (pp. 201–220). New York: Springer Publishing Company.

Nietzsche, F. (1927). *Thus spake Zarathustra.* New York: Modern Library. (Original work 1885)

Prigogine, I. (1996). *The end of certainty.* New York: Free Press.

Range, L. M. (1996). Suicide and life-threatening behavior in childhood. In C. A. Corr & D. M. Corr (Eds.), *Handbook of child death and bereavement* (pp. 71–88). New York: Springer Publishing Company.

Schopenhauer, A. (1957). *The world as will and idea* (Vol. 3). London: Routledge & Kegan Paul. (Original work published in German in 1883)

Sheets-Johnstone, M. (1990). *The roots of thinking.* Philadelphia: Temple University Press.

Shneidman, E. S. (1985). *Definition of suicide.* New York: Wiley Interscience.

Sperling, M. (1969). Migraine headaches, altered states of consciousness and accident proneness: A clinical contribution to the death instinct theory. *Psychoanalytic Forum, 3,* 69–100.

Symons, J. (1927). Does masochism imply the existence of a death instinct? *International Journal of Psychoanalysis, 8,* 38–46.

Wass, H. (1995). Appetite for destruction: Children and violent death in popular culture. In D. W. Adams & E. J. Deveau (Eds.), *Beyond the innocence of childhood* (Vol. 1, pp. 95–108). New York: Baywood.

6

Dying: Toward A Psychological Perspective

She said she wanted him to hold her, and share this time with her. They had always shared their lives, and now she felt alone. . . . She started to cry. . . . She wanted to share the time remaining with him. Time was so short. They were losing what was left. She couldn't get those days back.

—Sharon Thuell

How far can an intellectual effort diminish pain? I think my experience this night (and on several similar occasions) qualify me to write: *Yes, decidedly!* It can throw fairly severe pain into the background and keep it there pretty steadily for an hour or two. . . . It is rather cheering. It pulls one together, and seems to indicate that what I called the collapse of Will-Power or the structure of personality is not finally destructive.

—William McDougall

How do we think, feel, act, and interact as we die? And as we live with companions who are dying? This is the first of two chapters that explore these questions from a psychological perspective. Here we look at the flow of experience, behavior, and interaction during the course of a final illness. The following chapter focuses on the deathbed scene.

We begin by acquainting ourselves with the terms that are most often used to describe the course of experience and behavior as the end of life approaches. Next, we briefly consider the types of perspective that might serve as guides to understanding and helping. This is followed by a concise review of psychologically oriented theories about dying. A new approach is then offered in the form of multiple partial models, each focusing on a specific facet of the dying person's situation. We conclude with a consideration of the dying person's own model of life and death. Particular attention is given to the journal written by a famous psychologist during the last months of his life.

A CHOICE OF TERMS

The available terms are not always precise, appropriate, and unbiased. *Dying* is by far the most familiar of these terms, rich with associations and direct in its message. Perhaps the meaning is all too clear because this term had barely crossed the threshold of public and professional acceptance before it was again banished. Dying, like death, is too plain-spoken a word for some tastes. *Terminal illness* has triumphed as the politically correct term since the medical establishment became a significant factor in the death awareness movement. With this phrase we are able to shift the emphasis from the dying person to the illness. This term not only attenuates the emotional impact, but also supports continued medicalization of the dying process, along with all the decision making and power relationships implied.

Four other terms have come into frequent use: *life-threatening condition, end-phase, end-of-life issues*, and *critical care.* Here we will speak of *dying* when we are concerned with the total person within his or her total life situation. We will speak of *terminal illness* when attention is focused on symptoms, prognosis, and management. It will be useful to speak of a *life-threatening condition* when there is a possibility of recovery or remission. There is often much similarity in the experience of an illness that will prove to be fatal and one that will be survived. People may live for years with serious medical conditions, so it would be inappropriate to describe them as dying. It will also be useful to speak of the *end-phase* of life because the failure of multiple body systems often leads to intensified symptoms and markedly diminished functional capacity. *End-of-life issues* refer to concerns and decisions in many spheres of life, ranging from instructions for medical and nursing care to funerary and financial arrangements. *Critical care* has gained a foothold as a specialty in nursing and medicine, supported by a growing body of research and the development of training programs. This term is welcome for its official recognition that dying or life-threatened people deserve and require special attention, but it also can contribute to the continued isolation of death and dying within the overall health care system. Even with all these terms and distinctions, we may find that no generally accepted term quite describes the diverse, complex, and shifting realities encountered as life edges toward death.

A CHOICE OF PERSPECTIVES

Psychologists have long been aware that we bring something of our own experiences, hopes, and fears to the situations we encounter, even when we assume we are being purely "objective." Psychologists have also urged that we become keenly aware of our own mindsets and emotional triggers to reduce the possibility of hasty misperceptions and actions. Accordingly, we will reflect a moment on personal and role-specific perspectives.

The Personal Perspective

Many of us have personal perspectives on dying and death. We may have seen a family member or friend move from health to illness and from illness to death. We may have had medical problems of our own that provided a hint of what it might feel like to become progressively debilitated. Some of us know that we are living with a suspended death sentence, a vulnerability that could lead to a fatal outcome at some unknown time in the future. Furthermore, most of us have been exposed to images of dying from the popular media, including a mixture of sentimental and melodramatic farewell scenes.

Our personal perspectives have been influenced by childhood experiences. Did the grown-ups take our concerns seriously, or did they try to evade and distract us when death was in the air? Did adult behavior teach us that dying people remain in the bosom of the family, or that it is so horrible and mysterious that we should not even speak of them? Few of us know just how much and just in what ways we are influenced by images and feelings we acquired in childhood. Occasionally we may have a memory flash in which we suddenly grasp the connection between our present day attitudes and events that occurred in childhood, and as interpreted by a child's mind. At other times we may experience a surge of panic, revulsion, or anger whose links with early exposures to dying and death are not immediately apparent to us.

It would be going too far, though, to assume that everybody has a personal perspective on dying. Being exposed to something does not necessarily mean that we have integrated this experience into our view of self and world. People differ in their inclination and ability to see connections. We may tend to act situationally, or we may mediate response to immediate circumstances by scanning both past experiences and future expectations for guidelines. This difference in style of approaching the world can be consequential. One person, for example, turns away from a dying friend and literally bolts out of the room because the scene is disturbing to her senses. Another person is also upset by the sights, sounds, and smells of the sick room, but this reaction is more than balanced by everything that has bound her in friendship. The first woman is experiencing a reaction to the immediate situation; the second woman has a perspective in which she can integrate the shock and distress of this encounter. Differences in perspective also vary as people face the prospect of their own death. Some people bring to this challenge a strong and enduring perspective that has always included the mortality factor. Others are still seeking for meaning and purpose as they face terminal illness. Personal perspective on dying is a variable, then, not a constant or a universal.

Role-Specific Perspectives

There are also perspectives on dying that are influenced by education, role, and responsibility. Clergy may be called upon both as representatives of the sacred and as counselors for troubled minds. The clergyperson's personal perspective on dying is expected to function within the established framework of theology and custom. Dying usually is to be conceived as a transition from one form of existence to another.

Some clergy have added the perspective of a trained counselor, and some the breadth of faith to minister to people of more than one denomination. Challenges facing clergy today include moral issues associated with euthanasia and their stance toward people dying without religious belief.

By contrast, nurses and physicians are not given an overarching worldview as part of their professional education. It us up to each nurse and physician to bring a personal perspective to the stressful situations they encounter. This personal perspective, however, may coexist uneasily with the time-pressured functionalistic approach that is characteristic of health service delivery today. Nurses are particularly vulnerable to stress in the care of dying people because they are expected to carry out physician orders and obey regulations even when their perceptions and feelings would prompt them to do things differently. Frustration with the discrepancy between their own caring impulses and the restrictions of the system prepared many nurses to welcome the hospice approach when it crossed the Atlantic from Great Britain. Physicians struggle with the still-powerful code that patient death equals physician failure, and sometimes with the impulse to minimize contact with dying people and their families. Despite significant differences, clergy, nurses, and physicians are likely to have both their personal and professional perspectives put to the test as they try to fulfill their responsibilities to terminally ill people.

Anthropologists and sociologists seldom have bedside responsibilities to test their perspectives or caregiving skills. Both are likely to construe dying primarily from the standpoint of the community. Dying is a form of status passage. The dying process can generate instability and conflict (as when contenders vie for the position that is being vacated or the goods that will be distributed). Cultural values are either affirmed or weakened by the way people die and how we treat them during their final passage and the subsequent memorial rites. How we die and how we behave toward the dying, then, is an index of a society's own health status. Anthropologists and sociologists often notice things about the dying process that escape the attention of those who are engaged in providing direct services, and the reverse is also true.

Psychology has pretty much avoided death in both its theory-spinning exercises and research programs ever since breaking away from its parental tradition of philosophical speculation. The particulars of psychology's studied resistance to studying dying and death have already been discussed (chapter 1). There are still many chambers in the house of psychology in which one can function productively without giving dying and death a tumble. Clinical and counseling psychologists, however, often are called upon to serve people whose lives are in the grip of death, whether through suicidality, grief, or concern about their own survival. The psychologist may experience the stress of a family's response to the terminal illness of their child, a youth's life-threatening sexually transmitted disease, or an elder's long struggle with failing health. The counseling and therapeutic techniques they have learned may prove useful, but fall short of providing a comprehensive perspective. Does psychology tell us enough about life to tell us enough about dying and death?

In what follows I make several guiding assumptions based upon my own clinical and research experiences and what I have learned from the work of others:

- It is useful to develop a high level of competency in at least one of the fields of knowledge and skill that can be called upon to help dying people. By contrast, it is risky merely to skim the surface of one or more fields and then apply superficial ideas and fragmented facts to real life situations.

- It is useful to learn enough about at least one other contributing field in order to free ourselves from overdependence on the only knowledge base and perspective that happens to be at our disposal. A psychologist who can also see a family's coping efforts with their terminally ill member from the view of a nurse or social worker, for example, is in a position to be more helpful.

- We do have to know something about the physical side of the dying process, whether or not that subject is congenial to us. What is likely to happen next in this condition? What actual choices does the physician have in providing pain relief, and what are the possible difficulties with each of these options? How are this person's mood and activities being affected both by the deteriorating physical condition and by medications and overall management? At the very least, a basic knowledge of terminal illness at ground level will enable the psychologist to communicate more effectively with other careproviders as well as patient and family.

- The temptation to devise special theories specific to dying should be resisted until we have thoroughly explored the possibility of understanding the last phase of life within a broader perspective that offers a rich and encompassing view of human thought, experience, action, and interaction across many situations.

• In selecting or developing a psychological perspective we should be open to illuminating observations from other fields of inquiry as well, and we should have a decent concern for the ways in which our particular view may be challenged by others.

• Living and dying are not that simple—so perhaps our theories should not be that simple either.

So much for my little list of "shoulds" that you can accept or reject as you see fit. Now we turn to the admittedly limited array of available psychologically oriented perspectives on dying.

A CHOICE OF THEORIES

We begin with the two models of the dying process that have had the most influence among those who are highly engaged in educational, research, and clinical activities related to the dying person. These models differ markedly in extent and nature of influence, and as well as in method, data base, and focus. They also share a basic commonality, however, as we will see.

Awareness and Interaction

Sociologist David Sudnow (1967) jolted many slumbering minds with the observations reported in *Passing On: The Social Organization of Dying*. Focusing on emergency-room interactions he found that the attention received by people in life-or-death situations was significantly influenced by hospital staff's perception of their age, presentability, and social status. Today we are no longer surprised when studies continue to confirm that medical response to the dying person is influenced by other than medical factors (Schulman et al., 1999). With Sudnow's unsettling contribution, if not before, we realized that patterns of discrimination throughout life tend to follow people to the grave—and beyond (Kastenbaum, Kastenbaum, & Peyton, 1978).

The psychology of prejudice and social influence immediately became a prime approach to bring to bear on interactions during the dying process—in point of fact, however, little use has actually been made of this approach.

Sandwiched around Sudnow's book were two other substantial contributions that were also drawn from hospital-based observations. In *Awareness of Dying* (1966) and *Time for Dying* (1968) Barney G. Glaser and Anselm L. Strauss reported the patterns of interaction they noted in six San Francisco area hospitals. Glaser and Strauss would soon become prominent throughout the total spectrum of social and behavioral science research with their advocacy for the *grounded-theory* approach. Their development of useful descriptive models grounded by direct observations is well exemplified by their analysis of hospital-based interactions involving dying people and their caregivers.

The set of awareness-and-interaction types identified by Glaser and Strauss in their first book has become an enduring part of our knowledge base. Each type of awareness and interaction involves a dying person and a family member or professional careprovider. The patients may be aware or unaware of their fatal prognosis and interested or reluctant in communicating about it. The other interactants similarly may be aware or unaware of their fatal prognosis and interested or reluctant in communicating about it. Four basic types emerge from the possible combinations of awareness and communication patterns:

1. *Closed awareness.* The dying person does not realize that he or she is dying and the careprovider or other interaction partner is not going to tell them. This is a keeping-the-secret context of communication (or, rather, noncommunication). It is of great psychological interest because of the tension involved in trying to interact positively with a dying person while at the same time avoiding a disclosure that one fears would be devastating.

2. *Suspected awareness.* The patient surmises that he or she is not being told the truth, all the truth, and nothing but the truth. There is an effort to check out one's growing belief that the progress of the disease cannot be reversed or halted. The other interactant may or may not suspect that the patient is suspecting, but in any case is resolved not to let the truth slip out.

3. *Open awareness.* Both the patient and others are willing and able to share their knowledge and concerns. This does not necessarily

mean that they have extensive discussions of dying and death. Rather, it means that everybody involved feels free to bring up the subject whenever it seems necessary or useful to do so. The open awareness context is almost invariably accompanied by less tension and conflict than either of the first two that have been noted.

4. *Mutual pretense.* This is perhaps the most subtle and certainly the most often discussed type of interaction context. The patient knows he or she is dying. The visitor knows the patient is dying. Both pretend that they don't know. Furthermore, both may be aware that the other person is pretending, too. The mutual pretense act is difficult to sustain; one or the other person may be caught off guard or under pressure and let the horrifying truth escape.

Interjecting a psychological perspective here, often we can see that family members, friends, and health careproviders are attributing some of their own anxiety to the patient. "*I* would not know what to do. *I* would feel terribly upset if she knew that I knew. . . . " Many terminally ill people, conditioned by their experiences with the illness and supported by their own maturity, are more prepared than their interactants to face the facts. Moreover, the situation can be complicated by uncertainties and changes in the patient's condition. What we knew of a life-threatened person's condition last week may not hold true today. What looked to be a strong sign of improvement or deterioration may look differently to another person at another time. The underlying reality is often sufficiently unclear, uncertain, and unstable, suggesting that nobody's version of the truth is beyond question (Kastenbaum, 1998).

In their follow-up book Glaser and Strauss focused on the time line between illness and death: actually, the time*lines*. Some pathways to death take a quick trajectory, others are lingering. Their observations regarding *Time for Dying* (1968) are still very much worth readers' attention. Most germane here is the emphasis given to type and phase of physical illness and the frequency and kind of interactions that are likely to occur. Psychiatrist E. M. Pattison (1977) later offered a complementary descriptive model that also emphasizes the relationship between the phase of the illness and the individual's awareness and concerns. These and other observers have effectively drawn our attention to the need to consider both physical condition and interaction context even if our primary interest is in the dying person's thoughts, feelings, and values.

Stages of Dying

Two types of stage theory had been available long before the modern death awareness movement made itself known. Medical people recognized that many illnesses passed through several phases, some reaching a point of no return. Stages also figured in cultural and spiritual views of the life course. Life could be seen as a journey with a number of normative way stations (e.g., the child, the lover, the parent . . .) until the soul was ready to depart from the body (Cole, 1992). The dying process itself was dissected into no less than eight stages in the Buddhist tradition (Gyatso, 1985). By far the most familiar stage model of dying today, though, is the version offered by Elisabeth Kübler-Ross (1969) in a book that brought the plight of dying people to the attention of the general public as well as health care professionals. She offered observations and comments based on her interviews with hospitalized men and women who were considered to have life-threatening or terminal conditions (it is not clear how many were actually dying). For many readers this was the first opportunity to learn something of the world as experienced by dying people. Also, for many readers, the organization of these experiences into a sequence provided a coherent and convenient guide. It was a relief to learn that people don't just come apart as they encounter the rigors of terminal illness—there is a pattern, a plan.

The five stages are almost too familiar to repeat here, but perhaps we can all do with a reminder. At the outset we note that these stages are regarded as normal responses, not as neurotic or psychotic symptoms. People move from one stage to the next, but may slip back and forth a little along the way. Not everybody makes it through the entire sequence (a similarity with the otherwise very different Buddhist conception). Kübler-Ross (1969) enhances her basic stage model by observing that hope can thread its way throughout the sequence. It is not fixed or guaranteed at any one particular stage.

Stage 1: Denial. The sequence begins with exposure to the fact that one has a fatal illness. This news is stunning. One feels paralyzed, numb, suspended. The initial shock reaction is quickly followed by a longer (though variable) period of denial. It can't be true! I can't be dying! Repeating the bad news or coming across further evidence still does not get through. The dying person is "in denial."

Stage 2: Anger.   For most people, the denial does not last forever. The shock and numbing wears off, and one's reality sense demands that facts be faced. Resentment and rage now becomes the prevailing mood. "It's not fair!" is a characteristic response at this stage. The anger is often diffuse and can shift from one target to another. The patient may snap at loved ones, health care personnel, and other innocent parties, or even revile God. Not surprisingly, the dying person in this stage can be a difficult and puzzling individual who may inadvertently drive away the people he or she needs most.

Stage 3: Bargaining.   Anger does not last forever, either, as a general rule. The dying person now becomes more strategic, willing to make a deal with fate. The proposed deal might be for God to allow them to live until a certain event (e.g., a child's graduation) has occurred or milestone (e.g., anniversary) reached. In this stage the person has rekindled a measure of hope and self-efficacy: perhaps there is something I can do about this!

Stage 4: Depression.   The rally fades, however. One's physical condition continues to worsen. Weaker, more fatigued, and less able to function, one becomes vulnerable to depression. Now the psychological picture becomes darker and more complicated. There may be shame and guilt, a sense of unworthiness. Fear of death becomes more openly experienced and expressed. This is a very bad time indeed; perhaps the worst of times.

Stage 5: Acceptance.   The struggle is over. There is nothing more to be done. One can only wait for the inevitable. Although the term "acceptance" may suggest a profound philosophical orientation, it more often refers instead to a sense of depletion. Kübler-Ross noted that patients in this stage seem to be resting a little after all their previous efforts, and readying themselves for the ending as best they can.

What is most useful in this model, most worth incorporating into an informed psychological perspective on dying? The following facets seem most well founded and useful:

• People attempt to cope with the rigors of a life threatening or terminal illness in a variety of ways. The same person is likely to use several different responses over time. Family, friends, and professional careproviders therefore should not assume that the same response will persist throughout the dying process but, rather, should be sensitive to changes.

• The responses are triggered by a communicational interaction: somebody has delivered the message that nobody wants to receive. We should therefore be aware of the powerful effect both of the telling and of the hearing. An obvious implication is that the communication should take place within a context of mutual trust and respect that is structured to be most appropriate for a particular patient and family. One would avoid the dysfunctional technique used by some physicians—giving the bad news at their convenience, and then pretty much disappearing to avoid further clarifications and discussion. The increasing frequency of sit-down conferences with patient, family, and the health care team probably owes something to Kübler-Ross' emphasis on the impact of breaking the bad news. Although others have also made this point, the fact that it is salient in stage theory may well have contributed to improved communication processes.

• The responses of dying people to their difficult situation may themselves be difficult from the standpoint of others, such as, anger and depression. By recognizing the source of these moods and communications we can avoid overreacting to them or even punishing the dying person with our own anger or withdrawal.

• It is also useful to be aware that hope may persist or become renewed even when the dying person seems to be in the grip of negative emotions. Here Kübler-Ross's observations are consistent with what many others have noted as they observed and reflected on the human capacity to preserve hope under a variety of oppressive circumstances. Maurice Farber's (1968) theory of suicide emphasizes the saving grace of hope and the self-destructive consequences when hope is lost.

• The psychological reaction to dying and death is affected by changes in physical condition. This point is not developed or well detailed in her presentation of stage theory, but it is clear enough that the exhausting struggle and the continuing loss of function contribute to the shift from anger and bargaining to depression and a final phase that is characterized as acceptance or depletion.

These, I think, are the major contributions of the Kübler-Ross stage theory. Problems and limitations will be touched on below. Above and beyond the theory *per se*, Kübler-Ross did much to encourage urgently needed attention to the quality of life for dying persons and their families.

Two Theoretical Perspectives Awaiting Further Development

Many other types of theoretical approach are possible and may be heard from eventually. Here we touch on two perspectives that have been introduced to the dialogue on dying but which have not yet been developed to their full potential.

Coping with Dying As a Life-Span Developmental Task

Life can be regarded as a succession of problems to solve or tasks to complete. These challenges start in early childhood and continue through the adolescent and adult years. When we pass the test at one checkpoint we are able to move on to the next challenge with energy, confidence, and wholeness. If we fail to solve the core problem at one checkpoint, we will be flawed and unprepared for the next challenge. This is pretty much the perspective that is shared by life-span developmental theories. Eric H. Erikson's (1959) epigenetic theory is the most influential of such theories, being widely taught in social science and education courses. Several other life-span theories were already in circulation, but most of these gave only limited attention to the later adult years. Erikson's approach earned its special status not only by encompassing the challenges of the later adult years but also by taking cultural factors more thoroughly into account. Robert N. Butler's (1963) concept of the life review supplemented Erikson with its emphasis on the challenge of self-evaluation as one approaches advanced age and death. In recent years there has been a general movement toward coping or task theories that encompass the entire life span and cross the invisible line, if cautiously, to the dying process.

Charles A. Corr and Kenneth J. Doka have recently offered perspectives on dying that draw on mainstream life-span developmental task theory. Corr (1992) suggests that dying people must cope with four types of challenge: the physical (satisfying body needs and reducing distress); the psychological (feeling secure, in control, and still having a life to live); the social (keeping valued attachments to other individuals and to groups and causes); and the spiritual (finding or affirming meaning, having a sense of connectedness, transcendence, and hope). Doka (1993) describes "phase-specific" tasks that are encountered from the prediagnostic situation to recovery (if the life-threatening illness is brought under control).

The Corr/Doka perspective offers several potentially valuable guidelines:

• The dying process does not have to be—and in fact, should not be—walled off as a special domain. It is more useful to consider dying within the compass of the total life span and as a normative event rather than a deviant or pathological episode.

• Dying people may still have things to accomplish. One does not cease coping and striving; indeed, one calls upon all available resources to accomplish the final set of tasks.

• The life-span developmental task approach encourages attention to a very broad range of problems and thereby reduces the temptation to view the dying process within a narrowed and possibly oversimplified perspective. In particular, this wide spectrum approach may help to protect the holistic situation of dying people and their families from excessive medicalization.

• The idea of having to achieve something when we are aging and, again, when we are dying seems to resonate well with the product and goal-directed character of our society. We have become accustomed to taking tests, demonstrating productivity, and meeting challenges in order to receive both the approbation of society and our own approval. People who have become achievement and success oriented throughout their lives may find it logical and meaningful to apply this approach to the very end.

Meaning in Life and Death: The Existential Perspective

Existentialism offers a challenge to mental health approaches that emphasize achievement and adjustment. An apparently "successful" life may be shallow, conformist, and lacking both depth and purpose. The anguish experienced by Tolstoy's dying Ivan Ilych (1886/1960) surged from his belated recognition that he had not really lived, but had only played the role of a semi-important person who did what he thought others expected of him. Most existentialists would hold that the way in which we die has much to do with the way in which we have lived. A life of evasion and compromise increases the difficulty of ending as a whole person. Despair or terror come not so much from the prospect of death as from the failure to have lived an authentic and fulfilling life.

Friedrich Nietzsche (1954) and Soren Kierkegaard (1940) are among the powerfully unsettling thinkers who offered existential perspectives before that label had itself been introduced. Neither emphasized the dying process, but both criticized superficial styles of living that contributed to a despairing end. Jean Paul Sartre (1956) brought *Being and Nothingness* into focus in a book that is often considered the foundation of modern existential thought. Again, though, the focus was not on the dying process per se. Sartre took suicide to be the core issue: why should one *not* end a meaningless existence?

Existential thought came to the fore after World War II, emerging from the widespread devastation in Europe. Variously grief-stricken, numbed, or enraged, many survivors were also shaken by the meaningless of violent, senseless deaths. The questions became: what does a human life mean if death is so meaningless? Are there really any rules to live by, any guiding lights, any authentic value in civilization? People answered these questions in various ways, covering the spectrum from renewed religious faith to atheism and alienation. Indeed, existentialism became a death-haunted psychological philosophy defined more by its questions than its answers.

Perhaps the two most influential existential contributors to a psychology of death were Ernest Becker (1973) whose thoughts were discussed in chapter 5, and philosopher Walter Kaufmann (1959; 1976). Both remain valuable sources for psychologically relevant existential philosophy, though neither offer a detailed perspective on the dying process as such. Nevertheless, the broad outlines of an existential perspective on dying can be discerned:

- The issues of meaning and purpose are at the core of both living and dying. Palliation of physical symptoms is certainly a high priority, but psychological or spiritual suffering may be intense when dying persons feel that neither their lives nor their deaths have any substantial meaning.
- Similarly, it may be important to accomplish certain end-of-life tasks, but the key is not so much the tasks themselves as their meaning, their value to the individual. We should not become

so preoccupied with the many details of the dying process that we overlook their significance to the person. For example, a ritual that seems inconvenient or unimportant to one may bring a sense of affirmation and comfort to another.

- Open and honest communication is essential, but this is not likely to develop unless family, friends, and professional careproviders have come to terms with their own existential issues. We cannot really be open with the dying person—in fact, we cannot really be *with* the dying person until we have dissolved the denial trance that is so prevalent in everyday life.
- Our relationship with mortality does not begin when we learn that we have a fatal illness. Throughout our lives we have entered into some kind of relationship with the prospect of nonbeing, whether by evasion, denial, dissociation, fantasy, or even an identification with death. Our spiritual biography is therefore intrinsic to the way we come to final terms with death.

WHAT SHOULD WE TAKE FROM THE AVAILABLE THEORIES?

We pause now for a brief review and evaluation of the theoretical perspectives that are most salient at this time.

Method, Data Base, Verifiability

The awareness and interaction perspective introduced by Glaser and Strauss is the only theory grounded on systematic observations of terminally ill people within the hospital situation. Little statistical information is presented in the reports from these ethnographic studies, but the researchers seem to have sampled many patient-staff interactions in several hospital settings. Their descriptions of interaction types are clear enough to be subjected to verification by other observers. Competent researchers can discover for themselves what types of interaction occur within a particular setting, and how these types are related to the trajectory of the patient's illness as well as to other factors. Glaser and Strauss do not make claims or generalizations that go beyond what others might observe for themselves. Their model would be more useful if extended to larger units of the total health care environment within which the various type of interaction occur (e.g., the ward, the service, the overall hospital system).

The stage theory is based on interviews as conducted and interpreted by one person. Again, the report does not provide statistical information (e.g., the number of people with what types of condition at what medical phase, etc), but seems to be drawn from a fairly large number of patient contacts. There are methodological and interpretive problems that stand in the way of accepting the stage model as an accurate depiction of the dying process. These problems include:

• The existence of the five-stage sequence has not been demonstrated, either by Kübler-Ross or by independent research. In her original report there is no evidence that the same person did in fact pass through the stages. There is no doubt that some dying people do behave just as described by Kübler-Ross, but that these responses comprise a universal sequence is a much different assertion and this has not been supported by subsequent observations.

• The theory *attributes* various states of mind to patients that were not supported by evidence other than their mostly verbal responses in interview situations controlled by the psychiatrist.

• The stage interpretation neglected the patients' total life situation, including, for example, relationship support and conflicts, family obligations, specific effects of their illness, and the management and communicational milieu to which they were exposed (e.g., an anxious and denying institutional climate). A patient "in denial" might be responding to a denying milieu; a patient in the "stage of anger" might be upset because she has not received adequate care or been kept well informed about her condition.

• The line between description and prescription is blurred. Are the stages to be considered as natural and therefore value-neutral occurrences, or *should* people be moved along efficiently in order to reach the final stage?

• The stages generally were assumed to be self-evident—not only did they not require verification, but there was no clear way to put them to the test. We should see these stages, and so we do.

The stage theory of dying provided guidelines at a time when people were just learning to talk about death and work up the nerve to be with dying patients. By and large, it was the failure of the research community to examine and test the theory that contributed to its uncritical acceptance. *On Death and Dying* (Kübler-Ross, 1969) is a classic contribution, but can be appreciated without placing heavy reliance on the five-stage model.

Life-span developmental task theory was discussed in some detail in chapters 1 and 2 as well as here. Many developmental psychologists now find it useful to consider the entire course of human life from birth through the later adult years as their frame of reference. The data base has grown substantially over the past three decades through the application of both quantitative and qualitative research methods. Not much has been done, however, to test the proposition that human life should be regarded as a more or less fixed succession of tasks. One can have a thriving and well-informed life-span developmental perspective without insisting on the concept of stage-related tasks. Even the most respected life-span stage theory (Erikson's) has not been well confirmed by empirical research. The data thin out even more when we focus on dying as a series of tasks. We can choose to *interpret* various observations in terms of tasks, but no studies have been directed to testing either the validity or the usefulness of this theory. At this point the developmental task theory of dying is in some danger of joining other models that have never been put seriously to the test of careful empirical research.

The core assumptions of an existential approach are difficult to test through traditional research modalities. As noted in chapter 5, for example, a key existential assertion is that both societal customs and individual lifestyles are formed by the intense need to deny our mortality. One can find evidence for a death anxiety → denial pattern in many situations, but that is a long way from demonstrating that this is a universal and primary characteristic. The more basic the existential concept, the more unlikely it is that it is open to empirical verification or rejection. Is the universe indifferent to our hopes, dreams, and loves? Are each of us essentially alone and responsible for our own fate? When you come right down to it, is life meaningless except for whatever meanings we ourselves can invent? These are philosophical issues very much worth considering—but perhaps not likely to be settled through the labors of social and behavioral scientists.

There are some implications of existential theory, however, that could be tested. Several studies (chapter 4) have explored the possible relationship between death anxiety and one's sense of meaning, purpose, and life fulfillment. Family members and hospice staff who have frequent and intimate contacts with dying people do learn something about the values that are cherished and the meanings that are sought or affirmed. We might learn much that is useful by attending to the meaning-structure through which dying people attempt to understand their situation and, in so doing, help to bridge the gap between existential theory and the experience of dying.

Where the Theories Agree

Setting aside for a moment the difficulties and limitations of the available theoretical perspectives, we can reflect on their major points of agreement (for another review of the literature see Corr, Doka, & Kastenbaum, in press). All emphasize the importance of communication, including the art of active listening. All recognize that our response to terminal illness is neither simple nor static: we deal with a complex and changing situation with whatever resources we can muster. All see the final phase of life as a part of the whole, not as a pathological episode. All suggest that the quality of life for a dying person can be protected and enhanced by sensitive human contact. Some perspectives also emphasize the continuity of personality: the person is no less important than the terminal condition in shaping the final experiences. At least one perspective emphasizes the importance of self-knowledge and coming to terms with one's own mortality if we are to be helpful to dying and grieving people. Taken together, these perspectives have the effect of ending the exclusion of the dying person from our conceptualizations of human experience and behavior. Our theories can only be the better for that.

A MULTIPLE-PERSPECTIVE APPROACH

It may be useful to consider another approach to understanding the dying process, actually, a converging set of partial models. I will not be suggesting that any one of these models is adequate for encompassing the situation of the dying person. Each may have something distinctive to offer, however, and could supplement any of the theoretical approaches already described. Furthermore, it is possible that by converging and combining these partial models we can develop an improved guide for describing, understanding, predicting, and helping. The partial models will be described briefly one by one before we explore the possibility of an integrated multiperspective approach.

There is a unifying theme that underlies these partial models. All are attempts to discover how much we can learn about the dying process with the "dying" left out. Admittedly, this is a strange-sounding proposition. It may appear less bizarre, however, if we take seriously the belief that dying is part of living—and living, therefore, a significant part of dying. Much that occurs during the dying process also occurs during other experiences and in other situations. This suggests that we may actually know more about the dying process than we realize. We can learn what has been learned about the many other challenges that have something in common with the situation of the dying person. Moreover, we can make new observations when we bring these perspectives to bear. There is a secondary advantage to this approach as well. We are less likely to attribute every behavior and communication to the terminal illness or dying. Perhaps this would also make us less likely to consider the dying person as a special case who requires a special theory.

But we will not actually ignore the dying of the dying person either in theory or practice. As an approach to theory development, we set aside the dying while we explore other paths to understanding. We then return to the total situation—dying included. In practice, I do not forget for a moment that I am with a dying or grieving person. In the development of theory, however, I offer myself—and you—the opportunity to consider many other aspects of the situation.

Partial Models of the Dying Process: An Overview

Seventeen partial models will be presented for your consideration. The models are identified in Table 6.1 and will be described briefly here.

Each of the first four partial models directs attention to a psychological situation that often is produced by the effects of a terminal illness— but which also can occur in other situations in which there is not a terminal illness.

TABLE 6.1   Partial Models of the Dying Person's Situation

Model	Brief description
1. Restricted Activity	I can do less and less
2. Limited Energy	I must conserve what is left of my strength
3. Illness & Body Image	I do not feel as I should feel
4. Contagion	You act like you would catch something bad from me
5. Disempowerment	I have lost the ability to influence you
6. Attributional Incompetency	You think I can't do anything right
7. Ineffectuance	I cannot make things happen the way I want them to
8. Stress Response	My defenses have become so intense that they are causing problems of their own
9. Time Anxiety	I fear it's too late to do all I must do
10. Loss and Separation	I am losing contact with everything that is most important to me
11. Disengagement	I feel ready to withdraw from interactions and responsibilities
12. Journey	I am going some place I have never been before
13. Closing the Book	I am doing everything for the last time; it will soon all be over
14. Performance	How am I doing? How do you think I am doing?
15. Endangered Relationship	I fear I am losing your love and respect
16. Struggling Brain	My mind is not working as it should; The world is slipping away from me
17. Storying	I must come up with the best possible story of all that has happened, is happening, and will happen

1.   The Restricted Activity Model

The dying person experiences a restriction of activity: "I can do less and less" is the basic psychological response. There are many other situations in which activity is restricted, sometimes increasingly so. Chronic illness and disability limit the free-ranging activity of many people who are not terminally ill. There may also be an intense feeling of activity restriction in the absence of physical dysfunction. A child protective services worker, for example, may become tense and frustrated because rules and resources do not allow her to offer timely assistance to those in need: the "system" restricts her from action. Barriers to action and the resulting enforced passivity can increase stress while at the same time limiting the outlets for tension reduction. There is also reason to think that restricted activity can stimulate fantasy and/or obsessive review as the mind tries to become an alternative theater of action.

2. The Limited Energy Model

The dying person experiences a lack of energy both for the requirements of everyday life and for responding to important challenges and opportunities: "I must conserve what is left of my strength" becomes a rule that cannot often be disobeyed. Limited energy, however, is often experienced during or following a passing illness, as well as pregnancy. A person who is depressed for any reason is also likely to feel unable to muster energy. Fatigued people (e.g., parents of lively infants and toddlers; firefighters after long exertion) also experience periods of time in which they find their energy banks temporarily depleted. Among the common psychological responses to energy depletion are (a) alarm that one is no longer a vibrant and adventurous person; (b) guilt that one has difficulty in meeting obligations to others; (c) ambiguous feelings about the unacceptability and yet the lure of passivity. The strange freedom of enforced passivity can threaten those who have made themselves into active, can-do people in part as a reaction to the temptation of idling. Meanwhile, those who interact with a person who is following the energy conservation rule may imagine themselves rejected or unappreciated because they do not recognize the powerful influence of fatigue and reduced energy.

3. The Illness and Distorted Body Image Model

The dying person experiences disturbing feedback from a body that has become less functional and more the source of pain and other symptoms: "I do not feel as I should" is likely to be the primary response. This may develop into the perception that "I am not as I should be" and then into "I am not me." A split may deepen between the perceiving mind and the object of its perception, the altered and altering body. There may be competition between the image of "who I was" and "who—or what—I am now." Others may notice confusing, even apparently irrational behavior from the person whose sense of self is being challenged because of changes in body appearance and feedback. For example, there may be sporadic efforts to escape mentally from the shell of an unacceptable body. This kind of situation is often experienced during the course of illnesses that are not terminal, as well as during periods of convalescence and healing. Aging is a slow normative sequence to which people respond with varying degrees of apprehension, alarm, depression, and ego-splitting. Some people are at war with their body images when they put on weight or acquire any other blemish to their ideal self. There are a variety of possible psychological responses to the perception that one is caught inside a troubling and unattractive body. These responses range from intensified cosmetic and grooming efforts to use of alcohol and other drugs to dull the perception

4. The Contagion Model

The dying person may feel that he or she could be the source of danger to others or that "You act like you would catch something bad from me." In point of fact, most people with a life-threatening illness do not pose a risk to others. We will not "catch death" from our friends who are afflicted with such major causes of death as cardiovascular conditions, cancer, or chronic obstructive lung disease. There is, however, a common fear of interacting with dying people that comes from two sources: (a) that fact that in the past some types of often-fatal illness *were* highly contagious, such as, tuberculosis and an especially virulent form of influenza; and (b) magical thinking that death is external and contagious, rather than an intrinsic part of the human condition (Kastenbaum, 1993). In practice, an unreadiness to deal with one's own mortality and a hesitancy to interact with a dying person may activate the irrational judgment that "death is catching." The contagion factor, then, often is not part of the actual illness, but can be part of the interpersonal situation and its effect on the dying person. We can tutor our understanding of the contagion fear with dying people by drawing upon experiences with nonfatal contagious illnesses. But we can also learn something by considering circumstances in which certain people are treated as though dangerous or unpalatable when no illness at all is involved. All too many examples are available in the annals of social stereotyping and discrimination. We don't want to be seen with "those people," do we? (And, perhaps, they don't want to be seen with us?) We understand something about contagion if we have ever felt that others did not want to be with us because this association somehow damaged them, or if we have ever withdrawn from another person for that reason.

The next three partial models have in common the perception that one can no longer function well in the sociophysical world. There is something distinctive about each model, however, that deserves particular attention.

5. The Disempowerment Model

The dying person may feel marginalized by family and society, having been stripped of status for decision-making and persuasion: "I have lost the ability to influence you." For some people this is a precipitous loss: a top echelon manager may be taken out of the loop; a family matriarch or patriarch's opinions may no longer have the force of authority. Dying people may lose their place at the table, both figuratively and literally. Disempowerment occurs in many other situations. A corporation is swallowed up by another corporation and the previous managers may find themselves either without a job or sharply reduced influence. A widow may discover that her social status and influence have been markedly reduced upon the death of her husband. Artists, performers, or politicians may find themselves on the outs after a period of success and acclaim as public opinion and taste prove fickle. Many people experience disempowerment because they have grown older and thereby entered the zone of the "senior" who is supposed to retire more or less gracefully to the sideline. When we perceive ourselves as being subjected to disempowerment we might respond in a variety of ways—resistance and anger, depression and withdrawal, confusion, flights into fantasy, to mention just a few. The psychological distress of dying people can be understood to some extent as an attempt to retain or regain the power of social influence. This can take the form of using one's illness and impairment as a power strategy if all else seems to have failed. Becoming more sensitive to the situation of a person who is attempting to cope with a loss of control and influence could help family, friends, and professional careproviders to respond more effectively.

6. The Attributional Incompetency Model

The dying person may become aware that he or she is being treated as though possessing no knowledge, intelligence or skills: "You think I can't do anything right." People are always making attributions about other people. Often we make attributions on the basis of class stereotypes, such as, what we expect from a person who speaks with a particular kind of regional accent or has a particular level or type of education. These attributional stereotypes may be accurate or way off the mark with respect to the other person's actual motives, knowledge, and skills. Nevertheless, the attributions themselves are part of reality and influence our interactions and decisions. We have all been on both the sending and receiving end of attributions (especially in our youth), so we should all know what it is like to feel that we are being misunderstood and dysvalued. It would be helpful, then, to recognize that much of a dying person's anguish can derive from being considered incompetent. This attribution can quickly intensify and expand after the first few observations that a person has changed through the course of the terminal illness. The guiding assumption that the dying person is less competent becomes very easy to reinforce when every sign of fatigue or slight clouding of consciousness is taken as further proof—while evidence of the person's clear understanding and good judgment are neglected.

7. The Ineffectuance Model

The dying person may be in a situation that is so different from previous life experiences that he or she does not have either a cognitive model or a coping repertoire available: "I can't make things happen the way I want them to." In this respect, dying is an ineffectuance situation. It can be useful, then, to learn from the way we try to understand and cope with the entire class of ineffectuance situations. What other ineffectuance situations might we have encountered long before coming to our deathbeds? Did we feel at a loss on our first day at kindergarten? On the first day of a new job? On the first day that retirement meant we did not have to go to work? On our wedding day or night? On taking our first essay test? On having our first significant interaction with a person who was much different from the people we knew? On our first hospitalization? For some of us many or all of these experiences have the quality of an ineffectuance situation: we hadn't had to face these challenges before and didn't know right off what we could or should do. We differ in the type and number of situations that induce a sense of ineffectuance, with most of us becoming more generally competent through continued maturation and experience. Some of us have had so much experience with disability or illness that we have already learned to cope with many of the challenges that we are likely to encounter in our terminal illness. Nevertheless, the dying person tends to encounter many "firsts," and many of these of a challenging nature. We may have an improved understanding of the dying person's situation if we recognize that previous cognitive schemata, behavioral skills, and interactive strategies may not have been adequate preparation. The dying person who seems unmodulated, disinhibited, labile, and anguished may be responding not only to the prospect of death, but to the unnerving immediacy of an ineffectuance situation. With this possibility in mind, we may be in a better position to help the dying person master much of what for the moment seems so new, different, and overwhelming.

8. The Stress Response Model

The dying person may experience stress from many sources, physical, psychological, social, and spiritual. Much of his or her energy may therefore be expended in trying to cope with relentless and intensifying stress: "My defenses have become so intense that they are causing problems of their own." Much of the dying person's anguish can be understood as the consequence of an all-out effort to protect one's self from the effects of multiple and prolonged stress. Furthermore, the people who are most in contact with the dying person are also likely to be experiencing a high level of stress, therefore inadvertently contributing to an interpersonal system that can be dominated by tension and strain. Hans Selye (1956), the bioscientist who laid the foundation for modern approaches to stress, distinguished between general and specific stress. All sources of stress (e.g., cold, thirst, hunger, pain, noise) produce some common effects as the organism attempts to defend itself. There are also specific responses to each particular source of stress. A hungry animal or person, for example, will behave differently than one who is being subjected to painful levels of noise. The dying person must deal with many specific stresses, requiring adjustments that may be at cross-purposes with each other while at the same time contributing to an increasingly high level of general stress. Most significantly, perhaps, is the probability that the dying person's response to stress itself becomes a source of further stress, fatigue, and anguish. This would place the dying person at the final phase of Selye's general adaptation syndrome, the one in which the organism has become permanently disabled and may even cause its own death through the extreme and protracted use of the very strategies that were intended to prolong life. Alert and sensitive caregivers might be able to devise stress-reduction strategies that reduce the strain on the dying person's own psychobiological responses and would also recognize the broad spectrum of possible sources of stress, including loneliness, threats to relationships, role loss, identity crises, and challenges to vital meanings of life.

9. The Time Anxiety Model

Dying people must contend with a foreshortened future that drastically limits their opportunity to complete projects and obliga-

tions as well as to restructure their most significant intepersonal relationships: "I fear it's too late to do all I must do." There may be numerous end-of-life issues of a practical nature, such as deciding on the distribution of the estate, making other financial and legal arrangements, and giving instructions for funeral and memorial events. There may also be responsibilities of an individual and symbolic nature, for example, an elder's desire to complete a geneology or family history. Furthermore, some of us go through life with a compulsion to do and achieve with our eyes always on the clock and calendar. We live in a society that rewards obedience to time strictures and that encourages us to squeeze many obligations and projects into a limited time frame. Many people among today's elderly population still function within the harness of time-consciousness that served them well during their careers. Similarly, some people bring their need "to get things done" to the final phase of their lives. The better we understand the role of time anxiety in our lives—and the more adept we become in reducing this anxiety—the better we will be able to assist the dying person who now has an indisputable reason for being concerned about squeezing a lot of life into a little time.

10. The Loss and Separation Model

The dying person has already lost much and faces the loss of everything: "I am losing contact with everything that is most important to me." Over a period of time the person may lose connections to his or her previous life in every realm of functioning. The workplace may be lost along with its opportunities to demonstrate one's skills and engage in pleasant social interactions. Sexual relations may be lost along with the intimacy, tension relief, and sense of satisfying the partner. Loss of the ability to drive may be followed by loss of the ability to walk without assistance. Each actual loss can intensify anxiety about the losses still to come. For many people it is the loss of relationships that is most crucial. (Some have the compensating belief that reunion with lost loved ones will be found in the next life.) We can improve our understanding of the dying person's situation by learning from the many other types of loss and separation experience. How do people cope with such situations as leaving home for college, moving from one country to another, changing jobs, or leaving the good old gang upon graduation or marriage? None of these situations are close to the experience of dying, but all raise such issues as the resolution of ambivalence, the symbolic continuation of interrupted relationships, and the process of leave-taking. The death-awareness movement has stimulated increased attention to the importance of a meaningful leave-taking for both the dying person and those who will be left with the memories. Whatever else dying may be, it is certainly the very model of loss and separation.

11. The Disengagement Model

The dying person may believe that he or she has already lived the full life and is now content to let the world go by: "I feel ready to withdraw from interactions and responsibilities." Disengagement theory was introduced to the social sciences by Elaine Cumming and William E. Henry (1961) as a way of understanding the shift from middle adult to later adult life. According to this formulation, we become most fully engaged with society—most responsible, most obligated—during our middle adult years. Eventually we realize that we will not be living forever and that, in fact, time is starting to run out on us. We respond by stepping back from social obligations to spend more time on our personal interests and needs while, at the same time, society gently but firmly shows us to the door. After a period of transition, we re-engage with society, still participating but in a less active and compulsory manner. The theory was important for some years in gerontology, but has had mixed results from research and is no longer dominant. Nevertheless, disengagement theory does offer a potentially useful partial model for the dying process. A person may already have withdrawn much of his her or involvement with society prior to the terminal illness. Death may not be experienced as a powerful threat by a person who feels that his or her "real life" has been over for some time. Some of the other partial models described here (e.g., Disempowerment, Time Anxiety) may not be applicable. By understanding how people deal with the pressure or temptation to disengage in a variety of situations we may learn something important about the orientation of some dying people.

12. The Journey Model

The dying person is leaving all that he or she has known of life and moving toward a destination that is both universal yet profoundly personal: "I am going some place I have never been before." Some people are keenly aware of dying as a journey. Death can be viewed not as the destination, but as the port of entry into a new and more radiant form of life. As one elderly woman told me from her hospital bed: "All of life is a journey to a better life. Dying is just one more leg on the journey." Other people are not as sure about the destination, but agree that dying is "as natural as anything else; you can't say 'I'll only take this part of life and not all the rest that comes with it.' " This man, survivor of his second heart attack, had travelled through much of the world and considered dying to be "one more trip—and not necessarily the worst!" The *idea* of journey is deeply embedded in many if not all world cultures. Youth's adventures and ordeals enroute to adulthood are often portrayed as journeys, and, in fact, often do involve travel. Many rituals (notably those involving initiation into a new status or group) are symbolic representations of a journey, complete with challenges to test one's character and qualifications. Eastern thought has offered the conception of human existence as a journey not only through one's lifecourse development, but also through realms of spiritual enlightenment and into subsequent reincarnations. At the very least, it would be useful to learn if the idea of dying as part of the journey of life is salient for the dying people with whom we come into contact. This can provide a shared frame of discourse to strengthen communication throughout the dying process. Moreover, thinking of dying as a journey can help to replace the stigmatization of the terminally ill person (e.g., as incompetent, contagious, or powerless) with the more positive concept of a traveller on a daunting road to a new land. The value of providing companionship along the way may also become more evident.

13. The Closing-the-Book Model

The dying person becomes more or less aware that the book of life will soon close: "I am doing everything for the last time; it will soon be all over." There is abundant preparation for the final closing of the book. Most of us have repeatedly experienced the literal closing of a book after reading the last page. We have also experienced the end of the semester, perhaps heaving away all the books. In a more symbolic way we have closed the books on our high school and perhaps our college experiences and on any number of tasks and projects. We are also practiced in completing an episode in our lives, even though a similar episode may be expected in the future. For example, we may have completed our gardening for this season, cleaning and putting away the tools. Next year, though, we expect to open the book of our garden to a new chapter. How we interpret "closing the book" situations throughout our lives may have a bearing on the way we respond to the end of our lives as we move into the final chapter. The terminal phase of life may also reawaken our memories about previous endings. Perhaps we will feel a confidence born of many successful completions followed by the ability to go on with our lives. Perhaps we will feel conflicted and confused because we have had such a difficult time in accepting closures in the past. Many people would appreciate companions who, by active listening, help them to put their closing-the-book thoughts and feelings into focus. A systematic life review might be valuable to one person, while another requires only the opportunity to share a few thoughts and memories with a treasured companion. In my experience, it is not unusual for a dying person to seek a little assurance that he or she has earned the right to close the book on a good life without regrets and without the obligation to continue the struggle in order to demonstrate courage and character.

14. The Performance Model

The dying person is not only responding to stress and loss, but is also enacting a drama. There will be some degree of awareness that he or she is in fact performing: "How am I doing? How do you think I am doing?" The term "performance" is sometimes taken to mean a kind of show that has an element of pretense or artificiality, such as an actor reciting a memorized script but trying to behave as though the words were coming spontaneously. Here, though, we are thinking of performance as this concept is used in communication theory. Many of our actions—real actions in real situations—also are performances, enactments of who we are and what we believe. For example, the college student who gives a formal talk while chewing gum, smiling inappropriately, and wearing a baseball cap (backwards, of course) might be regarded as performing immaturity. The police officer who devotes his own time to helping troubled children is performing compassion and community spirit. The dying person may not have any intention of "performing" in the theatrical sense of the term, but may nevertheless be aware that others are observing and evaluating. Indeed, dying people may carefully observe and evaluate their own behavior. "Am I letting people down by complaining too much or not being responsive enough?" "Am I scaring people away?" "Am I showing the wrong side of my personality and destroying the reputation I worked all my life to earn?" The dying person may feel compelled to perform as expected (or as he or she believes is expected), and may suffer additional anguish when unable to do so. Sensitive companions and careproviders could relieve some of the dying person's burden by recognizing and thereby not imposing their own implicit expectations for performance of "the dying role." We may also improve our ability to participate in the drama of the last phase of life by understanding what it is that the dying person is attempting to perform and why.

15.   The Endangered Relationship Model

The dying person may dread the symbolic as well as palpable loss of significant relationships: "I fear I am losing your love and respect." The previously cited observations of Glaser and Strauss (1966) attest to the relationship anxiety that dying people and their companions are likely to experience. The mutual pretense form of communication is a particularly vivid example of the extent to which people may go to avoid moments of confrontation and disturbance that could disrupt a relationship. Threats to a valued relationship are troubling at any time, but much more so when one is facing the stress of a terminal illness. A person may be able to cope with the distress and dysfunction of the illness, but be devastated when friends and family appear to be withdrawing. On a more subtle level, one may fear the loss of relationship with one's own former self: "*I* am not me anymore: *I* don't want any part of this *me*." The perception of actual or potential rejection by self and others can lead to heightened suicidality: "I will destroy the sick, useless, and unacceptable me—that will make everybody else feel better." We bring to our terminal illness a lifetime's worth of experiences with relationships that have continued and developed over the years, but also with some that failed or turned negative. The endangered relationship model invites attention both to the individual's history of relationship maintenance, growth, and loss, and to the relationship issues that are most significant in the immediate situation. These may include the possibility of resolving long-standing family quarrels to bring people together again and sharing memories, even secrets, that can affirm and strengthen existing relationships.

16.   The Struggling Brain Model

The dying person may be experiencing fluctuations and flaws in mental functioning: "My mind is not working as it should; the world is slipping away from me." Much of what has been said about the other partial models of dying has assumed that for the most part the individual is alert and able to communicate. This, of course, is not always the case. For some people it is the failure of brain function that is most responsible for the impending death (e.g., massive head trauma in an accident). More often the neural problems are part of the total impairment syndrome. Cardiovascular conditions, for example, may result in a diminished supply of blood and therefore oxygen to the brain. There may also be specific impairments to blood circulation within the brain. Many people experience episodes of clouded consciousness or confusion as the result of medications. Furthermore, the enforced passivity and reduced stimulation that often accompanies a debilitating illness may well have negative effects on cognitive functioning. The dying person's ability to process information may also be diminished by reductions in acuity in one or more sensory modalities. All in all, the dying person's brain may be engaged in a desperate struggle to maintain its integrity within a context of stress, deprivation, and loss. Whatever we can learn from the coping difficulties of people with a variety of brain syndromes could be useful in understanding the situation of those dying people who are similarly afflicted. Expert palliative care—including environmental enrichments and supportive interactions—can moderate the struggling brain facet of terminal illness by reducing the need for medications and providing meaningful communication. Before we become too dedicated to psychological interpretations of the dying person's situation we might remind ourselves that consciousness and thought are subject to influence by whatever influences brain function.

17. The Storying Model

The dying person may have a difficult time making sense not only of the illness-related experiences but of the way in which the present situation might be integrated into his or her total life: "I must come up with the best possible story of all that has happened, is happening, and will happen." We belong to a species that loves to hear stories. Many of us also enjoy creating and telling stories. The significance of storytelling is much deeper than entertainment, however. Storying is one of our most effective ways of organizing information for meaning, memory, and communication. Not only incidents but tone, character, and moral implication are conveyed through narrative structures. A memorable and powerful story may contain any mix of factual and fictional elements. What is most important is the strength of the narrative structure that arranges these elements into an affecting pattern. The need to weave the elements of our own lives into a coherent and meaningful pattern is intensified by loss, stress, and threat. When society perceives itself as endangered there is an upsurge of rival stories about the threat. When we are grieving the death of a child we may repeatedly ask ourselves why "it had to happen" and suffer not only for the loss but also for the lack of a credible story that puts the loss into perspective. Today more people are living longer with their final illnesses. There is more time to think about "what it all means" and to search for a pattern that encompasses one's total life, indeed, perhaps the very meaning of life. Some dying people are much concerned with finding or creating a story that summarizes and distills the meaning of their lives—and this quest is being carried out under the most difficult circumstances.

THE DYING PERSON'S OWN THEORY

Theoreticians are not the only people who have theories. We all have ideas about why things happen as they do. We may be able to share these ideas fluently when called upon, or we may not be quite sure what we think until the time comes when we have to make critical decisions. Perhaps, then, we should give more attention to the dying person's own theory. We have already made a start by identifying storying as a partial model of the dying process. This model is only partial, though, when we are taking the viewpoint of an external observer. From the external standpoint we can select as many partial models as we consider promising. It is quite different from the dying person's view, however. As the end of our lives approach most of us are holding or seeking an integrative conception: a model that contains all that is worth including of possible explanations. In other words, the partial model of storying opens into any number of integrative individual accounts of the meaning of life, dying, and death. It may be difficult to learn how a particular dying person envisions his or her world, but without at least making the effort we limit ourselves to whatever preexistent models we happen to have on hand. Here we will explore one example in a little detail and touch on several others.

A Dying Psychologist Observed by Himself

William McDougall, MD, a biomedical researcher, political scientist, and independent-minded behaviorist, was among the founders of social psychology. Imported from England to replace the late William James at Harvard University, McDougall became one of the nation's most distinguished psychologists but did not fit comfortably into the aggressive behavioralism that was making its mark in the United States. He scored a victory in a famous debate with archbehavioralist John B. Watson emphasizing that we are not "empty organisms" that can be easily manipulated and shaped by environmental stimuli.

McDougall and his new American colleagues baffled each other. He was puzzled and hurt by their cold and occasionally hostile attitude. For their part, his feisty young American colleagues saw the tall, reserved, and learned McDougall as an intimidating foreigner who represented the kind of philosophically oriented psychology that they were rebelling against. (Many years later several of these psychologists told me that they had pegged McDougall wrong; in E. G. Boring's words, "We took McDougall to be an arrogant fellow who looked down on us—actually, he was a shy and goodhearted person who had just as much trouble making sense out of us."

McDougall moved to a more hospitable environment, becoming chair of the Duke University Department of Psychology in 1927. He became a valued mentor and role model for his colleagues and students and continued to contribute significant articles and books. A decade later he felt himself ready to write his *magnum opus*, the book that would present to the world his mature vision of social psychology as the foundation for all sciences through a systematic analysis of the United States. The world needed all the help it could get at that time. Like his senior contemporary Sigmund Freud, McDougall was painfully aware of flaws in modern civilization that generated tension, suicide, murder, and war. He saw World War II coming, and with it a massive threat to the survival of civilized societies everywhere.

And then he learned that he had cancer. Not long afterward he would learn that his condition was terminal. There were probably just a few months to go. Quickly he decided to cancel his classes to avoid putting his students in a bind should he be unable to complete the semester. He also had lost the opportunity to write the book that might have crowned his life's work. What he could do was to observe and comment on his own final days. McDougall intended that his journal be shared with colleagues at some indefinite time in the future. When he died in 1938 (2 months after starting the journal) psychology was locked into its avoidance of dying and death. It was unlikely that his final words would be read or understood. Years later his son Angus McDougall, a librarian at Duke University, kindly made a copy of the journal and invited me to use it as I saw fit. McDougall's journal was published along with my commentary (Kastenbaum, 1995–1996) at a time when more people were ready to attend to the observations of a dying psychologist. We revisit McDougall's journal here as an illuminating example of a dying person's own implicit model of the dying process and its meanings. What follows now is a summary and illustration of McDougall's comments as he observes his own rapid decline.

1. *"A vague pain widely diffused and vaguely localized in the lower abdomen."* McDougall introduces us to the history of his illness. He had been afflicted with partial deafness for many years, and recently suffered further loss of hearing, having to compensate for this as best he could. More ominous, though, had been the increase in vague symptoms of discomfort that he had been experiencing for more than a decade. Reluctantly, he had to upgrade his appraisal from "discomfort" to "pain" and seek medical attention. He knew the condition could prove to be fatal eventually, but thought that the "ups and downs" might continue for a while so he considered himself to be having "on the whole, a very tolerable existence . . . for months and perhaps years," especially with the "extreme kind devotion" of his wife and son. At this point McDougall was coping well with progressive physical decline and distress. He did not, however, consider himself to be a dying person because there were still medical treatments to try and his own adjustments seem to have been useful.

2. *"The pain seems to fill and to constitute the whole of Consciousness. . . .* Much sooner than expected, however, McDougall's pain became severe. In fact pain became a visualized reality "in the shape of a vague dim white ball, every other Cns function being arrested; that is a kind of sleep but sleep of a terrible kind. The topic of speed on the road had been discussed at the breakfast table." From this point onward McDougall would be living with severe and occasionally overwhelming pain as his companion. As a physician/psychologist, McDougall remarked on "the astonishing degree of our ignorance of pain, of pain in general, and of cancer pain in particular." As a suffering person, McDougall wondered how long his pain could be even partially controlled by the available drugs and how long he

could bear the agony. We should not overlook a cryptic statement that seems just to have been tagged on to his visual description of the pain: what did he mean by "the topic of speed on the road?"

What did "speed on the road" have to do with anything? McDougall was telling us ubiquely that he had raised the possibility of hastening his death (most likely by overdosing on morphine). This was the first and last mention of suicide as a way out of his suffering. A few days later he learned—indirectly—that his doctor has known that "case is hopeless" from the beginning. "It has not made much difference to my outlook because I had been forced to same general conclusion. . . . On q. whether it was wise to keep back the facts from me so long, I pretend to no opinion. There are pro's and con's on both sides, about offsetting each other."

3. *"Have I, properly speaking, achieved anything?"* McDougall accepts the evidence of his own and his physician's observations without a glimmer of denial. He is dying, and there is not much time left. Immediately he focuses on the issue of self-evaluation: what has he achieved and what has he failed to achieve? McDougall concedes that "I have decently filled a number of academic posts and played a quite respectable part in keeping going the academic routine." This does not count for much with him, though. The academic world does not seem to have valued his contributions very highly, and may well forget about his work when he is gone. But it is not enough to muse about his achievements in a general way. McDougall now devotes several pages of his journal to a year-by-year review of his most important research and scholarly work, from his 1897 studies of cross-striated muscle through his two pioneering books on social psychology a decade later and the 1908 introduction of his famous instinct theory, and on to many later works as well as several other projects still in various stages of development. All in all, he was inclined to think of himself as a failure because his achievements had not matched his scientific ambitions and had not won a secure place in history (though he had not completely given up hope on that score). There are a few positives, however: he has lived the life he has chosen, choosing his own friends and residing "in pleasant and beautiful places."

4. *"I married almost suddenly for love pure and simple."* McDougall considers himself "outrageously lucky" in his marriage and family life. There is something more than curious, though, in the very

brief discussion of his personal life. McDougall's narrative throughout
the journal is almost always controlled and objectivistic. It comes as
a surprise when he describes his pain in such a vivid manner, and it
comes again as a surprise when he speaks of his marriage in a rhap-
sodic and impulsive manner. However, this rare mood of exposed
personal feelings does not survive even that sentence. Here we italicize
the second part of the sentence that throws cold water on the romantic
ardor of the first: "I married almost suddenly for love pure and simple,
*and though I did not utterly lose sight of eugenic considerations
I do not know that these would have sufficed to modify my course
of action in the least, had they seemed to demand changes."*
McDougall has changed immediately from a moment of rapture recalled to a stiff and distancing perspective. He then continues to write
one of his most extended entries, devoting it to the subject of eugenics.
A better world requires better people. The best way to get better
people is to beget them through the union of genetically superior
and flawless mates. Here we find a way of thinking that becomes
increasingly evident throughout this dying man's journal: our lives are
to be evaluated within a social-moral perspective. One is lucky, indeed,
outrageously lucky, to find happiness in one's personal life. It is far
more important, though, to be socially responsible and strong enough
to meet the highest standards. This demanding and austere moral
perspective on life has no obvious connection to religious belief, which
does not surface in his journal.

   5.   *"From that time my will-power seemed completely col-
lapsed."* The triggering event was his decision to cancel his classes
because of "very severe pain" and concern that he could not complete
the semester. As already noted, this cancellation also dissolved his
dream of writing that one more and most important book. McDougall
then has something else to say about will power that seems to be
directed both to his personal situation and the world at large. What
keeps either an individual personality or the spirit of a nation together
might be called *will power*, the resolve to withstand the forces of
strain, chaos, and violence. He refers to the crisis of will power being
faced by a Europe at war again and his personal struggle with cancer.
What should a dying person do? The same as a nation in crisis: "follow
a *strong* course."

   His "strong course" included the determined effort to remain conscious and alert, a thinking person, despite severe pain. "How far can

an intellectual effort diminish pain? I think my experiences . . . qualify me to write: Yes, decidedly! It can throw fairly severe pain into the background and keep it there pretty steadily for an hour or 2. . . . It is rather cheering. It pulls one together, and seems that what I called the collapse of Will-Power or of the structure of personality is not finally destructive."

McDougall's Implicit Theory of Dying

McDougall reports his final weeks of life through a "split screen" self. Indeed, his journal begins with the phrase, "I find myself . . . " Often he devotes his limited energies to classifying, analyzing, and making lists—all well practiced modes of processing information, but not the stuff of direct human experience. His theory of dying is implicit in his selected observations and interpretations (discussed in more detail in Kastenbaum, 1995). We discover that evaluation of his career achievements is more at issue than his interpersonal relationships. He has very little to say about the important people in his life, and most of these comments are framed in the perspective of social-moral evaluation rather than personal feeling.

A theory of dying is also a theory of life and its meanings. However, it is not necessarily a theory that encompasses *all* of a person's life and its possible meanings. McDougall chooses not to include his childhood and youth. He chooses not to reflect on his courtship, marriage, and parenting experiences, nor his relationships with colleagues and students. This psychologist with his highly developed analytic ability chooses to exclude nearly all of his early experiences and life-long relationships from consideration as he reviews his life with death in near prospect.

Religion and the question of a life after death are also ignored. These omissions are striking for two reasons. What McDougall excluded are precisely the topics that are dear to current theories of mental health and human development. A dying person is supposed to review early experiences, resolve relationship issues, and come to terms with death. From this standpoint, McDougall is not dying according to the book. Just as curious is the fact that McDougall's own theoretical approach in psychology emphasizes *purpose*. He was opposed to the kind of behaviorism that viewed people as simply the middle term between stimulus and response. We live through our purposes, our intentions, and these derive both from our biological nature and our individual personalities as formed in unique sociocultural situations. He might have reflected on religion and death from the unique perspective of a dying person, but he did not. We can see already that McDougall's implicit theory of dying does not accord either with the traditional religious orientation that might have been expected from his background or with his own psychological theory.

McDougall did have an immediate and highly stressful problem that could not be ignored: increasingly severe and relentless pain. He made use of the pain-relieving modalities then available, but would not accept being "snowed under." The issue became McDougall's intellect and will power against the pain. He transformed his personal struggle into a general theory of individual and society: we must attain and maintain the highest possible "structural integrity." McDougall is both inside and outside of his experiences as a dying person. His ordeal and violence-threatened society's have much in common.

Never does McDougall permit himself the luxury of slipping into denial or fantasy. One exerts will power as strong and as long as possible—but bodies will fail and peace will give way to war. We can strengthen ourselves. We can resist stress and chaos. Our power and efficacy are limited, though, even with the most resolute attitude. Furthermore, there is luck and chance to consider. In fact, much of what affects the course of our lives is not so much purpose and planning as luck and accident. McDougall was ahead of most psychologists of his time in recognizing the implications of new developments in physics and mathematics. We do not live in a strictly determined universe, nor can the individual's most profound desires and most clever thoughts insure that all will be well. He does not seek religious, magical, or scientific solutions to his predicament. "Why me?" is a question he never asks. There is no conspiracy at work, nor does the frustration of his career goals signify the displeasure of God. It is terrible to suffer so much and sad to see death coming so soon—but that's just the sort of thing that happens in a universe that we cannot control.

One of McDougall's concerns does accord well with developmental task theory. Has his life (meaning his scientific career) been successful? Will his work endure? Interestingly, this person who has apparently dispensed with a religious perspective has nevertheless subjected himself to stringent evaluation. He is not only both the observer and the subject, but also the judge and the defendant. McDougall's objectivism perhaps saves the day. He knows that he cannot know for sure what will become of his ideas and reputation. He also knows that he could not have done more in the time that was available to him and that he does not have to beg or earn "redemption" for any shortcomings. He did what he did, and perhaps he fell short of his own ambitions, but one simply must live—and die—with that.

Despite the self-imposed task of evaluation, McDougall's implicit perspective on dying does not otherwise accord with today's prevailing guidelines. He does not observe himself passing through psychological stages during his final illness (nor does the reader note any such progression). He does not find it necessary to resolve relationship issues, come to peace with God, or persuade himself that death is anything other than death. I do not like to repeat myself, but in the more extensive analysis of McDougall's journal, I attempted to reconstruct his implicit theory of dying in the following words, and this statement might be useful right about here. (Please bear in mind that this *is* an attempt to extract McDougall's implicit theory and therefore not in his own words, although some of his key phrases are included.)

What, then, is life in prospect of death? I will tell you what it is for me. First, it is life that is most interesting. Death is the word we use to describe the outcome *of structural collapse.* I do not bother much with the concept of death in my life story; it is merely the point at which it is useless to do any further *overhauling* of the system.

The prospect of death, though—that is worth our attention because it provides an occasion to evaluate how well we have lived our lives according to our own criteria and expectations. We may fare poorly or well in this self-evaluation. The crucial point is that we do follow the *strong course of action,* that we do apply *our intellectual effort* as long as we have breath. How we live on in the memory of others is also important, although this is quite out of our control.

Control? It is not wise to become too attached to this concept. Yes, I have always valued control, and I seek control now. But please remember that I have also acknowledged the reality of *luck* or chance, the limits of what we can predict and what we can control. My strong course of action is to draw upon *strength of purpose* and *effort of intellect* as far and as long as these resources can take me. And as for the rest? I do not pretend to understand what lies beyond my understanding, nor demand such assurances as the world is in no position to provide. This is my construction of life with death in near prospect and my plan for getting through it as best I can. What is your construction and your plan? (Kastenbaum, 1995, pp. 162–163)

McDougall's implicit theory of dying may or may not resonate well with our own. It certainly deviates appreciably from the theories that have gained some popularity in recent years. Our own response is not nearly as important, however, as our willingness to recognize that the dying person does have an implicit theory, and that we can be more informed companions if we understand and respect this perspective rather than projecting our own ideas or automatically applying existing models. Perhaps we can also appreciate the intrinsic value of developing, testing, and sharing one's view of life while in final transition.

A Sampling of Other Personal Models of Dying

Much more briefly we will acquaint ourselves with several other implicit models of dying.

Sara

Sara was a spontaneous and high-spirited person who liked to run not only her own life but everybody else's. It was unusual for her to feel tired and out of sorts. Medical tests revealed that she had cancer that had spread to the brain. It soon became evident that her condition was terminal. Her implicit model of dying could be capsulized in just a few words: "Get it all in while you can!" She decided to regard dying as a brief last act that should be crowded with the kind of life she enjoyed—which included plenty of shopping, dining out, and giving others the benefit of her opinions. With the help of devoted friends, Sara did have this telescoped type of life, though it required continued bursts of energy that seemed unlikely given her physical condition. The time anxiety and relationship failure models seemed most salient in her own perspective on dying. The former she could handle with the philosophy that she would run until she dropped, and that would be that. The latter was more difficult because her husband, traumatized by her illness, had become more distant, not knowing how to relate to her, fearing he might say or do the wrong thing. Finally, as a friend noted:

She said she wanted him to hold her, and share this time with her. They had always shared their lives, and now she felt alone. She started to cry. . . . She wanted to share the time remaining with him. Time was so short. They were losing what was left. She couldn't get those days back. (Thuell, 1995)

Sara's effort to live intensely in the present and put aside both the past and the future had carried her for several months, but now she needed to draw strength from the most sustaining relationship in her life. Her model of dying did see her all the way, but it contributed to a stimulating sense of active life until almost the very end.

Rita

Rita lived alone in an apartment she had furnished attractively. She had been through five surgeries and was paralyzed below the waist from metastases to her spine. Bald from radiation, her weight down to about 95 pounds, and unable to sit up straight, she showed the ravages of her long struggle with cancer. Rita's mind remained quick and she insisted on being in control of the situation. During a period of time when hospice was still an unfamiliar concept, Rita was being pressured to return to the hospital. She would have no part of that and made it clear that she would live until she died in her apartment. Despite much opposition from the medical establishment, she had her wish, thanks to nurses whose "conspiracy" with her included serving a martini for her at 5 o'clock (alcoholic beverages having been prohibited). "Life's little pleasures," she would say.

Rita's model of dying centered around the importance of being one's own self. She was not becoming a different kind of person just because she was dying, and her life did not suddenly belong to anybody else. Rita was not a contentious person except when others threatened to take her life away from her. She had warm relationships with the people in her life and became close to the visiting nurses as well. Death was inevitable, so there was not much that needed to be said on that score. Dying was hard—especially her restricted activity—but it did not require a transformed view of life, just some help from others to remain one's own self to the end.

Michael

Michael was a 21-year-old who characterized himself as "permanently unemployed" except for "many hours at the beach with many women." He was 6 foot 2, a mellow young man who usually offered an engaging smile to whoever he met. Nurses came to know him when he was admitted for diagnostic studies of his headache complaint. They learned that he loved to laugh and had absolutely no ambition, but also that he had spent his childhood in foster homes and had nothing that could be described as a family. Physicians discovered that Michael's headaches were caused by cancer that had spread to the brain. They hoped to save his life and tried everything. He accepted all the interventions with few complaints despite the discomfort and other side effects, which included extreme nausea and vomiting, as well as infection in the surgical wounds. Physicians and nurses had quickly become attached to Michael and became emotionally involved in trying to keep him alive. Meanwhile, as a nurse observed, "he continued to play his guitar poorly, and play poker well."

Michael espoused a simple philosophy of life: "Enjoy. No worry." This had contributed to making him a popular companion. Death? He would smile, sometimes laugh. "That's not for me!" He seemed truly to believe in his immortality. He had always been alive. Why shouldn't he stay alive? Things would work out. Michael did not see himself as in need of salvation or in jeopardy of punishment. He did not compare his deeds to a high standard of achievement. Life was something you took day by day, and expected to continue. Was he "in denial"? This would be a tempting conclusion. However, it would also be a distortion. Michael had not suddenly been shocked and numbed by the onset of his terminal illness. He was getting on with his life pretty much as usual, except for the inconveniences of an illness and its management. His terminal illness neither evoked a latent worldview or led to a transformed perspective. Should we perhaps insist that he had been living in denial all along? This would be a gratuitous assumption unless we were willing to engage in a lot of soul-searching ourselves. It is not so unusual for young men to believe in their immortality. It is not even so unusual for many other people to take life as it comes without being harnessed by future hopes, expectations, and fears. Michael is not likely to be the only person we come across who finds a simple model of life sufficient and has little interest in abstractions such as death or remote possibilities, such as dying.

This brief sampling of the individual's own model of dying will have been counterproductive if we immediately start to classify them and emphasize common features. My point is quite the opposite: How well can we discover, understand, and respect every person's implicit model of dying in all its uniqueness?

REFERENCES

Becker, E. (1973). *The denial of death.* New York: Free Press.

Butler, R. N. (1963). The life review: An interpretation of reminiscence in the aged. *Psychiatry, 26,* 65–76.

Cole, T. R. (1992). *The journey of life.* Cambridge, UK: Cambridge University Press.

Corr, C. A. (1992). A task-based approach to coping with dying. *Omega, Journal of Death and Dying, 24,* 81–94.

Corr, C. A., Doka, K. J., & Kastenbaum, R. (in press). Dying and its interpreters: A review of selected literature and some comments on the state of the field. *Omega, Journal of Death and Dying.*

Cumming, E. M., & Henry, W. E. (1961). *Growing old.* New York: Basic Books.

Doka, K. J. (1993) *Living with life-threatening illness.* Lexington, MA: Lexington Books.

Erikson, E. H. (1959) *Identity and life cycle.* New York: International Universities Press.

Farber, M. L. (1968). *Theory of suicide.* New York: Funk & Wagnalls.

Glaser, B. G., & Strauss, A. L. (1966). *Awareness of dying.* Chicago: Aldine.

Glaser, B. G., & Strauss, A. L. (1968). *Time for dying.* Chicago: Aldine.

Gyatso, Tenzin, the 14th Dali Lama. (1985). *Kindness, clarity, and insight.* (J. Hopkings, Trans.). Ithaca, NY: Snow Lions Publications. (Original work published 1980)

Heckler, R. A. (1994). *Waking up alive.* New York: Ballantine Books.

Hollinger, P. C., Offer, D., Barter, J. T., & Bell. C. C. (1994). *Suicide and homicide among adolescents.* New York: Guildford Press.

Kastenbaum, R. (1993). Reconstructing death in postmodern society. *Omega, Journal of Death and Dying, 27,* 75–90.

Kastenbaum, R. (1995–1996). "How far can an intellectual effort diminish pain?" William McDougall's Journal as a model for facing death. *Omega, Journal of Death and Dying, 32,* 123–164.

Kastenbaum, R. (1998). *Death, society, and human experience* (6th ed.). Boston: Allyn & Bacon.

Kastenbaum, R., Kastenbaum, B. K., & Peyton, S. (1978). Sex discrimination after death. *Omega, Journal of Death and Dying, 8,* 351–359.

Kaufmann, W. (1959). Existentialism and death. In H. Feifel (Ed.), *The meaning of death* (pp. 39–63). New York: McGraw-Hill.

Kaufmann, W. (1976). *Existentialism, religion, and death.* New York: New American Library.

Kierkegaard, S. (1940). *The concept of dread.* Princeton, NJ: Princeton University Press.

Kübler-Ross, E. (1969). *On death and dying.* New York: Macmillan.

Leenaars, A. A., Maris, R. W., McIntosh, J. L., & Richman, J. (Eds.). (1992). *Suicide and the older adult.* New York: Guilford Press.

Nietzche, F. (1954). *The portable Nietzsche.* New York: The Viking Press.

Pattison, E. M. (1977). *The experience of dying.* Englewood Cliffs, NJ: Prentice-Hall.

Satre, J. P. (1956). *Being and nothingness.* New York: Philosophical Library.

Selye, H. (1956). *The stress of life.* New York: McGraw-Hill

Schulman, K. E., Berlin, J. A., Harless, W., Kerner, J. F., Sistrunk, S., Gersh, M. B., Dube, R., Teleghani, C., Burke, J., Williams, S., Eisenberg, J. M., & Escarce, J. J. (1999). The effect of race and sex on physicians' recommendations for cardiac catherizations. *New England Journal of Medicine, 340,* 618–625.

Sudnow, D. (1967). *Passing on: The social organization of dying.* Englewood Cliffs, NJ: Prentice-Hall.

Thuell, S. (1995). *Sara and Bill.* Tempe, AZ: Arizona State University, Department of Communication, Unpublished archival report.

Tolstoy, L. (1960). *The death of Ivan Ilych.* New York: New American Library.

7

Deathbed Scenes

I've seen a Dying Eye
Run round and round a Room
In search of Something-as it seemed

—Emily Dickinson

Helen, mother, please take me out. Come on, Rosie. O. K. Hymes
would not do it; not him. I will settle . . . the indictment. Come on,
Max, open the soap duckets. Frankie, please come here. Open that
door, Dumpey's door. It is so much, Abe, that . . . with the brewery,
come on. Hey, Jimmie! the Chimney Sweeps. Talk to the Sword.
Shut up, you got a big mouth! Please come help me up, Henny. Max,
come over here . . . French Canadian bean soup . . . I want to pay.
Let them leave me alone. . . .

—Dutch Schultz

The dying man's clothes are ripped off, an intern has slammed her
fist into his chest as hard as she can, and now she starts to push
down on the dying man's breastbone, rhythmically breaking his ribs.
A medical resident sticks a metal hook in the man's mouth and lifts
his head and neck off the table with the hook as he places a large
tube in the man's throat. Another intern sticks a large needle into
the dying man's chest, just below the collar bone; then, cursing, he
pulls it out and sticks it in the dying man's neck. All the while there
is shouting, maybe even laughing. . . .

—James S. Goodwin & Jean S. Goodwin

Poet Emily Dickinson witnessed several, perhaps many, deathbed
scenes. She described herself as having been schooled in "a
science of the grave" by her religious upbringing. How we

behave in our deathbeds is a predictor and perhaps determinant of the fate of our soul. The person who welcomes death is a good candidate for "a heavenly destiny." The person who struggles against death is not ready to go because his or her soul is not at peace with God. "The Dying Eye" is searching for a special Something: a vision indicating that all will be well.

Arthur Flegenheimer was better known as the notorious gangster, Dutch Schultz. He has a secure place in history as one of the most violent killers in an era of violent crime. His deathbed scene took place in Newark City Hospital on October 24, 1935. Burning with a 106 degree fever (secondary to a gunshot wound), Schultz summoned person after person to his rescue. Unlike Dickinson's composed and confident deathbed Christian, Schulz was neither ready for death nor at peace with God. Nevertheless, he, too, was searching for—Something.

Most people say they would prefer to die peacefully, often adding "in my sleep." The violence of a "code" procedure obviously is at odds with this wish. Resuscitation efforts, however, are not intended to assure a peaceful deathbed scene, but to keep the person alive. Sometimes they work.

Deathbed scenes have long been the stuff of poetry, literature, drama, and cinema, as well as a test of religious faith. Images of deathbed scenes (factual, fictional, or some place inbetween) can influence us throughout our lives: "I don't want to die *that* way!" "I hope I can have such a beautiful death."

Four of the most direct ways in which death presents itself to the human mind are integral to the deathbed scene: (a) a pointed reminder of our common and personal mortality; (b) the observable transition from life to death; (c) the person becomes a dead body; and (d) the pain of separation and loss. To put it another way: death is no longer theoretical. The deathbed scene is the border, the edge, the precipice. What strengths do we possess as individuals and what strengths can we draw from companions and culture that can offer comfort and meaning as the deathbed scene runs its course? These are some of the questions raised about the deathbed scene that deserve the attention of psychologists and others concerned with the human condition. We begin with a consideration of the ways in which deathbed scenes are shaped by our own hopes, fears, and mindworkings.

DEATHBED SCENES AS SYMBOLIC CONSTRUCTIONS

Deathbed scenes are enacted in our minds both before and after they occur in the "real world." Anticipated scenes. Remembered scenes. We may anticipate a deathbed scene for days and remember it for years—and yet feel detached or disoriented during the actual episode. Deathbed scenes are symbolic constructions that draw upon both idiosyncratic personal experiences and culturally available themes, events, and meaning fragments. In this sense, the deathbed scene is comparable with a variety of other occasions that bring people together to observe or participate in a shared event. There is no scene quite like a deathbed scene, but all societies have established scenes with which instructive, if limited comparisons can be made, such as initiations, graduations, weddings, and retirements. These ceremonies mark rites of passage and attempt to secure safe conduct from one status (e.g., youth) to another (e.g., adult). The deathbed scene has the potential for being constructed as one of the most significant rites of passage, but often this potential is not realized in practice. A person may die alone. The only human contact before and after the passing may be the rituals required by the medical system. This person may have died not only without significant human contact, but without leaving the trace of a memory, without a story.

We begin here with one example of the way in which the many elements and events that occur over a period of time can become transformed into a deathbed scene.

Creating the Story of a Death

One person is dying. Others are providing care, making observations, communicating, trying to understand what is happening and trying to deal with their own stressful experiences. All these anticipations, observations, communications, and stressors do not of themselves constitute a coherent story of a death. Furthermore, the participants may not have a firm sense of the deathbed scene while it is in progress, and the "same" death might be represented very differently over a period of time.

A Typical Sequence

Here is one typical sequence that I have noticed, primarily from reviewing hospice case histories with the assistance of the nurses who were most closely involved in their care. This is not the only way in which deathbed scenes are constructed, nor is it necessarily the way we should construct them. It is simply a sequence one discovers fairly often when people have been looking after a family member who is in the end stage of a terminal illness.

1.   The dying person is characterized as rejecting nourishment by mouth. Respiration labored. Low-grade fever. Urinary incontinence. Questions raised about adjusting medications: effective symptom control in one sphere might produce side effects in another. Family tense, subdued, looking to each other and to staff for clues as to how to respond. Many isolated observations such as these are made, noted in the record, sometimes shared among the caregivers.

2.   *Slipping away.* "That must be what is happening!" The guiding principle emerges that the dying person will quietly and painlessly ease from life. The family now has a firmer sense of its role: "We should *keep watch,* while professional caregivers preside and consult." Be available. Be caring. But, mostly, watch and wait.

3.   No: that's not what is happening at all. An alternative interpretation has appeared. "There's *crisis* just ahead. Something terrible might happen that we would never forgive ourselves for. But something marvellous might happen also. And it can all depend on us." This change in the story line can be prompted by either a positive or negative development, such as the dying person has become more alert and communicative, or the medications no longer seem to be effective in controlling symptoms. The family must be at full alert, and see to it that the health professionals are also prepared to do all that can be done to influence the course of the struggle.

4.   These alternative constructions—slipping away versus crisis—also take their turns as alternating constructions of the situation. If there are many participants in this scene, we may find some who favor one interpretation and some the other, while a few "swing votes" alter their views whenever there is a new real or apparent development.

5.   Several months after the death, most of the family have agreed upon a fairly stable and consistent construction of the events and their

meaning. Contributing to this stability is the fact that "it's over," thereby providing most of the elements needed for an enduring mental representation. (This stability can be challenged, however, if some discordant and unexpected fact turns up later.) Furthermore, the family survivors are liberated from the pressure of the ongoing events with their ambiguities and uncertainties. Everybody can reflect upon the deathbed scene, no longer being seized by it as an urgency of the moment. (The professional caregivers who were involved will have achieved their own sense of closure, usually more rapidly.)

Storying the Deathbed Scene

This sequence started with a set of factual observations that did not add up to much. Things were happening. Assessments were being made. The dying person was behaving like this; people were feeling like that. There was no dominant story or construction, however. (We are focusing now on the experiential state of the family; the pattern often would differ for the professional caregivers.)

We are seldom at our best when forced to function in a demanding situation without the guidance that a persuasive story, belief, or myth can offer. In this early phase of the sequence, the family is more likely to have difficulty in reconciling "deathbedness" with their ordinary life routines. There is a lack of clear delineation and definition. How should I behave differently? In what ways can I continue to go on with my normal life while "this" is going on? The family at this point is likely to be cautious and inhibited for the most part because the signals are that not clear to them. (This prevailing tendency may well be interrupted when peaks of anxiety occur.)

The "no story" situation seldom lasts very long. We need stories. And we are gifted in the making of stories. The particular sequence described here continued with the emergence of two competing interpretations of the situation: crisis versus slipping away. Some of the observed and agreed-upon facts loaned themselves to either version. However, once the main storylines had been formulated, the participants could emphasize observations that favored either the slipping away or the crisis interpretation. Furthermore, each new development could be evaluated within the frame of both competing stories as the dying person's physical, emotional, and communicational status changed. Given a story—given two radically different stories—the family tends to be more active and purposeful, taking life into its own hands again, even if sometimes at cross-purpose with each other and even with themselves.

The deathbed scene as such does not exist until it has been given the breath of life by the story-maker's imagination, whether one especially persuasive individual or the totality of a group's experience. The *elements* of the deathbed scene are real enough: labored respiration, fever, impaired communication, and so on. It requires an act of narrative imagination, however, to create the overall construction of the deathbed scene. In the sequence we have briefly considered here, the competing stories were seen as though emerging from the participants' ongoing observations and experiences. However, on further analysis we would discover that the central ideas had been preexistent. Our shared culture had already provided the participants with usable symbols and meaning-modules that include *keeping-watch-for-a-slipping-away* and being *on-guard-during-a-crisis*.

Suppose that we met a family member some time after this deathbed scene. Expressing our interest in the experience, we would be likely to hear a coherent narrative in which many of the elements have been preserved. Some aspects and some moments would be given more prominence than others. There would also be a sense of development, conflict, and destination or denouement. The multitudinous observations and experiences would at last have added up to something: to a compact and meaningful symbolic structure. This "package of meaning" would be easier to keep in mind and to share with others, as distinguished from the unstable mixture of elements and experiences that one experiences while the events were in progress. In this sense, the "true deathbed scene" emerged after a preliminary period of selection, choice, and refinement.

Let's take this process one step further. A colleague at work reveals that a person in his or her family has a terminal disease and is not expected to live much longer. The person who has already experienced a death in his or her own household may now be in a position to be helpful as a good listener and companion. The survivor who possesses an authenticated deathbed story ("This really happened to us") might also choose to offer it as a model for others. The colleague with a dying family will then be alerted to certain deathbed scene anticipations. Whether for better or worse (or a little of both), this person may view subsequent developments from a particular framework—and attempt to behave in accordance with this model.

Consider, for example, the caregiving daughter of an elderly hospice patient whose long-absent sister had charged back into the home with the conviction that a deathbed scene was a crisis that must be managed like a five-alarm fire on an oil tanker. This view had been inspired by what she had been told (or what she had taken from) another person's report of a deathbed scene. This "raging inferno" view of the dying process did make things more exciting at home and stimulated thoughts and feelings that might not otherwise have surfaced. Nevertheless, after a period of competition between story-lines, the serenity of the dying person and the low-key competence of the hospice personnel moved the balance toward the slipping away version. The caregiver daughter came away with her own version of the story:

> I had been out of the room just a moment. I was coming back from the kitchen with fresh water, just in case he wanted another sip. And then just like that he died. One moment he looked peacefully asleep. The next moment he was gone. It was almost as though nothing had happened, but now it was all over. The first thought you had was that now nothing more could hurt him, and then you found tears running down your face like they would never stop.

Deathbed scenes are not simple, peripheral, or inconsequential. As symbolic constructions, they enshrine emotionally significant facts and values and become an enduring part of our memories, hopes, fears, and dreams. Additionally, these symbolic constructions can have vital implications for actions that are taken while the dying person is still with us. We will explore this process below through the question: who owns the deathbed scene? First, however, we will find it useful to establish a more balanced approach to deathbed scenes—the quasi-objective perspective that so captivates behavioral scientists. (This, too, is a symbolic construction, of course, but we will pretend not to notice.)

DEATHBED SCENES AS BEHAVIOR SETTINGS

It may seem odd and perhaps even cold to think of deathbed scenes as behavior settings, but so they are, although they are also much more. Here we will consider place; time, timing, and sequence; and people as elements of the deathbed scene.

Place

A deathbed scene occurs in a particular place. The more carefully we identify and observe this place, the better our opportunity to understand what is happening and perhaps even why. Consider this set of alternative descriptions:

- A geriatric facility
- The intensive care unit (ICU) of a geriatric facility
- A private side-room on the ICU of a geriatric facility
- The bed screened off by curtains in a private side-room on the ICU of a geriatric facility.

Although all identify the same behavior setting, they differ markedly in the information provided. I have known many people whose physical deathbed scene could be described by any or all of the above. In the memory of Mrs. G. S., here is the way in which one person's place of death could be reconstructed.

For the purposes of the death certificate, it was sufficient to state that G. S. died at Cushing Hospital, a facility for the aged operated by The Commonwealth of Massachusetts. For public notice, a local newspaper reported that she died in a nursing home. This notice was not quite accurate, and omitted include the name of the particular facility, probably because a death in a state hospital was considered to be not very acceptable. This briefest of behavior setting specifications (either Cushing Hospital or "nursing home") was as much as the public expected or required. There was a psychological subtext, though:

"Who dies?"
"Old people."
"Well, that's a relief. Where do they die?"
"Some place else. Not in our homes, not in our beds."

Bare-bone descriptions, then, suit us well when we do not really want to know too much, and when our main interest is that the scene occurred some place else. For most people, the most significant thing was not the precise scene itself, but its location: right across the town dump, where old age and death could be sequestered behind a chain link fence. Physical boundaries and barriers. Psychological boundaries and barriers.

For contrast, consider the most elaborated of these brief descriptions. The expanded information tells us that Mrs. G. S.'s death had been expected by the staff, or, at least, had not come as a surprise to them. She was at three removes from most other residents of the facility: (1) transferred to ICU, (2) moved to side-room, (3) screened off. Each of these boundary-markers also could be regarded as road markers on the final steps of her life's journey. Separately and accumulatively, they had the double function of providing specialized care for Mrs. G. S., but also of protecting the hospital community at large from her "deathness." Many others would die in the weeks, months, and years ahead. However, it was felt necessary and proper to encapsulate the acute deathness of Mrs. G. S. and thereby keep the rest of the hospital an (illusory) death-free zone. The relatively differentiated description of her physical deathbed scene tells us, then, of a death anticipated, a specialized staff available to provide comfort and care, and an attempt to divide the hospital community into the living and the dying—just as the general community tended to view the facility itself as the place where old people went to die.

At this point it might be tempting to move away from Mrs. G. S.'s death place. It was not a very appealing physical setting: small, clinical, sequestered, apt to make us feel claustrophobic and ill at ease. But isn't that precisely what we must try to identify and understand? The narrow confines of the ICU side-room and the space-taking equipment and supplies severely limited the number of people who can be present. Furthermore, the location—deep within the mediconursing core of the hospital—made it difficult for potential visitors to approach. It was not a casual place, like the dayrooms on "home wards," or the "Times Square" sector with its recreational facilities, coffee shop, and other amenities. One must pass through a boundary of tension into a specialized area in which "civilians" are neither welcome nor comfortable. The location and the parameters of the physical setting often convey information about how the deathbed scene is conceived, who exercises control, and what types of actions and communications are to be countenanced.

We change the setting now. Here is a family home. A man is dying too soon: he was a vigorous person in his early sixties. Nobody in the large, multigenerational and multi-in-lawed family had been prepared for his rapid decline and, now, his imminent death. Let us ignore everything else—as we would not do in the actual situation—and focus upon one physical element. He is dying not just at home, but in the guest room often used by visiting grandchildren. And he is dying not just in that room, but in a bed that has taken on heirloom status after use by several generations of children and grandchildren. Unlike Mrs. G. S, Mr. L. L. was in a physical setting that made it easy for people to come and go. It was a familiar location, and "house rules" rather than "hospital rules" applied. He remained integrated into family patterns of interaction, communication, and affection until the end.

But now he has died. And there's that bed—the bed that he died in. *What is to become of it?* When the family returned home after the funeral, discussion eventually turned to the bed. There was a general feeling that they would have to get rid of it. In fact, the "kids' room" itself had become the "where-Dad-died" room and emotionally off-limits. A surprising thing happened that night. Two grandchildren decided on the spur of the moment to sleep in the death-bed. The next morning they reported that they had felt that Grandfather had been close to them and liked having them there. They also ate a good breakfast. This action had the effect of decontaminating both the room and the bed. They would remain part of the family's shared memory of the deathbed scene, but it had overcome the risk of being exclusively the physical setting of the deathbed scene.

One further example will introduce the concept of "placeness" as a psychological complement to place. The following passage is excerpted from a young woman's depiction of the deathbed scene as she expects it to occur after she has had a long and fulfilling life:

> My death, as I picture it, occurs in my own bedroom, not a hospital room. The surroundings are comfortable and familiar. It seems foolish to me to consider the decor of the room, however that's what pops into my mind first. This I believe reflects my desire to die content. The bed, higher than the average, has a beautiful floral spread with matching sheets and lace pillow cases. The carpet, drapes, and wallpaper are softly colored and create an open and fresh feeling. The atmosphere in the room will be accented by the weather outside. The season is mid-Spring, a sunny morning with a light, warm breeze and birds singing outside. The importance of the type of day to me signifies a sense of freedom or the lifting of burden.

The loving attention to detail is obvious. This young woman is describing a well-imaged scene. Her sense of herself as an individual is affirmed by the particularities—the colors she has selected, the type of day it must be. But the place itself is unknown, indeed, unknowable. She cannot predict where she will be living many years from now (and with a husband she has yet to meet). But she does have a well-developed sense of placeness. The deathbed scene is both located ("my bedroom") and indeterminate (what part of the world?). What really matters is "placeness," the comforting and individual quality of the scene—wherever it might happen to be.

Time, Timing, and Sequence

A deathbed scene moves through time at a particular time. Again, we can choose to notice little or much as the following set of brief examples indicate:

- Mr. W. B. E. died at 10: 30 A.M., September 8, 1985.
- Mr. W. B. E. died at 10:30 A.M., September 8, 1985, *after a long illness.*
- Mr. W. B. E. died at 10:30 A.M., September 8, 1985, after a long illness, *culminated by a farewell scene of nearly 24 hours.*
- Mr. W. B. E. died at 10:30 A.M., September 8, 1985, after a long illness, culminated by a farewell scene of nearly 24 hours *that came at the right time (Mr. W. B. E., wife, and friends Mr. & Mrs. B.), but prematurely for the visiting hospice nurse.*

The first of these reports establishes a coordinate between Mr. W. B. E.'s death and the matrix of public or social time. It is the moment he has left the company of the living, and the moment that a particular behavior setting has become a place of death. This report satisfies bureaucratic requirements for converting Mr. W. B. E. into a statistic, but accomplishes little else. The second report indicates that there had been an extended passage, a period of time in which Mr. W. B. E. lived with his dying. Possibly some or all of this time was shared with others. Possibly there was a scene of parting at the end. Possibly.

Most reports of a death are limited to the first or second types that have been exemplified above. This is true not only of routine newspaper reports, but also of the records maintained by health care providers. Occasionally we will learn that a newsworthy person has died peacefully in the company of three of his or her ex-spouses, a press agent, and Waldo, the wonder pig. Typically, however, the temporal pattern of the death and what might or might not have made it a scene are ignored.

I have reviewed thousands of "closed" as well as current hospital and nursing home charts. Seldom can the reader reconstruct even the most basic elements of the (possible) deathbed scene. Who was with this person as he or she died? Anybody? What type of communications occurred? Did the dying person attempt to speak? Did a nurse—or perhaps a custodian who just happened to wander in—take the dying person's hand? Did a relative pause in the doorway, then turn away with tears in her eyes? *I mean: who was there and what happened?* It is rare that questions such as these can be answered from the available documentation. I have noted this lack of documentation in celebrated research hospitals as well as underfunded and understaffed nursing homes. And, despite its impressive record of health-related research, the Veterans Administration quietly backed away from its promise to conduct a preliminary self-study of deathbed scenes. Left to itself, the U.S. health care system prefers not to notice how people think, feel, and communicate at the point of death. Hospice organizations are not necessarily exceptions to this rule. Although often much more sensitive to the needs of the dying person and the family, hospice staff are apt to feel under pressure to do paperwork necessary to comply with regulations, and have little incentive or training for observing the deathbed scene as such.

The expanded time-of-death descriptions given above are seldom available from medical records and similar sources. We usually learn about deathbed scenes only by having been there ourselves, or by managing to do research despite the numerous obstacles. Some years ago we discovered that a modified psychological autopsy method could help us understand how the last moments might be related both to personality and lifestyle, and to the circumstances and events that a person had moved through as the end approached (Weisman & Kastenbaum, 1968). The many nurses, physicians and other caregivers who participated in this investigative process shared with us in our growing appreciation for the end-phase of human life. We realized (sometimes too late) that having known the person a little better previously could have helped us to offer more sensitive and appropriate care at the time that a behavior setting was becoming a deathbed scene.

But let us continue with Mr. W. B. E. to see how closer attention to time, timing, and sequence can alert us to the significance of a deathbed scene. The hospice nurse was taken aback when he crossed Mr. W. B. E.'s threshold for the first time. An enormous polar bear rushed at him, toothy jaws agape. Fortunately, the bear's attack was restrained by its placement in the wall. Mr. W. B. E. had been a vigorous and independent-minded man who spent many years hunting, trapping, and prospecting. Now in his mid-seventies and exhausted by his battle with cancer, he had become house-bound and reconciled to death. "I've had a great life," he told the nurse, "no regrets." Following the initial examination, Mr. W. B. E. had first one and then another request for the nurse. "Can you talk my doctor into letting me drink a shot of whiskey now and then?" This was quickly accomplished. "Thanks. Now I want you to promise that you'll take a last snort with me when I croak." The nurse, a very light drinker, agreed that he would join the clan (patient, wife, and another couple who had been friends for years) in a "last snort" if circumstances permitted. ("I prayed it wouldn't be in the early morning hours when so many seem to pass away: a shot of whisky at that hour might finish me, too!")

Consider what has already been brought forward in this situation: The dying person has conceived of his own deathbed scene and is making plans for it. This is not to be a scene in which the central player intends to be unaware or passive. Furthermore, he has a devoted "supporting cast." Wife and friends indicate that they are with him all the way. There *is* to be a deathbed scene, and it is to be scripted or constructed in advance. And it is to be a sort of celebration—of the way one man has chosen to live and end his life, affirmed and amplified by his closest companions. Ensuing contacts made it clear that the old friends had moved in with the couple for a "last house party" that would signify the end of an era for all of them. Everybody seemed ready for Mr. W. B. E.'s death, except the nurse. Impressed by the patient's resilience and, perhaps, not yet willing to let him go, the nurse believed that he would hold on for some time yet.

All too soon (from the nurse's perspective) his beeper signalled a call from Mr. W. B. E.'s wife. They had been gathered around the dying man for nearly 24 hours, telling the old stories together, but it looked as though there wasn't much time left. The old man was pleased to see that the nurse had returned to keep his promise. "Fix the drinks, lover." As his wife placed a drink in every hand, all except the nurse burst out with an X-rated toast to the good life. The old man winked and died.

This concluded the deathbed scene as anticipated. But there was more to come. The nurse performed the obligatory ritual of checking the man's vital signs and confirming his death (to be later certified by a physician). Another action remained to be taken. Unlike thoughts and communications about death, a deathbed scene results in a corpse, and something must be done with it. The nurse placed a call. Some time later, two men arrived at the door, their business vehicle parked outside. As they approached the bed and started to place hands on the corpse, the deceased's "good old buddy" halted them: "Say, what's the rush? Can't you see he hasn't finished his drink?" Sure enough, there was the shot glass still in the dead man's grip, and still containing whiskey. "A man in his condition needs a little extra time to finish his drink. You can see that for yourself!" The two men retreated in confusion and sat in their van for a while. When they returned, they noticed that there was now only a drop left in the whiskey glass. Again they started to take the corpse, but again were angrily confronted by the buddy. "One last sip—can't you wait for his last little snip! What kind of guys are you, anyhow!" After a longer interval, the two men ventured to return again, saw that the glass was now empty, and removed the corpse without further incident.

The rough humor of this incident was viewed by Mr. W. B. E.'s wife and friends as a lively performance of his deathbed scene that he would have heartily appreciated (although a view not likely to have been shared by the corpse handlers). Whether the reader responds with outrage or amusement to this incident, it does represent the type of deathbed scene that is at least partially crafted in advance and requires the willing participation of others. Time is important in the prepared deathbed scene, time to anticipate and prepare. Timing and sequence also matter. Had the hospice nurse entered the picture a little later, for example, he might not have become so much a part of the unfolding scenario. The deathbed scene, like any other, is vulnerable to unexpected events, coincidents, and breakdowns. It is also subject to variant interpretations: such as the death coming too soon from the perspective of the nurse, but not the man and his companions; and the total scene appearing either appropriate (insider's view) or bizarre (outsider's view).

Satisfaction with the knowledge that "Mr. W. B. E. died at 10: 30 A.M., September 8, 1985" would have deprived us of the opportunity to "witness" this rather elaborate and unique deathbed scene and the story that the old prospector started and his friends completed.

People

A deathbed scene could involve only one person. Many people have died alone, whether far from others or socially isolated. Usually, we do not know what was experienced by the person who died without companionship. Occasionally, however, we are given access to some of the person's last thoughts:

> Lay in bed . . . all day.
> Life? is so boreing. Back into the same rut. No lights in Chev. Joe has got car. Truck wont start, stereo quit, caint sleep. Women left me. I feel like shit. (Leenaars, 1988, p. 237)

and

> My love for you has always been the deepest and hopefully I'll see you again. You are my miracle. I have accepted the lord Jesus as my saviour but I know that he wouldn't condone this. I accept the just dues and pray that maybe you wont hurt anymore. Make our kid something! You and Jesus I pray can forgive me for copping out. . . . If I see mom I'll see that Joe is taken care of + I will try to be with him too! . . . Eternity is the best way of saying how long I (?) love you. . . . May the lord bless + keep you + forgive me for something I have no earthly rights to do. (Leenaars, p. 241)

These suicide notes tell us that their authors were not entirely alone. They may have been the only visible person in their behavior setting, but in their minds they were playing scenes that involved other people. Both facts are significant: (a) the person was alone; (b) the person thought and experienced as though interacting with others. The second note is especially rich with its inclusion of "you," "our kid," "Jesus," "mom," and "Joe." If all scenes are symbolic constructions, then all begin in the mind, whether or not they also "play" in shared time-place.

Reports of Near-Death Experiences (NDEs) often describe interactions that seem to have been locked within the individual's private experiences. The individual later may report encounters with his or her own unresponsive body or with a "spiritual being of light." Even if there are other persons within the same physical setting, they will not have detected and probably will not have suspected that this vivid scene had been enacted.

There have been numerous reports of people emerging from a deep and sometimes prolonged period of unresponsiveness. Sometimes one has the impression that they did have interactions and experiences within their own phenomenological spheres even though these were denied expression. Sacks (1968) has described dramatic examples of this type among people who were stricken by encephalitis at the end of World War I and then regained their minds when successfully treated many years later. A study of our own that was reported in previous editions of *The Psychology of Death* is also germane. Three student research assistants made two-daily observations for a 3-day period on more than 200 hospitalized geriatric patients. Four types of low-level behavior syndrome were established on the basis of these observations. The lowest level syndrome was characterized by the following set of observations:

Type I

1. In bed
2. Supine
3. Mouth open
4. Eyes closed or with empty stare
5. Head tilted back
6. Arms straight at side
7. Absence of adjustive movements, fidgeting, speech, verbalizations, etc.
8. General impression of having been placed or molded into position.

As can be seen, there was virtually no behavior to describe. People who consistently fit into this category appeared to be static objects within their behavior settings.

A simple behavioral intervention was carried out for patients in all of the low level behavior categories. One member of the observational team would slowly approach the patient, then take the patient's hand

and hold it gently, introduce him or herself, and speak to the patient by name. This intervention was repeated twice a day for 3 days. Nearly half of the Type I and Type II patients responded to such an extent that they were reclassified into a higher category; a "priming effect" was observed in which the repeated brief contacts seemed to increase the patient's readiness to respond to a subsequent contact. Apparently the prolonged lack of interpersonal stimulation had contributed to their nonresponsive orientation, although all were also neurologically impaired as well.

Of particular interest here was a transitional phenomenon that was not mentioned in the earlier report. In "coming up," some patients behaved as though they had been engaged in a continuing interaction with the contact person. We had the impression that a kind of "shadow play" interaction had been taking place, at least sporadically, within the minds of these previously unresponsive people prior to their "awakening." For example, an old man who had not been known to speak in the past several weeks responded to a research assistant's hand-embrace on her third visit. He pressed her hand, stared at her for a moment, and then spoke to her comfortably as "Irene." For several minutes he nodded and chatted with perhaps the same Irene he had been visiting with previously in his clouded reveries.

Often we have no way of knowing whether or not an unresponsive person is still experiencing life at some level. It is virtually impossible to rule out the null hypothesis: lack of responsiveness does not prove lack of phenomenological experience. We do know that many people have reported having had experiences while apparently nonresponsive after they have recovered from a life-threatening condition. Awareness of this possibility has prompted some nurses, physicians, and other caregivers to speak with a nonresponsive dying person as though this person were still capable of experiencing and understanding. And many of us who have had experiences with anesthesia can recall that "in between" state of mind in which our thoughts and interactions move across an unstable boundary between fantasy and reality.

A dying person may also experience private or phenomenological deathbed scenes in addition to events that actually occur in shared time-place. An old woman (in the same geriatric hospital) was as lucid and well oriented as ever despite her declining health. Two days before her death, she said her good-byes to her visiting sister and brother-in-law while I also happened to be with her. She set aside their objections that she was not about to die by reporting a dream from the night before: mother, father, and the whole family had been there by her bedside which was also, at the same time, the old family homestead in Wyoming. Everything was going to be fine. They were keeping a place for her. This woman had a controlled and "proper little deathbed scene" with her living kin, but also a more expansive and heartening deathbed scene on the level of dream-experience.

Emily Dickinson was never able to satisfy her curiosity when she sat by a dying person who seemed to be thinking and feeling Something and even interacting with Somebody. The same is true today. I have little doubt that some of the dying people I have been with were experiencing a meaningful interaction that was beyond my power to observe. Perhaps that is just as it should be.

Nevertheless, when we think of a deathbed scene we are most likely to visualize one or more intimate companions gathered around the dying person in "real" time and place. Being with the right people is often specified as the most desired component of the deathbed scene. Terminally ill people who have selected the hospice care option give high priority to having the companionship of one or more people who are precious to them. Sometimes there is a core person whose presence is sought on a continuous basis, while others are to be seen, farewelled, and then encouraged to depart. It is not unusual for a terminally ill person to express the wish that a certain person *not* be included ("How can I die in peace if She is strutting around, giving orders and putting on airs!").

One of the best studies on farewelling was conducted by Australian sociologists Allan Kellehear and Terry Lewin (1988–1989). They found that 81 of 100 terminally ill cancer patients expressed the desire for a leave-taking opportunity with people who were significant to them. Not everybody intended to wait for the last minute; some had already said their farewells or were planning to do so well before the end. Those who preferred a relatively early farewell scene were usually motivated by the desire to do so while they were still in relatively good health. Another advantage seen in the early farewelling was the opportunity to give little gifts and remembrances: one woman, for example, made many small dolls while she lay abed and gave these to friends on their last visit.

However, the classic vision of a farewell scene in their final hour was contemplated by most (73) of Kellehear and Lewin's respondents.

They often wanted to have their very last words with their spouse, children, and closest friends. But why did some people prefer not to have farewell scenes, either early or late? Mostly, they did not want to upset themselves or other people: "From these persons' viewpoints, final farewells would make 'the end' too intense and dramatic, over-drawing attention to the fact of imminent death" (Kellehear & Lewin, p. 285). Two respondents felt that there was no point to having a farewell scene because they would be meeting each other again in the afterlife. As though agreeing with this logic, two other people who described themselves as nonreligious declared that that was no point in saying good-bye because they would not be saying hello again.

The individual differences reported in this study are worth keeping in mind. If we assumed that everybody wants to have a deathbed scene, we might inadvertently force this arrangement upon those who would prefer to end their lives without a conspicuous final scene. It is also possible that some people would discover that they really do want the comfort, affection, and companionship of a farewell scene after they have had the opportunity to express and revise the negative scenario that has been troubling them.

A thorough discussion of the people-dimension of deathbed scenes would also take into account such factors as:

- Barriers to being together: such as, a roomful of bulky and noisy equipment; intrafamily conflict; competing responsibilities, such as child care; travel time and expense, and so on.
- Unresolved problems in the relationship between the dying person him or herself and others, such as, disapproval of the other person's lifestyle, recriminations over past misdeeds.
- The place of the dying person within the entire family and friend-ship configuration, such as, is this the king or queen pin of the entire network, or somebody who had been "written off" by the family many years ago, and so forth?
- The personal meanings and implications of the death for the survivors, such as, is this person dying of an illness to which others believe themselves vulnerable; is this person's suffering perceived as a foretaste of what others will undergo when their time comes?

We will give further consideration to the people-dimension of the deathbed scene in much of what follows.

WHO OWNS THE DEATHBED SCENE?

This question offers us a way of looking at some of the uncertainties, ambiguities, and conflicts that arise around deathbed scenes today. Paradoxically, it is when life and death become most concrete, palpable, and immediate that fantasies, imaginings, and dogmas are also likely to escape their leash. The drawn face resting on the pillow is real and immediate in a way that "death talk" is not.

Here we will consult several deathbed scenes and give particular attention to the concepts of perceived control, efficacy, and comprehension, all of which figure mightily in the contest for ownership of the deathbed scene. We are especially keen to grasp control when we feel it slipping away, to demonstrate efficacy when we sense helplessness, and to proclaim understanding when we are but a gasp away from bewilderment. Everything that the deathbed scene threatens to take away from us—composure, security, comfort, power—we may seek to replace through culturally available compensatory devices or idiosyncratic improvisations. The deathbed scene also tempts those who would take advantage of another person's helplessness for sake of their own ego gratification. A few examples follow.

Moral Claims

Deathbed scenes have had a long association with religious belief and practice. The early Christian message emphasized triumph over death. By the thirteenth century, however, the dread of damnation had become more vivid to many believers (Aries, 1981). The deathbed scene became regarded as a spiritual crisis. Would the poor sinner be condemned to unremitting torment or was salvation still possible? "Life's final moments . . . took on a new intensity" (Le Goff, 1984). The fundamental idea of the deathbed scene *as* a scene owes much to this intensification of fear/hope dynamics some 8 centuries ago. The deathbed scene was no longer simply the expected and natural "tag end" of life, but had become a "final exam" that determined our grade and fate.

This view had retained its power 400 years later when Jeremy Taylor wrote his classic *Rules and Exercises for Holy Dying* (1651).

The exercise he proposed was more formidable than any latter day aerobic work-out program: we must think each day of that moment when our life will end and become subject to divine judgment. "He that would die well, must all the days of his life measure up against the day of death." Specifically, he recommended that as we lie down to sleep at the end of each day we conduct a diligent examination of our actions, "the disorders of every day, the multitude of impertinent words, the great portions of time spent in vanity. . . . " Each day was a life in microcosm, and each evening a rehearsal for the last fall of darkness. The expected deathbed scene had become perhaps even more salient in our minds than the final scene itself.

Our major example here comes from a point less distant in time. We are in 19th-century London, a tumultuous city caught up in the raging industrialism that offered new opportunities but also left many physical and psychological casualties. John Warton, doctor of divinity, will publish a set of three posthumous volumes entitled *Death-Bed Scenes* (1826). He is on his way to one of them now. Warton does not know Mr. Marsden, nor has the dying man invited him, but this is of no consequence for he knew himself to be "a humble instrument in God's hands for the accomplishment of his gracious purposes of love and mercy."

Warton observes that Marsden's "nose was pinched, as if by the hand of death; and, if he had been still he might well have been supposed to be a corpse. But there was something at work within him, which would not let him rest for a single moment. He turned his face from side to side . . . and his eyes betokened enquiry and alarm." This "piteous sight" instantly convinces Warton that the dying man had either been abandoned by wife and daughter who must have fled from his forbidding countenance, or that he had banished them himself. (Neither hypothesis has to be checked against reality: as usual, Warton understands a situation perfectly the moment he beholds it.)

The interaction begins with Warton's comment, "I am truly sorry, Sir, to see you in so deplorable a condition." Marsden answers immediately and sternly: "Why to be sure, this room is not a fine one, nor am I lying in a fine bed." Impregnable to ironic humor, Warton delivers a verbose explanation of what he had meant, concluding with reference to "this grievous disease, which seems to have brought you almost to death's door, and this uneasiness of mind which again makes you so restless."

These solicitous comments enrage the dying man who snaps: "You know nothing about my mind, whether it is uneasy or not. What business have you here, to make observations upon *me*? Who sent for you? I'm sure I didn't—what you are come for?" These foolish questions do not provoke the gentle doctor of divinity. He offers to forgive the dying man for his intemperate response and adds that "at such an awful time as this . . . the mind should be set quite at ease with respect to all worldly affairs; and every moment should be devoted to the thinking of God, and of your Saviour, and of the world to come which will have no end."

Marsden, whose heart is proving as "impenetrable as the granite-rock," does not leap to the invitation offered by his unscheduled visitor. In fact, he mutters to himself, "They pretend that you have a right to plague us, when we might die quietly without you." Warton just keeps on talking. When he pauses for breath a moment, the dying man seizes the opportunity to speak his own mind: "Now you have had your say, now you may go; I want none of your help for body or soul."

For a moment, Warton is too shocked to reply, but he recovers and warns Marsden of his "terrible danger," "fearful precipice," and a plunge into an "eternity of woe." He even favors the dying man with one of his favorite phrases: "O think, whilst God spares you time to think, think what it is to die, and *he* your enemy!" Surprisingly, Marsden does not warm to these comforting words. "None of your preaching, away with it! You would be kind to me, you say; be gone then! That is the only kindness for which I will thank you. Go to those who will listen. . . . "

Warton responds valiantly to this challenge. He speaks lovingly of fire and brimstone, gnawing worms, stinging scorpions, and furious devils "exulting in the torments which they will inflect upon you." This impassioned oration has a tremendous effect—upon Warton himself, who bursts into tears at the beauty of his words. Marsden? "Have done with your whining and your jibber-jabber. I hate all your trumpery." But no such ingratitude can deter the doctor of divinity once he is well launched into his mission. He continues to barrage the dying man with visions of the judgment that God will surely bring against him and the horrible suffering that will follow. Warton works diligently to "make him condemn himself out of his own mouth . . . " a technique that is "generally product in the end. . . . "

Warton's account of his word barrage against the dying man goes on page after bruising page. Marsden never gives in, so Warton eventually turns away "slowly and reluctantly from the sickbed." Still persistent, he confronts the wife and daughter, doing his best to bully them into awakening the fear of God's retribution in the dying man. He reports partial success with this strategy because, after a while, "Mrs. Marsden trembled exceedingly." Continuing to give unstintingly of himself, Warton returns to belabor the dying man and his family again until the very moment of his death ("He expired with a single but a terrible groan!"). Warton uses this occasion to fall upon his knees and ask grace "for ourselves, that we may live well, and die happily."

Warton offered testimonies such as these to posterity, firm in the conviction that his moral claims justified any stratagem one found necessary to employ in the deathbed scene. It was proper to wear the dying person down with long, convoluted, and impassioned argument. It was proper to shame, threaten, and condemn. It was proper to ignore the dying person's or family's own ideas, values, experiences, and needs—what could these matter when compared with the "dreadful spectacle" of eternal torment? Although many of the other dying people visited by Warton also resisted his advances, he never seemed to pause for once and wonder, "maybe this person's right; maybe I should respect his/her own wishes."

Warton's example may appear extreme, but he is not the only person who has been armed with the belief that he or she possesses the right, and the obligation to change other people's lives as they lay dying. He is valuable to us today as the protagonist of a cautionary tale—to what excesses moral arrogance can lend itself. A person as steadfastly locked inside his own beliefs as Warton would not find welcome in a hospice program. Dame Cicely Saunders, founder of the modern hospice movement, has set the pattern by providing opportunity for faith to be affirmed and expressed spontaneously and in an infinite variety of ways. Indeed, it was a dying Jewish man who she credits as inspiring her to start the hospice movement in earnest (Saunders, 1993), and her influential care programs provide benefits to people with a broad spectrum of religious beliefs, including agnostics and atheists. In keeping with this philosophy, it has been found that hospice volunteers often pray—but privately, for their own guidance and spiritual well-being (Schneider & Kastenbaum, 1993). They would be appalled at a modern-day Warton who tried to thrust himself upon dying patients and their families.

Religious and moral positions have become increasingly salient in recent years with the emergence of the physician-assisted death controversy. There are people of faith on both sides of the controversy, including those health care personnel who would and those who would not participate in actions to foreshorten a person's life by active euthanasia. The religious and moral facets of assisted death are stimulating many people to rethink their own beliefs about the meaning of life in general. The psychologist's approach to the deathbed scene should be illuminated by awareness of the religious and moral issues involved (Leone, 1998; Wekesser, 1995).

Professional, Bureaucratic, and Legalistic Claims

Ownership of the deathbed scene has been passing from the moralist to the professional and the bureaucrat. Unlike Warton, today's "proprietors" seldom lecture or proselytze. Instead, they rely on standard operating procedure: "This is how we do things around here." The social psychology of the deathbed scene now has less to do with shared cultural values than with principles of organizational communication and behavior keyed to cost effective measures. The individual psychology has shifted from the personality and motivation of the caregiver to the ability to cope with conflicting demands in the time-pressured situations that have intensified with the complexity and financial stakes of current health care systems.

Consider one common behavioral sequence: a nurse enters the hospital room of a terminally ill patient and monitors the machines before even looking at the patient's face. Does this mean that the nurse values technology and bureaucracy more than people? And does it perhaps also mean that this nurse has deep emotional conflicts about relating to dying people? Probably not. People who relate more to machines than to people and who are unable to care for those in great need usually are not attracted to bedside nursing. It is far more likely that this behavioral sequence is but one of many in which nurses are expected to set aside their own feelings and values. The priorities and pressures of the health care system impose themselves upon almost everything the nurse does. Individual differences remain important, of course. Some nurses "vote with their feet" by abandoning their careers because they experience too much stress or find themselves too often in conflict with the standard operating procedure. We would often be far wide of the mark if we interpreted the behavior or nurses (and others) in the deathbed scene in terms of their individual motivation and personality dynamics when, in fact, they are responding to work environment pressures.

Here are a few further examples of the ways in which professional, bureaucratic, and legalistic claims influence the contemporary deathbed scene.

Workable Dead

A paramedic recounts some of his recent experiences.

> . . . a suicide in Sun City. He was about 73 years old. He'd had a very extensive history of chronic obstructive pulmonary disease. He took a 44-magnum, stuck it in the roof of his mouth, and just splashed his entire skull all over the headboard and the wall of this home. The wife had called us. There was a fire department on the scene who had started cardiopulmonary respiration on the gentleman. They had not done any of the advanced skills because they didn't have paramedics. But they called us; we landed (our helicopter) in the street. We go in there. I mean: this guy is dead. I mean, he is big time dead. They had been doing CPR on him for 35–40 minutes, and we had no choice at that point but to continue to put IVs in him, intubate what was left of his head, and all of the other things that we had to do.

This paramedic estimates that he had been in similar situations "hundreds, hundreds of times." Sometimes these were deathbed scenes in the literal sense; but people also die on the highway, in restaurants, and many other places. Whatever the location, the paramedic may be required to start or continue futile interventions. Several of the paramedics we interviewed have described these people as "the workable dead." There is no doubt in the paramedic's mind that this person is dead. There is no fantasy about heroic measures, either at the site or at the hospital, that might restore life. Yet the paramedic is obliged to carry out procedures upon "the workable dead" or risk serious legal repercussions. Many a person who has died at home in bed has become subject to postmortem interventions at the hands of paramedics who fervently wished they did not have to perform them.

"People panic, and they call us," another paramedic commented. "By the time we get there, they realize that their husband or grandmother or whatever is dead, and they are starting to adjust to it. The wife will scream, 'Don't do that to him.' But I have no choice about it."

This bizarre-sounding concept—"the workable dead"—represents an extreme interpretation of the situation in which some people pass from life to death. We often think of denial as a defensive strategy that is resorted to by individuals who are faced with overwhelming stress. But here is a form of denial that is supported by law, regulations, and the standard operating procedures of sophisticated health care providers—and that requires the enactment of ritualistic behavior upon a corpse. The fact that there is a reason for "working the dead" does not obscure its bizarre features nor its psychological effects on those who must perform and those who must witness the procedures.

And the reason? Choose between "don't let the slightest chance for recovery slip by;" "we have the equipment and personnel, so we have to use them;" and "prevent malpractice suits." All these influences operate to prevent or sharply reduce the exercise of good judgment by the people who are actually on the scene. Laws and regulations are tailored for the general pattern of human behavior: but we die as individuals in unique situations. Whenever a general rule gains priority over informed judgment within the situation, there the dying person and his or her companions lose a significant degree of freedom. (In some parts of the nation it is now possible to avoid "working the dead." In the Phoenix area one can complete a form and wear an orange arm band that signifies the individual's wish not to have such measures taken. Kansas has authorized the wearing of a Medic Alert bracelet for the same purpose. It would be well to check with local health authorities to determine if such provisions apply in your city or county. The situation of enforced interventions can also be avoided if family members are accepting of the life-threatened person's desire to be allowed to die when the time comes and therefore do not immediately call for paramedical assistance. Obviously, mutual trust and good communication skills are required for consideration of this alternative.)

Code Blue

This chapter opened with an excerpt from a vivid description of a medical team's attempt to save the life of a dying man. Goodwin and

Goodwin (1985) portray the "code blue" scene as it really is: not a cool, orderly demonstration of medical science, but a noisy scramble in which a crowded roomful of people seem to be engaged in violent assault upon a defenseless victim. This type of scene is both more and less distressing than the paramedic's encounter with the workable dead. Family members or passersby may be disturbed by the sight of paramedics carrying out procedures in full view. The measures taken by physicians and nurses after cardiac or respiratory arrest may be even more invasive and violent, but there is no audience of laypeople to be traumatized.

There is irony here. For many years, hospitals were feared as places in which it was all too easy to die. Today, and especially in major medical centers, it can be very difficult to die. The deathbed scene is becoming an option that must be exercised in advance. The living will came into existence as an instrument for avoiding aggressive and invasive interventions that have little likelihood of prolonging sentient and meaningful life. Some physicians and ethicists have been devising advance directives that are more specific than the living will and therefore might improve the likelihood of the individual's wishes being respected at the critical time (Last Acts, Web site). For example, a physician might order insertion of a feeding tube even though the patient has completed a living will document. Providing water and nutrition to a dying person is regarded by some health care providers as an attempt to prolong life, while others regard it instead as a way of making the final days more comfortable. Because of such ambiguities, a person may not experience the deathbed scene that had been envisioned, but, instead, become embedded in a prolonged life-support operation. Furthermore, advance directives may be overlooked entirely in the haste of the moment, and with new people on the scene.

What is the psychology of crisis intervention here? Why do physicians, nurses, and technicians rush to perform emergency resuscitation procedures? Why is a person deprived of the comfort and serenity that seems to be provided by a traditional companionate deathbed scene? We do not have an adequate answer to these questions, but I would suggest systematic attention to the following components of the situation.

1. *The excitement of crisis.* Emergency room personnel and paramedics often speak of the "high" or "rush" they feel when called

upon to exercise their skills in life-or-death situations. This direct psychophysiological reward—a sense of being intensely alive and challenged—may help them to continue with an otherwise stressful occupation. Some health care professionals prefer routine work. But some become "hooked on crisis." They are not indifferent to the outcomes of their efforts, but the intensity and excitement of all-out intervention can become an overriding factor.

2. *The element of suspense.* Will this person live or die? The question may be indeterminate for a brief and eventful period of time. Mere spectators become engrossed in observing a sporting event or a detective film because the outcome is not known in advance. How much more involved we become when we ourselves are active participants and the suspense centers around the life or death of an actual person who is here in our midst. The fact that a person sometimes *is* brought back from the brink of death establishes a pattern of anticipated reinforcements that is highly resistant to extinction. Did this patient die despite our best efforts? Have all emergency resuscitation efforts failed in the past few weeks? These negative outcomes will not stand in the way of response to the next code. The emergency response team knows that some people have been saved and others will be saved: no succession of negative outcomes is likely to undermine the staff's aperiodic reinforcement schedule.

3. The hospital is not regarded as an appropriate location for a deathbed scene. Technology and economy have both dictated that hospital stays should be brief. Emphasis should be given to assessment and treatment procedures that qualify under the prevailing cost guidelines. The modern hospital is no place for a person to be. It is a place of passage, more comparable to an airport terminal than a home. With a few exceptions, the hospital is not hospitable to any scenes (and those exceptions are largely under the control of the hospital itself). Staff are apt to feel either role-less of in role conflict if a family bedside scene develops. A deathbed scene just does not compute in the elaborate system of authorized services and fees.

Some people who are the subjects of resuscitation efforts would not have had anything resembling a deathbed scene even if these efforts had been withheld. For example, a person might suffer an unexpected cardiac arrest while seeming to be recovering from a surgical procedure. Even more unexpectedly, a code blue situation might arise while a person is undergoing routine diagnostic testing. In situations such as these, there may have been no basis for assuming the person's life was in imminent danger. There was no reason for the family to draw together around the bedside. Without emergency interventions, the person would have died immediately from a sudden collapse of vital functions. The intervention may or may not succeed, but, in either event, it was not the intervention but the sudden onset that deprived the individual and his or her family of the opportunity for a time together.

Attenuated Life, Attenuated Death

The paramedic's encounter with "the workable dead" can occur any place in the community; the "code blue" emergency procedure is enacted within a hospital room. In both instances, strenuous interventions are central to the scene. There is seldom time or opportunity for anything resembling a traditional deathbed scene. However, many other people die "sceneless" although there had been opportunity for human interactions and a final leave-taking. Often such endings have involved the attenuation of both life and death. The person is seen as being markedly impaired and in a nonreversible situation. The confused old woman in the nursing home will never again be young and vital. It is just a matter of when she will finally draw her last breath. The young man who left home on his motorcycle has been gone for weeks; it is only his body that receives the benefits of the respirator and the intravenous feeding.

There are three obvious reasons for the fact that most people in such situations do not have deathbed scenes: (a) they are most often placed in a hospital or custodial care facility rather than kept at home; (b) their actual or perceived inability to communicate tends to reduce the inclination of other people to interact with them; and (c) their plight could continue for an indeterminate period of time.

The geriatric patients who were classified as exhibiting "low level behavior syndromes" have had millions of counterparts throughout the nation during the succeeding years. An institutionalized aged person may be deprived of the opportunity for a death bed scene even if he or she is not unresponsive or confused. All too many reside in facilities whose staff has little training, time, or incentive for meeting the psychological and spiritual needs of the residents. The inadequate patterns of resident-resident, resident-staff, and resident-visitor communication do not provide a foundation for developing any meaningful scenes, including the final scene of life. There are more exceptions to this rule today, thanks to an influx of enlightened directors and staff and to a greater awareness of the needs of dying people. Nevertheless, each day many old men and women slip away without a companion at their bedsides.

Some people are maintained on life-support systems for a relatively short period of time at some point in their treatment. They recover, fully or partially, and go on with their lives. It is not accurate, then, to equate intensive life-support procedures with a "persistent vegetative state" (vital functions are maintained, but there appears to be neither cognitive function nor potential for recovery). Deathbed scenes seldom occur for those who die after a period of intensive life support. It is more typical for the person's death to be discovered during a routine visit by a nurse or technician. For other people, it is more a question of medical judgment and discretion: a nonresponsive patient is certified as dead this morning, a decision that could have been made yesterday or postponed until tomorrow.

There is a greater opportunity for a deathbed scene when a decision has been made to withdraw or forego life-support procedures. However, the outcome is not always as expected. This can be illustrated through two young women and their families whose tragedies attracted national attention, influenced public opinion, and came under judicial review. Karen Anne Quinlan did not recover consciousness after she lapsed into a drug-induced coma (a preliminary diagnosis that was later disputed and never fully resolved). Her parents maintained hope for recovery for nearly half a year, although the young woman had suffered severe brain damage and wasted away to about 60 pounds. Eventually they accepted the counsel of a priest who declared that it is not morally necessary to employ extraordinary means to prolong life.

At this point, the Quinlans were psychologically prepared to take leave of their (adopted) daughter. They had absorbed the shock of her sudden incapacitation, drawn support from their religious faith, and started the preparatory process known as anticipatory grief (Rando, 1989). The Quinlans asked the physicians to turn off the respirator. Instead of an interminable period of attenuated life/attentuated death, there could now be a time-limited, decisive ending. The

Quinlans could be with Karen Anne as she slipped away, and then fully grieve her death. But their request was denied. This refusal was based on the observation that Karen Anne was not "brain dead." There was still some electrical activity that could be detected through EEG tracings, although this activity was very weak. She was described as existing in a persistent vegetative state (and, for the first time, this term was introduced to the general public). The Quinlans then asked the courts to override the physicians' judgment, and in doing so invoked an argument based upon religious freedom. The court decided otherwise. Medical knowledge and opinion should prevail. And so, Karen Anne remained on the life-support system, and the Quinlans were faced with a continuation of their own stressful situation.

Who owned the deathbed scene in this instance?

- The person whose own life and death was at issue could not make her own claim because of severe incapacitation.
- The family had brought its claim forward, only to be rejected by two sets of authorities: the medical and the legal establishments.
- Freedom of religious expression had also been rejected as a decisive claim, although this right is considered basic to the American way of life.
- Although nurses provide most of the services and carry out most of the interactions with total care patients, there is no evidence that the experiences, thoughts, feelings, and opinions of the nurses were even given a hearing.

In this landmark case the ownership of the deathbed scene had been determined at two levels. The physician seemed to be confirmed as the rightful owner because of (assumed) superior knowledge. However, the judge emerged as representing an even more basic power: it was the court that decided in favor of the physician. Less visible but not less active behind the scenes was the hospital administration. The potential deathbed scene was a small part of the total sociophysical environment that comprised the hospital. The court decision had the effect of affirming a variation on the right of the landlord. When admitted to a hospital, a person should abide by the prevailing laws and regulations of the realm. Health care administrators (and their lawyers) around the nation could breathe a little easier: their prevailing policies seem to have been supported in this first court test.

This conclusion, however, was not to remain conclusive. An appeal was made to the New Jersey Supreme Court. This time, the judiciary found a different basis for decision. It was no longer the question of whether or not some flickering signs of life remained. The critical question was whether or not Karen Anne had a reasonable chance of regaining consciousness. The respirator could be removed, with court approval, if physicians agreed that the young woman could not recover consciousness. But this was not the only change. More than a year after she lapsed into coma, Karen Anne was removed from the respirator. Now, finally, there could be a true ending, a final being-with the lost young woman, and the belated opportunity for the Quinlans to move on with their own lives. Everybody's assumption was proven wrong: Karen Anne did not die. Although she remained as unresponsive and incapacitated as ever, her vital functions continued after the respirator was removed. There was no deathbed scene, no closure. Transferred to a skilled nursing home, Karen Anne remained in a vegetative state for more than 10 years until succumbing to pneumonia (June 11, 1985). Both her life and her death had become so attentuated over so long a period of time that the final cessation passed virtually without notice.

Many other people have been trapped in persistent vegetative states since the Quinlans' ordeal began. Their stories have had various conclusions, but have frequently generated questions about ownership of the deathbed scene and complications in the grieving/mourning process. We will consider only the recent case of Nancy Curzan. Victim of an automobile accident on January 11, 1983, this young woman had been attached to a life support system for almost 8 years. Physicians were in agreement that she would never recover consciousness and, as with Karen Anne, Nancy had also wasted away and developed contractures. The family asked to have her feeding tube removed; the request was denied. For the first time, the U.S. Supreme Court accepted the challenge of ruling on a right-to-die situation. By the closest of margins (5-4), the court rejected the family's appeal to override the opposition of the local hospital authorities and the State of Missouri. As in previous court rulings, sympathy was expressed for the family members. However, the court held that there was not sufficient evidence that the young woman had ever expressed her wishes regarding termination of life support efforts. The overall decision confirmed the validity of advance directives such as the living will, but at the same time rejected the argument that others knew what Nancy Curzan would have wanted done.

Again, a court decision did not result in the most expectable outcome. A local probate judge decided that there had been enough information brought forward to indicate that family and friends knew what Nancy Curzan would have herself chosen in this circumstance. He gave permission for removal of the feeding tube. Attorneys for the State of Missouri chose not to contest this decision. However, others did protest. A throng of protesters, not identified by the media, entered public areas of the Missouri Rehabilitation Center to demand that the feeding tube be reinstated. Some kneeled and prayed; others blocked a fire exit stairwell and were arrested. The philosophy of the protesters was not clearly articulated through media reports, including television coverage. Nevertheless, it was apparent that they were acting upon religious convictions and regarded the proceedings as an immoral assault upon the young woman and the deprivation of her right to live. Nancy Curzan did die a few days after the feeding tube had been removed. Family members and friends reportedly were in attendance upon her until the end.

Changing Perceptions of the Deathbed Scene

The ordeals of the Quinlans, the Curzans, and many other families have had a growing influence on both the reality and the image of the deathbed scene. The psychology of the deathbed scene remains in a transitional state at present. Among the factors involved:

1.   Increasing awareness that one's self or loved ones might be caught in a situation in which critical life-or-death decisions must be made; therefore . . .

2.   Increasing awareness of the end-phase of life in general, a topic from which most people have shielded themselves;

3.   Increasing interest in learning more about the available options in order to make advance decisions (request for living wills material escalated greatly after the Supreme Court's Curzan decision);

4.   Increasing communication among family members, friends, and health care professionals;

5.   Intensified but varying interpretations of the psychological status of the person who is in either a comatose or a persistent vegetative

state. For example, a person without experience in critical medical situations might be horrified by seeing a patient connected to a respirator, an IV tree, and a feeding tube. Gaspings, tremblings and other behaviors might be interpreted as signs of suffering and the entire scene as one of indignity, in-humanity, and humiliation. By contrast, an experienced critical care nurse might judge that the patient is actually experiencing little or no discomfort. There is some room for differing opinions, so the observer's frame of reference contributes much to the interpretation of the patient's psychological status (whether on a life-support system or not).

6.   Pursuing a series of negotiations and partnerships among all the people and special interests who contest for ownership of the deathbed scene. I have never met anybody who is on the side of pain, suffering, or extended vegetative existence. Situations have placed some people at odds with each other who would have preferred to reach common cause and be of mutual assistance. We are starting to see productive attempts to bridge the gaps between the frameworks and interests of hospice administrators, attorneys, physicians, nurses, families, clergy, and public advocates. At least some of the potential conflicts over ownership of the deathbed scene may be avoided through enlightened communication.

We do not want to overestimate the prevalence of heightened awareness, communication, and decision making. Many people remain outside the circle. Furthermore, this increased attention to the right-to-die situation has not necessarily led to careful thought about deathbed scenes in general. However, there is a discernible movement toward integrating the thought of the deathbed scene into our system of values, beliefs, and prospects. It is not likely that profound changes will occur swiftly and easily in our perceptions of the deathbed scene. More probable is an extended period of time in which as individuals and as a society we experiment with the idea of our death and ourselves. We will return to prospects for protecting and enhancing the deathbed scene after we have explored both our own mindsets and a sampling of final moments.

ANTICIPATED VERSUS ACTUAL DEATHBED SCENES

What is the relationship between deathbed scenes as rehearsed in the mind and as actually experienced? Students of two university courses focusing on death were asked to write detailed descriptions of their own deathbed scenes (Kastenbaum & Normand, 1990). They were instructed to envision this scene as it was *most likely* to occur. Respondents were invited to think of this scene as it might be filmed for a movie of their lives, thereby encouraging enough detail to guide the director, actors, and camera person.

After describing this scene, the respondents were asked to make any one change that would result in a happier scenario. Next, they were asked to alter the scene again by making one change that would result in a more distressing scenario. "Happier" and "more distressing" were both to be defined by their own thoughts, feelings, and values.

We found that most of these college students located their deathbed scenes in old age or very old age (more than 100 years). In fact, "old age" was given as the most common cause of death, followed by accidents. The typical respondent expected to die at home, although it was not uncommon to anticipate death in a hospital or in transit. Almost everybody (96%) expected to be alert, lucid, and aware of their imminent death. Except for those who expected to die in motor vehicle accidents, the respondents almost invariably expected to be surrounded by accepting, supporting, even cheerful loved ones. About one person in five specified that the deathbed scene would occur within the context of a large family reunion. Family members were the people most frequently mentioned as being on the scene; women were much more likely to mention the presence of friends than were men.

What about the dying process itself? Almost all respondents expected to die within a few minutes, hours, or days. Only one person described having experienced several months of coping with a specific illness (cancer). The dying process was not only brief, it was also almost completely free of distress. Very few expected to have pain or other symptoms. Four out of five respondents did not report any type of distress as part of their deathbed scenes, and only 6% expected to experience pain. Nausea and diarrhea/constipation were never mentioned in the total sample. (Male respondents never mentioned bleeding, loss of consciousness, numbness, head throbbing, or weakness; these symptoms were mentioned occasionally by females.)

The anticipated deathbed scenes were offered in more detail by the female respondents. The scenes reported by the males tended to be more generalized and less attentive to physical surroundings such as furnishings, music, time of day, and weather (spring and sunshine were the conditions most often specified by the women). Overall, deathbed scenes were portrayed in more personal and vivid ways by the typical female respondent, but the genders did not differ in most substantive respects.

It is interesting to note what possible events were *not* mentioned. There were very few deathbed scenes in which last words or parting gifts were exchanged. Life reviews on the deathbed, for all their popularity in tradition, folklore and film, were seldom mentioned. References to an afterlife were also rare. (Most respondents separately reported having a belief in afterlife, but, for reasons unknown, few integrated this belief into the specifics of their deathbed scenes.) Furthermore, most respondents did not mention having any thoughts regarding other people as they were dying, and many did not report on their own emotional state.

About one person in six expected to die in an accident. These accidents were seen as happening in the near future, often within the next few months. Like those who died in old age, death-by-accident was expected to be quick and without pain or other symptoms; furthermore, they also expected themselves to be alert and aware of their situations.

What about their self-revised deathbed scenes, for the better and the worse? The respondents found it much easier to create a more disturbing scenario. The most common additions were: pain, time, and being alone. It was evident that the respondents were well aware of the possibilities they had rejected while preparing their original deathbed scene descriptions. Although respondents could always think of a more distressing deathbed scene, they could not always think of one that was more comforting or satisfying than the original. The most popular addition was the presence of a particular person; also mentioned was the sharing of personal feelings with another person, and the further reduction of the time it would take to die. The few who had previously seen themselves as dying in a hospital now took advantage of the revision opportunity to relocate themselves to their home. Either as part of their revised deathbed scenes or as comments made afterward, many said that they could not really improve upon the first version because "I guess I imagined it as I wanted it to be—even though I was supposed to imagine it as it would be."

The results of this small study suggest that people with an interest in death-related topics are not ready to think about their own relationship to death on a reality level. The students included a number of active health care professionals as well as others who were preparing themselves for human service careers. Basically, most of them "knew better," but felt the need to shield themselves from the more disturbing possibilities inherent in a deathbed scene. I have observed the same pattern continuing in all my subsequent death classes, even when a student occasionally asks, "As we *expect* or as we *want* it to be?" "As you *expect*," I reply—and they go on to write a description of the deathbed scene they would like to have. Most of us seem to have a powerful need to envision our deathbed scenes in idealized terms, or at least this is true of those who have made dying, death, and grief a special area of study. I doubt that a more realistic set of descriptions would be created by samples drawn from the general population, although this possibility has not yet been tested.

Direct studies of dying people and their experiences differ markedly from the anticipated deathbed scenes that have been summarized here (e.g., Levy, 1987–1988; Mor, Greer, & Kastenbaum, 1988; Nuland, 1994). Dying people do experience a variety of symptoms, including some that were rarely if ever mentioned by the students. Thanks mostly to the hospice movement, there have been significant advances in pain relief and other types of symptom control. But the fact remains that the dying person is often exhausted after a long struggle with illness and disability, and may have to contend with a variety of other problems.

College students have difficulty integrating these facts into their own life-and-death expectations. Typically, they "forget" that the dying person's body is no longer a pleasure machine. This tendency is often revealed when discussion turns to the last days of one's life (apart from the deathbed scene assignment). Young men, in particular, may boost their spirits by speaking of sexual adventures; it is not unusual for both men and women to fantasy that they will be able to do things they have not had the opportunity to do before: such as sail a yacht, hike the Grand Canyon. While spinning out these scenarios, they express a kind of euphoria and innocence that is hard to attain without denying the realities of debilitating illness. Are college students alone in this evasion? Probably not. Fantasies about "healthy dying" (Kastenbaum, 1979) have floated above the hard realities of terminal care ever since the emergence of the death awareness and hospice movements.

These fantasies go far beyond the basic goals and objectives of people who are knowledgeable in the care of dying patients. At an extreme, there are people who assert that dying is somehow more pleasurable, exciting, or meaningful than our days of health and well-being. Some people have also melded reports of near-death experiences into this belief. A person who has recovered from a life-threatening condition might report having had an experience of transcendence, serenity, and mystical enlightenment. Uncritical thought fails to distinguish this transient and distinctive experience from the day-by-day experiences of a person whose body is slowly but surely failing.

We will have an opportunity to consider the practical significance of expectations in a variety of deathbed scenes. (My thanks to The Hospice of The Valley in Phoenix for the opportunity to review and discuss their experiences with terminally ill patients.)

Some Deathbed Scenes and Their Implications

Every hospice care program has had a great many experiences from which we might learn. Here we offer but a sampling.

Red-Towel Deaths: The Anxiety Crescendo

Think of a cohesive family that is attempting to cope with the impending loss of one of its members. It is a multigenerational family that has managed to stay close despite competing and distracting responsibilities. Now the patriarch is dying. He is nearly 80, but was active and vigorous until felled by recently discovered cancer. There has been time for the family to adjust somewhat to the prospect of losing him. Most of their energies, however, are being devoted to making him as comfortable as possible for the time that is remaining. One of his daughters had heard about hospice. After a family conference with the physician, it was decided to seek the help of a local hospice organization with the objective of helping him to end his life at home and without unnecessary medical procedures.

How are they doing? On the surface, the family is coping well with this challenge, supported by visits from the hospice nurse and a volunteer. However, both the nurse and the volunteer detect an escalation of tension within the family. "They're going, each of them, into their own separate little shells," observes the volunteer. "I don't know why; I can't see anything that's happened to upset them, anything that wasn't expected." One day the nurse receives a call from one of the primary caregivers, the older daughter. It is an unusual contact because the daughter does not seem her usual well-centered self, and does not seem to have a compelling reason for making this call. Visiting the home later that day, the nurse wonders aloud if something is troubling the daughter. After a momentary, "No, I'm just a little tired," the daughter becomes tearful and agitated. Yes, she and the whole family are worried sick. About what? "About Dad . . . bleeding out."

It turns out that one of the family members had been told by a friend of a scene that she had been told about: a man dying in the hospital with blood just pouring out of his nose and mouth. The family now feared that the same might happen with Dad. Until this time, the family had kept its anxiety under control through its caregiving activities and confidence in hospice, but also through its expectation that the final scene would be peaceful and dignified. But now it appeared that every member of the family was tormented by the vision of Dad hemorrhaging and suffering. Nobody wanted to dwell on this possibility, yet it could not be dismissed. This fear had not only became a personal burden to each person, but also made communication more difficult because of the tacit agreement that this terrible scenario should not be discussed.

The hospice nurse is in a position to offer information as well as emotional support. She assures the daughter that terminal bleeding is very unlikely, given her father's condition and the care he is receiving. Uncontrolled bleeding is even more unlikely. There are occasional "bleed outs," but in her own several years of hospice experience, the nurse has never seen one. The daughter relaxes. The family relaxes. Attention can once again be given to Dad as he is rather than as what-might-happen-to him, and to mutual support among family members, his wife, both daughters, and a son-in-law, as he slips from consciousness into coma and beyond over a period of hours. There is no bleeding.

"I brought a red towel with me, though, just in case," the nurse later reports. Red towel? "To absorb the blood without showing it by changing color . . . to make the last scene less stressful for the family."

Families and the dying persons themselves can have a variety of fears about the deathbed scene. Bleeding out is the fear that has been most common in the cases I have studied, but other fears might be more common in other samples. From a practical standpoint, it is advisable to provide opportunities for people to express whatever fears, doubts, and worries they might have about the deathbed scene. Sometimes, as with the "red towel" scenario, it is possible to provide informed reassurance. In other circumstances, the fears might lead to identification of certain actions that should be taken or avoided. In any event, open communication will tend to reduce anxieties that could interfere with the relationship between caregiver and dying person.

Fire Dreams: Suffering and Terror

Hospice doctors and nurses often have state-of-the-arts skills in providing relief for pain and other symptoms. This is accomplished in part by adroit selection, dosage, and scheduling of medications and in part by contributing to a socioemotional climate of security and trust. It is not unusual for pain control to be a major priority. Furthermore, it may be necessary to try several methods of control before adequate relief is achieved. What *is* unusual—and extremely stressful—is to discover that nothing works.

A woman in her late forties learns that she has cancer of the breast. After diagnostic studies and treatment efforts it becomes clear that the disease cannot be halted. She may have only a few months. Experiencing great pain, she and her husband call upon the services of a hospice. The usual medications seems to have no effect. Dosage is increased. Dosage is increased again. Other methods are tried. The woman continues to be wracked by pain. There is also a sense of terror associated with her suffering. Hospice continues its efforts. Hypnosis. Guided imagery. Relaxation exercises. Her suffering continues unabated.

As far as hospice staff can determine, the patient's home situation is strong and supportive. Her (second) husband is devoted to her and very willingly takes time from his business activities to look after her. She is a practicing Catholic of strong faith, and together they have served as foster parents for an abused child. Her memories of childhood are painful: she herself had been abused by her alcoholic father while raised as a strict Catholic by her mother. Basically, she does not like to speak of her troubled life before finding happiness with her second husband.

Month after painful month goes by. She holds on to life although the pain is relentless. A entire year passes—an unusually long period of time for a hospice patient. Still trying to find a way to ease her pain, the hospice staff now wonders if she has "a need to suffer . . . the pain is hard to explain."

And now the dreams begin. It is a persistent, repetitive dream. There is a fire, and she's running, running, trying to get away. Her husband hears her screaming at night, presumably during these dreams. She awakens in exhausted terror. More than once she reports, "it's like the fires of hell. I will be punished. I am being punished." The fire dreams become more frequent and intense. Meanwhile, she is feeling much weaker. "Am I dying? What's happening? Am I dying?"

Although the hospice team includes one chaplain and has access to others, it happens that another clergyman becomes a visitor to the home. Apparently, he is a good listener and a strong personality. She tells him of her dreams . . . yes, there had been a real fire incident in her childhood, and somebody had died, but, that was not the fire in her dreams. More and more, she feels that these are the flames of retribution. She must have been a bad person, going back many years ago; now she is facing the punishment.

After disclosing her fears to the pastor, she experiences a different kind of dream. Three angels appear at her bedside. The first angel calls her by name and tells her, "It's going to be OK." The second angel adds: "You're going to see somebody soon." The third angel concludes the contact by declaring: "You're not going to have any more pain. You're not going to need any more pain medication." The next morning she wakes up relaxed and refreshed, for the first time in more than a year. Her husband brings the medications. She refused them. "I don't need them any more." He insists. She insists. And then it become clear to her husband that she really does not have any pain. "The pain is over," she reports. "I'm going to have a great day."

The couple have 2 good days together. She is not only pain-free, but also serene and relaxed. The tense and drained husband benefits much from this reprieve as well. A hospice nurse is with them when she dies: "After all that pain, she had one of the most peaceful deaths!" The hospice staff is still astounded by the sudden cessation of pain after "the mound of medications she had been taking."

This experience suggests that intense and unresolved problems of long duration may contribute to alarming visions of the deathbed scene. Did the little girl who has abused by her father so many years ago somehow blame herself, as some victims of abuse do? Did her subsequent divorce lead her to feel uneasy as a "good Catholic"? Did the theme of punishment help to make sense of being stricken with cancer when at last she had achieved happiness? Questions such as these cannot be answered definitively. But it is clear enough that psychological or spiritual problems make some of us vulnerable to suffering that is in excess of our physical conditions alone. It is also clear, as indicated by her experience with the pastoral visitor, that a mature interpretation of religion can have the power to overcome anxieties generated by immature interpretations.

Suicide: Death As Preventive Medicine

Earlier we described how Mr. W. B. E. and his wife and friends had co-created a deathbed scene that was in harmony with their wishes. A key to this outcome was the fact that the dying man felt he had lived one hell of a life and was ready to take his leave. However, there are many other ways in which people attempt to exercise control over their deathbed scene. Here are two examples of an approach that employs death itself as a form of preventative medicine.

Ms. L. V. was an unmarried nurse in her thirties. Her life had centered around her work and several close friendships. She had more than the usual knowledge of terminal illness and care. The idea of becoming a hospice nurse or director appealed to her but she was very much involved in her current position in a hospital. This, however, is the way things had been. Now, incredibly, she was dying. With the help of friends she had been able to remain at home. By saving up her energies she could write letters, read, converse, and even continue working a little on a project she had started prior to her illness.

One day she asks her two best friends if they would do a couple of errands for her. These errands happen to be in different directions and each will take at least an hour and a half. They return to find Ms. L. V. dead. She has somehow managed the very difficult feat of (a) acquiring a lethal supply of morphine and (b) rigging up the IV to deliver the drug into her own veins. There was a note asking their forgiveness for this little trick. She wanted to quit before life became unbearable.

The friends experienced a very strong and very mixed response: surprise, sorrow, relief, anger. The anger was still there months later.

"It was as if she didn't trust us." They had no difficulty in understanding why this strong-minded person would want to control her own destiny, especially since she knew better than most people about the probable future course of her illness and debility. But they felt that a bond of mutual trust had been broken when Ms. L. V. had not informed them of her plans. One did observe, however, that the "suicide machine" had been rigged with the outside possibility of rescue: she had used a hemalock device that would have made it possible to quickly shut off the flow of morphine had either friend returned earlier and noticed the set-up. Many suicide attempts to include an "escape hatch," enabling the individual to share a little of the responsibility with friends, family, or fate.

By contrast, Mr. J. J., a man about 70, did not conceal his suicidal intent. He told the visiting hospice nurse that he had his own way of treating his condition—and then produced a large handgun from beneath a pillow. Life was hardly worth living any more. They had already told him to stop smoking and drinking. What would they want to take away next? He wasn't going to keep lying around until he rusts out, and the doctors could keep their knives and pills for some other sucker. The nurse secured his agreement to speak with the hospice social worker about his suicidal intention and, in the meantime, wouldn't he like to feel a little better? The social worker responded promptly to her call. The nurse put the intervening time to good use, and persuaded Mr. J. J. to shave for the first time in weeks. He was looking more comfortable and relaxed by the time the social worker showed up.

After a brief conference with Mr. and Mrs. J. J., the social worker left their home with the gun inside a plastic bag. The weapon would be held for him in a locked security box. Mr. J. J. had the receipt. Hospice had his promise that he would give them a chance to support the quality of life remaining to him. Mrs. J. J., who had hardly spoken during the whole visit, nodded approvingly to the social worker: "You're all right."

Next morning's hospice team meeting devoted considerable attention to the J. J.'s. A little later they learned that he had killed himself with his *other* gun (most probably brought to him by his wife).

In both examples, the two people chose to select the exact time of deaths that would likely have occurred within a few weeks. Neither person was experiencing much pain at the time and both had intimate companions for support, but they thought to spare themselves from increasing dependency and helplessness. Ms. L. V. chose a mode of suicide that was consistent with her profession and also somewhat more characteristic of women. By contrast, J. J. selected the "blast off" method that has long been more characteristic of male suicides. Officially, these deaths were similar in being suicides. However, the "floating off" morphine ending with its respiratory failure and the abrupt punctuation of a gunshot could hardly be more different in their expressions of individual personality. Their actual deathbed scenes were prompted by expectations of the kind of death that would await them after a further period of discomfort and decline. Would they perhaps have died as peacefully as the fire dreamer if they had achieved her sense of trust and acceptance? This we will never know.

Picking the Moment: Loving Withdrawal

Here are two examples in which the dying person seems to select a "right time" to depart this life.

Mrs. B. T. had been a widow for many years. She declined most offers of assistance from family members scattered around the nation. Before being afflicted by her final illness, Mrs. B. T. seemed to be deriving most of her satisfaction from the ability to function independently and just as she chose. There were two good friends in the picture, and she maintained contacts with the family through telephone, correspondence, and occasional visitations (usually by cold-fleeing relatives during the mild Arizona winters).

Now, at age 72, she found herself finding a losing battle with cancer. She bore up well for a while and had some periods of relatively good health. As time went on, however, the treatments as well as the disease exhausted her. The two friends—women about her own age—did what they could to make things easier, such as running errands and transporting her for blood transfusions. Eventually the widely dispersed family members learned of the serious nature of her illness. Mrs. B. T. held off as long as she could, but then accepted the offer of assistance from one of her nieces, Mrs. A. L. The older woman recognized that she had become "a stand-offish kind of person," and also that she resented having to become dependent on anybody.

The decision to seek hospice care was made by Mrs. B. T. herself. She could see that her condition was not improving and, putting various pieces of information together, judged that she did not have long to live. Her physician tried to dissuade her from this move. From his viewpoint, there were still more treatments that could be tried. Mrs. B. T., however, had become more sophisticated about medical matters and felt she was not being properly informed by her physician and that perhaps her physician had not kept himself properly informed about her condition either. A turning point was her observation that the nurses were having increasing difficulties with her frequently punctured veins and the physician's unwillingness to admit or discuss this problem. "Mrs. B. T. was a fighter," the hospice nurse later recalled. She continued to look for treatment possibilities even after enrolling in the hospice program. But she was also a realist, and, increasingly fatigued, decided against a possible trip to a "miracle clinic" in Mexico.

The most unusual development occurred in the relationship between Mrs. B. T. and her niece. Becky, the younger woman, was a spontaneous and high-spirited person, fond of pranks and teasing. The older woman had a serious, no-nonsense mien and a streak of compulsivity. "They should have driven each other crazy! But somehow they hit it off beautifully." Becky seemed immune to the dark clouds and frowning features that greeted her arrival and, by and by, Mrs. B. T. found herself enjoying her lively company. It was hard to stay gloomy around Becky.

For nearly a month Mrs. B. T. enjoyed some of the most rewarding interactions of her life. She appeared to be "younger mentally" and not beyond the occasional prank herself. Nevertheless, life was becoming more and more difficult and her functioning ever more limited. There was not much pain to contend with, but she felt drained of energy. The hospice nurse recognized "that I-want-to-die look."

With what seemed to be her last reserve of energy, Mrs. B. T. thanked Becky for all that she had done and commanded her to go back to her own family ("They need you, too. Your life is with your own children"). Becky obeyed. A few hours after her departure, one of the older woman's friends contacted hospice. The friend and a hospice volunteer by now well known to Mrs. B. T. sat by her bedside, each holding one of her hands. Mrs. B. T. remained conscious but silent, then sighed and expelled her last breath.

Mr. K. M. was a successful businessman who was also known for his community activities. Orphaned in childhood when both of his parents were killed in an automobile accident, he was especially responsive to the needs of children and could be counted upon for contributions of time, energy, and money. After helping transport materials for a junior high school science fair, he experienced what felt like a flare-up of an old back injury. It was shocking to discover that he had cancer, and at an advanced stage. Mr. K. M. was not in the habit of paying much attention to aches and pains.

Passing through the gauntlet of diagnostic and treatment procedures, Mr. K. M. learned that his illness was terminal. He adjusted to this grim prospect more readily than did his family, business partner, and many friends in the community. For a period of time there was division within the family, with the majority either urgently favoring continued treatment efforts or persisting in the belief that the doctors had made some kind of mistake. "We're all on the same page now—I think!" he told the hospice nurse. After another short stay in the hospital to stabilize his condition, Mr. K. M. returned home where family members were with him almost every hour of the day. The hospice nurse recalls that "They were there for him, but for themselves, too. They were all jealous of their time with him. He meant so much to that family."

During the 3 weeks following his entry into a hospice program, Mr. K. M. participated in many interactions that could have fulfilled a scriptwriter's every need for a deathbed scene. His often abrasive and smart-alecky business partner broke down and cried. Grandchildren sat on his bed and presented him with their crayon drawings. Even a girl friend from high school days (almost 40 years ago) showed up. There was time alone with his wife, each of his three children, and several others. Had he died during or after one of these interactions, the survivors would have had a coherent and meaningful deathbed scene to remember.

What actually happened was a little different. Rapidly tiring, Mr. K. M. also observed strain and tension on the part of others. He confided to the hospice volunteer that his family was becoming "frazzled" and neglecting their other needs. It was Mr. K. M. who suggested that he be placed in a respite care facility. "I love you all, but I just need to rest for a few days. So do you." Reluctantly, the family agreed, but only with the provisions that they could visit him and that he would come back home soon. Despite their hesitancy about having him leave their home and care for even a few days, the family immediately started to reorient itself toward some of its other pressing concerns (including an impending graduation). Satisfied that Mr. K. M. was comfortable in the respite care facility, his wife and a son allowed themselves to be shooed away for a while. He also asked a member of the respite care staff not to be disturbed for a while; he needed his sleep. That was his last communication. Apparently he died in his sleep within an hour or so after taking leave of his wife and son.

Mrs. B. T. and Mr. K. M. had taken advantage of multiple opportunities to communicate with the people who were important to them. They did not have rushed, emergency farewells to make: both had been in steady contact with family and friends. They did not feel a compelling need for a final interaction in order to convey messages or construct meaning. Possibly, some deaths require a "scene" more than others. Both of these people had, in effect, said their good-byes. They appreciated the loving care they had received and, in return, seemed to pick the right moment to leave.

The Last Minute Rally: One More Time at Bat

The last "type" of deathbed scene we will illustrate here is one that many others have noticed over the years. It is easier to describe than to explain.

In his youth, Mr. S. P. had a short career in professional baseball until felled by breaking pitches and his own resistance to taking advice. He had made a good living as a skilled construction worker, and liked nothing better than to demonstrate his talent and knowledge, especially in carpentry. His family had long since adjusted to the fact that he was "not much of a talker," although he could be an attentive listener if there was no televised sporting event as competition.

With the onset and development of his terminal illness, Mr. S. P. became sulky and hard to live with. He made what seemed like constant demands for personal services, and resented having his wife leave his bedside for any reason. Consequently, the family had to cope not only with the prospect of his death but also with the tensions and unpleasantness of everyday life in the home. Mrs. S. P. was not much of a talker either, but she understood that her husband's demanding behavior was an expression of his fear. She tried to assure him by her actions that she would not abandon him, but his fear-driven pressure was relentless.

By the time that hospice entered the scene, Mr. S. P.'s condition had deteriorated markedly. He was bedridden, haggard, tense, and minimally communicative. It was determined that he had been in pain for some time without telling anybody. After the hospice evaluation, Mr. S. P. was given new medications that relieved his pain and may have contributed to his somewhat more relaxed appearance. Nevertheless, he would respond to hospice personnel and volunteers with only monosyllabic utterances, and sometimes not even that. Mrs. S. P. and a daughter-in-law received guidance in caregiving procedures from hospice and carried out these responsibilities in a proficient manner. The daughter-in-law apparently was the voice of the household and brought the family's anxieties and questions to the hospice staff. The family caregivers seemed to benefit most from knowing that they were not alone with this challenge and not remiss in their services.

Mr. S. P. had stopped complaining, but had very nearly stopped communicating as well. There were times when he did not recognize family members. His mind was adrift. The medications were reviewed on the possibility that they were responsible for the decline in his mental state, but this conclusion did not appear justified. Apparently his longer and longer periods of sleep and drift would continue to lengthen until he was not there any more.

After several days of only minimal interactive response and very little intake of nourishment, Mr. S. P. was lying in a curled up position with his face to the wall. Upon entering his room, Mrs. S. P. at first wondered if he was still alive. Assuring herself that he was still drawing breath, she found herself saying: "Sunday's your birthday. Would you like a party?" She had not meant this as a sick joke; it was just a bizarre thought that popped into her mind and out of her mouth. No response, of course.

On her next visit to his bedside, however, she discovered her husband with his eyes open and searching. It was Mr. S. P. who started the conversation: "Bacon. Balloons. All the kids." And so the family decided that the next morning would be his birthday (moved up a day). The dying man remained alert and attentive to the proceedings. He proved able to take his small portion of bacon and eggs at the family table. After a rest he was again wheeled out to the dining room which had been festooned with balloons, ribbons, and baseball memorabilia. Somebody had even fashioned a baseball medallion in the frosting of the birthday cake. He observed the comings and goings of two young grandchildren with special interest, one of whom was especially taken with the wheelchair. The candles were lit twice so each grandchild could take a turn in blowing them out.

Mr. S. P. was not a smiling sort of person and nobody observed him smiling on this occasion either. After some eating and drinking had been accomplished, he looked across the table at his wife and said simply, "That was good." She could not remember the last time she had heard a compliment from his lips. Again exhausted, Mr. S. P. was gently returned to his bed. He survived the night, called for his wife in the morning (she was there already), and died.

Known as "premortem clarity," this type of temporary recovery from withdrawal and confusion was observed a number of times in connections with our psychological autopsy studies and has also been reported by numerous physicians, nurses, and relatives. It would be speculative to explain these awakenings on either purely psychological or purely physiological grounds, nor can it be assumed that all instances have the same cause. However, it is probable that heavy medication and a lack of opportunity for meaningful social interaction are both conditions that would work against premortem clarity. For Mr. S. P., his final scene can be thought of as occurring during the birthday party when his mind was again in focus and most of his family on hand. For some other people in similar situations, the deathbed scene is enacted while its principal player is mute and perhaps inattentive.

THE MOMENT OF DEATH

The deathbed scene may be enacted over days or weeks. What about the last moment? Those who conceive of the deathbed scene primarily as a test of religious faith or general moral character have long given special attention to the final moment of life. For example, many have believed that the soul is expelled with the last breath to continue its flight to the next destination. The words and gestures that are exchanged just before that final moment—and the expression on the dying person's face—all are part of this value-laden scene. Whether religiously oriented or not, most witnesses to a final moment are likely to be impressed by the sudden transition from life to death. The person seems much as he or she did just a moment ago—but also, entirely different.

Physician John Nuland's clinical description of a typical passing clearly shows how psychological and spiritual interpretations can come to the witnesses' mind. Note that the term *agonal* here refers to struggle, not pain.

The apparent struggles of the agonal moments are like some violent outburst of protest arising deep in the primitive unconscious, raging against the too-hasty departure of the spirit; no matter its preparation by even months of antecedent illness, the body often seems reluctant to agree to the divorce. In the ultimate agonal moments, the rapid onset of oblivion is accompanied either by the cessation of breathing or by a short series of great heaving gasps . . . the chest or shoulders will sometimes heave once or twice, and there may be a brief agonal convulsion. The agonal phase merges into clinical death, and thence into the permanence of mortality.

The appearance of a newly lifeless face cannot be mistaken for unconsciousness. Within a minute after the heart stops beating, he face begins to take on the unmistakable gray-white pallor of death; in an uncanny way, the features very soon appear corpselike, even to those who have never before seen a dead body. A man's corpse looks as though his essence has left him, and it has. He is flat and toneless, no longer inflated by the vital spirit the Greeks called pneuma. The vibrant fullness is gone. (Nuland, 1994, p. 122)

Nuland's description unites the psychological, spiritual, and biomedical dimensions of the last moment. There is also a traditional assumption that the dying person knows more about death. Furthermore, at the very last moment the dying person is vouchsafed a vision of the domain beyond life. It would follow, therefore, that a person approaching the last moment might be able to tell us something of death because of his or her closeness to the edge. History and literature are replete with examples of last words that are intended to instruct and inspire. These utterances usually draw their power both from the fame or notoriety of the dying person and the assumption that the words must be expressing an ultimate truth because of their finality.

There has been a lot of mischief associated with last words, however. Some of the most famous deathbed statements were invented by others to suit their own agendas. For example, Charles Darwin's supposedly said, "How I wish I had not expressed my theory of evolution as I have done." This was taken as a deathbed conversion to belief in religious dogma about the creation of the world and species. Actually, what Darwin said was "I am not in the least afraid to die." The misquotation was concocted by a person who had never been close to Darwin and did not see him during his final illness (Boller & George, 1989). The possibility that we will hear what we want to hear and interpret how we want to interpret will continue to exist whenever last words are taken as evidence for a particular view of life and death.

It is questionable to assume that people know more about death because their lives are nearly at an end (Kastenbaum, 1993a). A person who is standing directly before a high wall does not necessarily know more about what is on the other side than a person perceiving the wall from a distance. Nevertheless, dying people are in an unique position to view *life*. The shape and meaning of what they have experienced might be disclosed to them in a different way than ever before. The distinctiveness of the dying person's final words is also intensified by their function as leave-taking statements. It is not just the words themselves, but to whom they are spoken and why. Furthermore, these words may express a continued quest for meaning rather than a resolution. Elie Metchnikoff, the Noble-prize winning bioscientist who introduced the term thanatology, spoke on his deathbed of heading toward "the great Whatever." Cotton Mather, the stalwart religious leader of colonial America and a man of strong faith, also wondered what would be coming next.

"Banjo Bill" provides a remarkable contemporary example of a man continuing to explore the meaning of life and death up to his last breath. The elderly entertainer was receiving hospice care for his terminal cancer and, along with his much younger woman companion, was living with his sister and brother-in-law. When he felt that death was near he dictated a fond letter of farewell to all the people he had known throughout the years including, symbolically, all the audiences he had entertained. This was a smoothly worded letter expressing thanks and offering blessings to others while reporting his enthusiasm for finally having a chance to play "the big show" and hoping it would be a long-term engagement. This would have made an accomplished and well-received set of final words from a person with many friends and admirers. Banjo Bill was not finished, however. A few days later he felt death to be even closer and summoned his companion with her tape recorder to take another statement. This time the substance, style, and speech pattern differed markedly. He spoke critically of "this babbling world of fools" where previously he had thanked "one and all" for having been such a great audience. Speaking in rapid bursts of inspiration, Banjo Bill offered his own now-keenly felt vision of life, death, and God, as in this excerpt in which I have italicized as an astoundingly poetic statement that amazed those who thought they had known him very well:

> Gradually becoming as Christ, the son of God, the son of God, now moulding itself into the man and cleansing each and every soul. It has nothing to do with us, the few before us, and the few after us, will bring his new thoughts into the world, with no hardening of the heart. *The hardness of the diamond ideas, self by self, idea by idea, that is the diamond, the pearl, til the final great wonderful pearl of great force shining with all the pinnacle—the pearl of great price, eternal.* (Kastenbaum, 1993b, p. 115)

After a few more words he ended with a blessing: "All powerful, all presence . . . Go from here in peace. Amen. Thank you."

Here were remarkable last words from a person not previously noted as an intense and original religious thinker. Except—they were not quite his last words. The next day he was very tired and wanted only to sleep, but perked up when he learned that it was lasagna for dinner. Unfortunately, he soon experienced a seizure and could not speak for a while. He did recover his voice, though, and motioned for the tape recorder. While his sister held his hand and his lover embraced him, Banjo Bill spoke into the microphone:

> Don't squeeze me, don't squeeze . . . to me, from me . . . from me to all . . . Love, I love you . . . Bye, bye, all is well . . . Forever . . . In case . . . All, everybody, it's been great. I love you . . . you've all been good. I'll see you again.

The old entertainer then demanded an encore for his encore:

> One more time . . . I love you all . . . OK. (p. 116)

Banjo Bill's last last words had returned him to the human sphere. Apparently he said what needed to be said about God, and now he was free to express his love in a direct and characteristic way to the people who most mattered to him. His opportunity to offer not just one but three parting messages owed much to (a) his life-long ability to make and keep warm interpersonal relationships; and (b) competent palliative care that enabled him to think, feel, and communicate without pain.

How should we regard final communications? First, we would certainly keep in mind that the most significant communications might not be the very last words themselves, but, rather, the pattern of verbal and nonverbal interactions that have preceded them. Next, we would probably agree that people should not have to die alone. There should be companions with whom meaningful communication is possible, whether by conversation or a touch of the hand. Whatever protects consciousness and cognitive function while at the same time controlling pain is invaluable in improving the opportunities for final communications (a topic we will take up in the next section). Our own cognitive processes might or might not be able to interpret the final words adequately, especially if reference is being made to events that are obscure to us or the dying person is in touch with a private reality we cannot experience.

A biomedical perspective might discipline us to consider many last words as epiphenomena—essentially meaningless fantasies generated by a struggling brain. A spiritual perspective might inspire us to consider last words and gestures as evidence for the sacred and for a meaningful survival of death. What guidance might we find from a psychological perspective? We have already seen that psychologists have constructed death in a variety of ways and that each of us also constructs our own version as we develop personal views of the meaning of life through maturation and experience. Furthermore, we have also seen that there are a great many ways to conceptualize the dying process. It is difficult to escape the conclusion that the last moment of life derives much of its meaning, shape, and texture from each individual's distinctive view of the world. This would suggest that there as many realities as there are experiencers. The biomedical perspective is still in play: the physiological milieu must exert a tremendous influence on the dying person's state of mind—yet this is not the same as asserting that, for example, Banjo Bill's thoughts were either caused by his illness and medications or that these thoughts were *ipso facto* meaningless. The spiritual perspective also remains available. Developing an accurate and useful psychology of death is challenge enough; it would be less than scientific to assert that there is nothing beyond psychology that might answer to the name of spirituality. A sociocultural perspective would also be in order: obviously, individual perspectives on life and death do not develop within a vacuum. Not everybody in the same culture has the same experiences or creates the same outlook on life, however. It is the individual who develops and lives among people and, if fortunate, has loving companions at the end. A psychological perspective on deathbed scenes and the last moment of life is therefore not only plausible, but essential.

REVIEW AND PROSPECTUS

Deathbed scenes are narrative constructions that help us to preview and/or preserve mental representations of our most direct encounters with mortality. They are subject to the influences that shape all of our expectations, memories, and interpersonal communications. Unlike most other expectations and memories, however, the deathbed scene takes us to the very limits of our knowledge and experience. I learned this from the first old man who I saw gazing into the middle distance and gesturing to . . . (?) just before he died. I could see him but not what he saw.

On the behavioral and overt level, the deathbed scene can be described, analyzed, and even quantified should we choose to do so. The behavioral analysis of the deathbed scene can encompass the people, the place, and the sequence and timing of events, including communications and other interactions. I believe that we can learn much of practical as well as conceptual value by attending both to the deathbed scene as an objective behavior setting and as a set of competing symbolic constructions.

It is the choice and the competition among symbolic constructions that I would like to emphasize at this point. Whoever is most persuasive in telling the story of the deathbed scene is also likely to be most successful in claiming ownership. We have seen that religious, medical, legal, and bureaucratic establishments have been among the major competitors. Psychological, poetic, and mythic versions can also be powerful and, at times, the most persuasive. There is a highly variable relationship between enfranchised and narrative power. Hospital administrators and their attorneys have a strong power base that lends strength to whatever vision of the deathbed scene they happen to endorse. The bureaucratic vision does not have to be especially insightful, comprehensive, or compelling—but it will be influential simply because it is the symbolic structure that has been erected by the "ruling class." By contrast, the pastoral visitor who listened so skillfully to the fire dreams had no enfranchised power. And yet he somehow helped her to relieve her own existing symbolic structure of its torment (painful death as punishment becoming angelic safe conduct).

I think we will continue to see a lively competition for the most persuasive interpretations of deathbed scenes. If we look closely, we will also see that these interpretations tend to justify courses of action that have been advocated or already taken. Agree with an aggressive physician that every last intervention must be attempted and we increase the likelihood of ending up with a code blue scene or reasonable facsimile. Agree with the Alaskan prospector that a life belongs to the person who has lived it, and we increase the likelihood of holding a drink in our hands while good old buddies end their relationship with a hearty final blast off. Symbolic constructions and their fate in the marketplace of human communication are significant for their consequences as well as for their intrinsic substance and form.

We have also seen that our thoughts are tempted by both the muse of fantasy and the implacable bill collector of reality. College students and working health care professionals in good health often succumb to wishful thinking when confronted with the prospect of their own deathbed scenes. Many others have embraced the chimeric concept of healthy dying. People who have been active in the death awareness movement for many years have learned to recognize a type of enthusiastic recruit for whom dying and death provide an emotional rush and the answer and compensation for all that has previously gone awry with their lives. Fortunately, many who jumped upon the band or hearse-wagon as an escapist adventure have since found other fads to enjoy. There are certainly many ambiguities and uncertainties as we move toward the deathbed scene, and many occasions that can be spiced and illuminated by imaginative thinking. However, there are times when all are better served by hard and resolute attention to reality.

On the positive side, as a society we seem to have overcome some of our reluctance to acknowledge the reality of the deathbed scene. It has become a less frequent standard operating procedure to ostracize and conceal the dying person, although this practice is still encountered in some nursing homes and hospitals. A perceptive and deepening dialogue on the nature of the deathbed scene has started to replace the anxious insistence that people leave the tidal pool of life without making a ripple.

There are now signs that the medical profession is becoming more systematically involved in the improvement of quality of life for dying patients. Through the years there have been many individual physicians who were models of compassion and skill. It is heartening to observe increasing interest on the part of the mainstream medical establishment. Many were distressed by the results of a large-scale study which found that physicians often communicated poorly with their hospitalized terminally ill patients and often ignored their do not resuscitate (DNR) requests (SUPPORT, 1995). Furthermore, many hospitalized patients still were spending the last few days of their lives in severe pain. These were devastating findings of a physician-conducted study. Hospice care had been making its mark in the United States for two decades, clearly demonstrating that pain relief and accommodation to patients' wishes were realistic goals.

Worse was to come. The study had a second phase. Interventions were attempted to improve pain relief, physician-patient communication, and physician compliance with patients' wishes. The results: no change, no improvement. Whatever psychological factors were involved in the physicians' pattern of ignoring communications from dying people and making pain relief a high priority were factors that were resistant to change. This does not mean that change could not occur, but that it would not be easy. The SUPPORT study was a sharp poke in the eye for the medical profession. There are now a number of significant initiatives on the part of physicians and colleagues in related fields. It looks encouraging. One example is a recent study of quality end-of-life care (Singer, Martin, & Kelner, 1999). This survey of patients' wishes for the last phase of their lives was not especially remarkable for its findings: the life-threatened patients wanted (a) to receive adequate pain and symptom management; (b) avoid having their dying prolonged by invasive and useless procedures; (c) keep a sense of control over their own lives; (d) not be a burden on their loved ones; and (e) to strengthen their relationship with their loved ones. None of these findings would surprise people who have long been active in the care of dying people. What was notable, though, was the fact that physicians considered this issue important enough to conduct a study—and the establishment agreed by accepting it for publication in the prestigious *Journal of the American Medical*

Association. This study, along with some of the other medical initia-tives, seem a bit like reinventing the wheel. But perhaps the wheel had to be reinvented after so many years of ignoring the dying person and avoiding the deathbed scene.

Hospice is clearly making a difference in reclaiming the deathbed scene as a core human experience (Kastenbaum, in press). Advances in pain management have enabled many terminally ill people to maintain their interpersonal relationships and both to reflect on their lives and deal with the current situation. Reduction of cognitive clouding and confusion has also enabled more people to remain alert and responsive longer. Less pain and less apprehension about pain helps people to communicate about everything that concerns them—and also heart-ens others to communicate with them. Less sense of social isolation, the preservation of family bonds, and the moderation of depression are among other frequent accomplishments of hospice care.

If care of dying people and their families is now on its way to becoming a real priority, then psychological theory, research, and counseling may be more welcome than ever. We just need to know something about dying, the construction of death, and the dynamics of the deathbed scene—and a lot about our own lives and our arrange-ments with mortality.

REFERENCES

Aries, P. (1981). *The hour of our death.* New York: Knopf.

Boller, P. F., Jr., & George, J. (1989). *They never said it.* New York: Oxford University Press.

Goodwin, J. S., & Goodwin, J. M. (1985). Second thoughts. *Journal of Chronic Diseases, 38,* 717–719.

Kastenbaum, R. (1979). "Healthy dying": A paradoxical quest continues. *Journal of Social Issues, 35,* 185–206.

Kastenbaum, R. (1993a). Last words. *The Monist, An International Journal of General Philosophical Inquiry, 76,* 270–290.

Kastenbaum, R. (1993b). Is there an ideal deathbed scene? In I. B. Corless, B. B. Germino, & W. Pittman (Eds.), *Dying, death and bereavement* (pp. 109–122). Boston: Jones & Bartlett.

Kastenbaum, R. (in press). The moment of death: Is hospice making a difference? *Hospice Journal.*

Kastenbaum, R., & Normand, C. (1990). Deathbed scenes as expected by the young and as experienced by the old. *Death Studies, 13,* 201–218.

Kellehear, A., & Lewin, T. (1988–1989). Farewells by the dying: A sociological study. *Omega, Journal of Death and Dying, 19,* 275–292.

Leenaars, A. A. (1988). *Suicide notes.* New York: Human Services Press.

LeGoff, J. (1984). *The birth of purgatory.* Chicago: University of Chicago Press.

Leone, D. F. (1998). (Ed.). *Physician-assisted suicide.* San Diego, CA: Greenhaven.

Levy, M. H. (1987–1988). Pain control research in the terminally ill. *Omega, Journal of Death and Dying, 18,* 265–280.

Mor, V., Greer, D. S., & Kastenbaum, R. (1988). *The hospice experiment.* Baltimore: Johns Hopkins University Press.

Nuland, J. (1994). *How we die.* New York: Knopf.

Rando, T. R. (1989). Anticipatory grief. In R. Kastenbaum & B. K. Kastenbaum (Eds.), *Encyclopedia of death* (pp. 12–15). Phoenix, AZ: Onyx.

Sacks, O. (1968). *Awakenings.* New York: Dutton.

Saunders, C. (1993). An *Omega* interview. *Omega, Journal of Death and Dying, 27,* 263–270.

Schneider, S., & Kastenbaum, R. (1993). Patterns and meanings of prayer in hospice caregivers: An exploratory study. *Death Studies, 17,* 471–485.

Singer, P. A., Martin, D. K., & Kelner, M. (1999). Quality end-of-life care. Patients' perspectives. *Journal of the American Medical Association, 281,* 163–168.

Taylor, J. (1977). *The rules and exercises of holy dying.* New York: Arno Press. (Original work published 1651)

The SUPPORT Principle Investigators. (1995). A controlled trial to improve care for seriously ill hospitalized patients: The Study to Understand Prognoses and Preferences for Outcomes and Risks of Treatments (SUPPORT). *Journal of the American Medical Association, 274,* 1591–1598.

Warton, J. (1826). *Death-bed scenes* (Vols. 1–3). London: John Murray, Albemarle Street.

Wekesser, C. (1995). (Ed.). *Euthanasia. Opposing viewpoints.* San Diego, CA: Greenhaven.

Weisman, A. D., & Kastenbaum, R. (1968). *The psychological autopsy: A study of the terminal phase of life.* New York: Behavioral Publications.

Index

Absence, death and, 31
Activation vs inactiviation of death construct, 72–73
Adolescents, death constructions of, 76–80
Adult "mental gymnastics," death and, 72–74
African Americans, 131–133, 200
Aged people, 71, 99–100, 121–128, 148; *see also* Deathbed scenes
Aggression, death instinct and, 169–170, 185–186
AIDS, 134–135, 144
Aliveness and deadness, 38, 45–46, 51–52
Allport, Gordon, 185
Anthony, Sylvia, 48–51
Antipatory grief, 282
Anxiety, *see* Death anxiety
Anxiety buffer hypothesis, 138
Anxiety surge phenomenon, 153
Attenuated life and death, 281–285
Attitudes toward death
   Adolescents, 77–80
   African American, Japanese American, and Mexican American, 131–133
   irrelevance of death, 1, 16
   morally coded, 8–12
   objectivisitic, 4, 14
   pop psych (New Age), 23–24

Automaton, personification of death, 144–145
Awareness vs habituation or denial, 72

"Banjo Bill," death of, 303–305
Becker, Ernest, 109–110, 184
Behaviorism, death and, 13–14
Being and nonbeing, 45–46, 75
Beyond the Pleasure Principle, 169
Bereavement, in childhood, 40–41
Binary logic, children and, 54–55
Bird, dead, 42–44
"Bleeding Kansas," 161, 199
Bleeding out, 291
Bluebond-Langner, Myra, 55–56
Brain death, 5–6
Brown, Norman O., 173

Canadians, 136
Castration anxiety,   103
Catastrophic death, 84–85
Chang, Iris, 200
Childhood amnesia, 40–41
Children, dying, 55–61
Children's constructions of death, 29–62
Choron, Jacque, 181
Christian doctrine, death anxiety and, 105–107
Code blue, 253, 278–281
Compartmentalization, 73–74, 90
Concepts of death, stability of, 67–68

311

Index